PERPICH

November 2, 1982. "It was Election Day, and Rudy was back on the Range. He is visiting Julius 'Clipper' Fiola's barbershop on Chestnut Street in Virginia, Minnesota, the epicenter of political gossip on the east Iron Range. It was said that 'Clipper' worked and talked so rapidly that you could double-park and get a haircut without getting a parking ticket. Rudy didn't let 'Clipper' cut his hair, maybe because Fiola also had a reputation for looking at someone else and talking politics while cutting hair. Rudy went there for political gossip. After the election, the barber put a sign in the window that read, 'I saw Rudy!'"
  --Mark Phillips, Commissioner of the Department of Iron Range
   Resources and Rehabilitation and Perpich Party member

PERPICH
A Minnesota Original

Ben Schierer
With Lori Sturdevant

FOREWORD BY MARK DAYTON

MINNESOTA
HISTORICAL
SOCIETY PRESS

mnhspress.org   @mnhspress

The Minnesota Historical Society Press is a member of the Association of University Presses.

Manufactured in the United States of America.

10 9 8 7 6 5 4 3 2 1

♾ The paper used in this publication meets the minimum requirements of the American National Standard for Information Sciences—Permanence for Printed Library Materials, ANSI Z39.48-1984.

International Standard Book Number
ISBN: 978-1-68134-308-2 (paper)
ISBN: 978-1-68134-309-9 (e-book)

Library of Congress Control Number: 2024949163

To my mom, who taught me to be myself,
and to my dad, who had the patience to deal with it.

Contents

Foreword

Ben Schierer has written a superb biography of an extraordinary leader and a remarkable man, Governor Rudy Perpich. He chronicles Rudy's rise from the most austere conditions in a small northern town to the most powerful political position in our entire state.

I worked for and with Governor Perpich from 1976 to 1990. I learned so much from him over the fourteen years of our friendship. I learned the importance of creating job opportunities for Minnesotans. Rudy grew up on the hardscrabble Iron Range, where his father worked in one of the mines. As he put it, on mornings when his father's lunch pail was on the kitchen table, his dad was working. When it remained on the shelf, he was not. I can only imagine what that difference meant to him and his family.

So, when Rudy campaigned on "Jobs, Jobs, Jobs," he *meant* it. And he would go anywhere, literally anywhere, throughout our country and around the globe, where there were prospects of jobs for Minnesotans.

I also worked for Walter Mondale, when he was a US senator. Unlike Fritz, who was cautious and careful, Rudy was spontaneous and impulsive. He was a font of new ideas, his own and those he culled from others. I once said that working for Mondale was like waterskiing behind a cabin cruiser. With Perpich, it was like waterskiing behind a jet boat, where you were holding on just trying to remain upright!

I began my relationship with Rudy as a staff assistant, when he became governor in December 1976. In April 1978 he appointed me commissioner of the Minnesota Department of Economic Development. Unfortunately, my service ended when he was defeated for reelection that November.

During the next four years, I called Rudy about once a month, while he was working for Control Data Corporation and living in Vienna, Austria. When he returned to run for governor again in 1982, he and I were initially on separate tracks. I was the DFL Party's endorsed US Senate candidate. Rudy was running in the gubernatorial primary against the endorsed DFL candidate, Warren Spannaus.

When he narrowly defeated Warren, there were fears that his victory would divide DFL Party leaders and activists against him. The next day, I met publicly

with Rudy, endorsed him, and put my organization to work persuading the
DFL leaders who comprised the party's Central Committee to endorse him
the following weekend. They did, and he cruised to a decisive general election
victory. Unfortunately, I was defeated in my quest.

After the election, Rudy offered me another position in his administration,
as commissioner of the expanded Department of Energy and Economic Development. I served there until the end of his second term in January 1987.
Other than being governor myself, it was the best job I ever had. Thanks to
Rudy, the department had new resources to assist with development projects
throughout the state.

That was the great satisfaction of the job. I could be involved with entrepreneurs, private lenders, and local officials to finance projects. A year later,
I'd drive by the site and see the cars of Minnesotans who had jobs there. That's
as good as it gets!

Because "Jobs, Jobs, Jobs" was Rudy's highest priority, he and I worked
closely together on many possible economic development projects. He traveled throughout our country and the world to attract new and expanding
businesses and the jobs they could provide. He single-handedly recruited new
wood product companies to Minnesota, which added thousands of new jobs
to our state. He established "Medical Alley" to attract new medical products
businesses and touted Minnesota as the "brainpower state."

And he greatly strengthened our state's educational system, from elementary and secondary schools through colleges and universities. He had arrived
in first grade barely speaking English. He knew his education had opened the
door to his success, and he wanted to make those opportunities available to all
Minnesotans.

An example of his farsightedness and the vast benefits he brought to Minnesota was his convincing the Ghermezian brothers to build the Mall of America in Bloomington. Some people and press scorned Rudy for a venture they
did not understand. But the Ghermezians *did* come to Minnesota and created
what is now a world-renowned destination center and, after more than thirty
successful years, 4.8 million square feet and still expanding.

Another amazing achievement was his bringing Soviet Premier Mikhail
Gorbachev to Minnesota. Gorbachev announced that he would be coming to
the United States in June 1990. His itinerary included Washington, New York,
and San Francisco. Rudy invited him to add a visit to Minnesota and see our
country's heartland.

The Minnesota press and Rudy's Republican critics scorned his invitation
as a cheap election-year ploy. But then Gorbachev accepted! The public's excitement on an unusually cold June day was torrid. Nothing rivaling the visit
by this iconic foreign leader had ever happened in Minnesota.

Rudy and I shared a final campaign together in 1990, when he ran for re-election as governor and I ran for state auditor. This time, our outcomes were reversed. I was elected, and he was narrowly defeated.

Shortly thereafter, he and I had a falling out. He was requesting additional monies from a state pension, which I, as auditor, felt obligated to oppose. He never spoke to me again before his death in 1995.

Unfortunately, many of Rudy's remarkable achievements as governor were not properly credited to him during his lifetime. This book is vitally important for understanding an exceptional man and appreciating his remarkable accomplishments.

Someone once said of another titanic leader, French president Charles de Gaulle, that "He had the faults of his virtues and the virtues of his faults." Rudy Perpich also had his faults, like all of us, but many of them served to benefit the people of Minnesota.

Most importantly, he loved our state, and he was deeply devoted to serving all the people of Minnesota. If he sometimes pushed too hard, it was because he knew his time to make a difference was limited, and he wanted to make the very most of it. What some called a fault embodied a deep virtue.

While he now rests in peace, this excellent book powerfully brings his achievements back to life.

Mark Dayton
Minnesota State Auditor, 1991–95
US Senator from Minnesota, 2001–07
Governor of Minnesota, 2011–19

Prologue: Inauguration

"As I entered class that day, my father was unemployed, and
I spoke no English. And yet, today I have taken the oath
of office as the 34th governor of Minnesota. This could not
happen in many parts of the world."
                    —*Rudy Perpich, 1976 Inauguration*

In the early morning hours of Thursday, December 30, 1976, Minnesota's newly sworn-in governor joined his small inaugural party at the St. Paul Hotel. He'd asked for no official festivities. This party included only close friends and family, relaxing and telling stories. They weren't political insiders from St. Paul. They were gas station owners, dental assistants, and the sons of union miners from Minnesota's remote and often neglected Iron Range. But tonight, they were in the private company of the governor.

At the center of attention, where he always was, sat the man everyone knew as Rudy—with his larger-than-life personality, his big smile, and his swollen right hand immersed in a bucket of ice.

Rudy Perpich had been sworn in as Minnesota's 34th governor earlier that day, and he had publicly declared that he would stand until midnight to shake the hand of everyone who came to greet him. It was close to 1:00 A.M. before the line of well-wishers finally ended. Still, even after twelve hours of hand-shaking, Perpich was energized. He wanted to shake the hand of every person in Minnesota.[1]

The crowds had come to meet the man who'd been promoted to the top job from lieutenant governor after Governor Wendell Anderson resigned. They came from the Twin Cities and from small farming communities. They dressed in suits, working clothes, jeans, and formal wear. They stood in line for hours to wish Perpich well in his new position. As one observer said, "They represented large business, small business, special interest groups, organizations— but mostly they just represented themselves."[2]

Perpich's day had begun with a polka mass at the Church of the Assumption in St. Paul. Father Frank Perkovich, who'd won a lifetime achievement award from the National Cleveland-Style Polka Hall of Fame, officiated the service. He referred to the new governor by his familiar name of Rudy but also as the "father of the family of Minnesota." Perkovich's band, the Polka Mass-ters Orchestra, consisting of an accordionist, guitarist, bass player, and drummer, provided Yugoslavian ballads and church music to a crowd that overflowed the thousand-seat church.

After the service, Perpich, along with his wife, Lola; his daughter, Mary Sue; his son, Rudy Jr.; and his parents, Anton and Mary, was chauffeured to the inauguration, which was to take place at the state capitol at noon. Hibbing judge Gail Murray, one of the few female jurists in the state, administered the oath. Her inaugural role was a harbinger of the intentions of a governor whose appointments of women to the courts would reshape the state's judiciary, and who would appoint more women and minorities to official positions than any governor in Minnesota's history.

The capitol had the elbow room of a small-town gymnasium as several thousand people packed the marble rotunda and crowded the balconies to witness Perpich's remarks. The Hibbing High School Band fired up the crowd before and during the ceremony. Perpich wore a dark blue three-piece suit that he bought specially for the ceremony. As a student of gubernatorial history, Perpich joked with reporters that he was cautious about buying the suit. The last lieutenant governor to face similar circumstances in 1923 had purchased a new suit, only to have the then-governor change his mind about stepping down.

But Perpich's focus on his clothing purchase was more than superstition. His reservations about a new suit tied back to his childhood. So did much of what he said that day, and so did so much of what would become one of the most consequential gubernatorial tenures in Minnesota history.

Perpich had been raised in poverty in the iron mining location of Carson Lake, Minnesota. In high school, he always arrived early to shower before classes, something he could not do at home. For school pictures, he was among the many male students who shared one tie. A few years later, he purchased his father a necktie as a Father's Day gift. Anton Perpich scolded him for being so frivolous with money. When Rudy married, his father asked him to return a writing pen that had been his high school graduation gift, so that a younger brother could use it. For Rudy, a new suit was a big deal. Even as governor.

The political road to this moment was filled with setbacks and challenges. Perpich was defeated in his first attempt for the Hibbing School Board. He was booed in his hometown and across Minnesota when he became one of the first politicians in the country to voice opposition to the Vietnam War. But standing up to powerful interests was part of his political DNA, a trait he attributed to his father. Following an incident which caused damage to Perpich family property, a young Rudy had gone with his father to the powerful U.S. Steel's local Iron Range office to demand compensation and, more importantly, respect—something too seldom afforded to the working-class families who inhabited company houses, shopped at company stores, and played by company rules.

While waiting to be seen, they heard someone loudly remark from an inner office, "Let the hunkie wait." That "hunkie" was now the governor of Minnesota.[3]

As he took the stage, Perpich paid homage to the place from whence he came and the systems that allowed him to thrive. He pledged to work hard so future generations would have the same opportunities afforded to him and his brothers. Going against the advice of political advisers, Perpich had rejected a lengthy policy speech written for him detailing directives for his new administration. Instead, he offered a three-minute tribute to family, education, and the importance of the immigrant story to Minnesota's past and future.

> For this great honor I owe a debt of gratitude to the people of our state who provided us with an excellent educational system which allowed me, my brothers, and others of my generation to achieve the most of which we were capable.

Growing up in a house without plumbing on the edge of an open mining pit, his childhood instilled a deeply held belief in the responsibility of community, driven by his experience and those of his parents and other immigrants and their strong ties to family. Education had proven his "passport out of poverty" and fueled his core conviction that no child should suffer poverty as the result of the unemployment of their parents—as he and his brothers had experienced.

Public initiatives had allowed Rudy Perpich and his brothers to advance beyond humble origins. He received his education on the G.I. Bill and his first pair of eyeglasses through his elementary school.

> Forty-three years ago I entered kindergarten in a small school in Minnesota's Iron Range. At that time the nation was in the grip of the Great Depression. Millions were unemployed, many were ill-nourished or ill-housed, and few had any real economic security. As I entered class that day, my father was unemployed, and I spoke no English. And, yet, today, I have taken the oath of office as the 34th governor of Minnesota. This could not happen in many parts of the world.

Perpich reached the heart of his message: family. He proudly looked to his parents as the speech hit its climax, and the crowd rose to their feet as he paid tribute to the ones who had made this day possible.

But more importantly, I owe a debt to my dedicated parents, Mary and Anton Perpich. My father, an immigrant, was attracted to the United States by the opportunities he envisioned. My parents worked long hours under difficult conditions in order to secure a college education and assure a better way of life for their children. And I am very happy that they can both be here to see their oldest son become the governor of Minnesota.

CHAPTER 1

Heritage, Heroes, and Family

"It would be nice if we got married when it was still summer."
—*Mary Vukelich, Rudy's mother*

"Yes, it probably would be."
—*Anton Perpich, Rudy's father*

Few regions of Minnesota—or the nation—have produced the number and variety of major national personalities as the small town of Hibbing. From the heart of Minnesota's 110-mile-long Iron Range have come musicians Bob Dylan and Gary Puckett, athletes Roger Maris and Kevin McHale, and political and business personalities Jeno Paulucci and Vincent Bugliosi—all of Hibbing, plus Jessica Lange (from neighboring Cloquet) and Judy Garland (Grand Rapids). All were products of the public investment, ethnic diversity, and political radicalism that characterized the first half of the twentieth century in northeastern Minnesota.

Hibbing's unique blend of people, politics, and place would likewise make an indelible stamp on Minnesota's longest-serving governor, Rudy Perpich.

Iron Hills

Lying seventy miles northwest of Duluth, near Coleraine, and stretching northeast to Mesaba, the Mesabi Range runs through Itasca and St. Louis Counties in northeastern Minnesota, housing 4 percent of the state's population on 11 percent of the state's land. "The Range" originally referenced the region's high-grade iron ore but has come to signify the cluster of communities located within the region. Together, these towns and the area share a distinctive geological—but also political and social—formation that sets them apart from others in the state.[1]

Minnesota's Iron Range story began in 1890 when the Merritt family of Duluth discovered a large hematite ore deposit near Mountain Iron. Mining began soon thereafter. The first shipments left the region in October 1892.

The discovery attracted major industrial players to Minnesota. John D. Rockefeller was the first tycoon capitalist to enter the Mesabi drama. Several railroads serviced the Range in those early days, but the Merritts were dissatisfied with the Duluth and Winnipeg Railroad, feeling it was inadequate, and with the Duluth and Iron Range Railroad, feeling it threatened their own interests. As a solution, they proposed to build their own railroad line, the Duluth, Missabe, and Northern Railway, which would run to the docks of Duluth. They needed cash, however, and Rockefeller provided it. The deal would be their undoing.[2]

What money they had received ran out before the work was complete, and they needed more. Rockefeller agreed to help once more in return for stock in the railroad operations and in five of the mines the Merritts owned. The family agreed, and the Lake Superior Consolidated Iron Mining Company was formed. When the enterprise hit financial straits a final time, the Merritts were forced to sell their stock to Rockefeller. Rockefeller paid with what the Merritts alleged to be stock of two insolvent companies, and they filed suit for misrepresentation. Rockefeller countered, and, in the end, the Merritts were put out of the iron ore business.

Rockefeller now owned several mines and the railroad he needed—but not the steel mills he wanted to create a final product. He needed a partner, and he wasn't the only tycoon with eyes on the Iron Range.

Henry Oliver, whose furnaces in Pittsburgh required a steady supply of ore, first visited Minnesota in June 1892 for the Republican National Convention in Minneapolis. Seeing the value in a steady and independent source of ore, he formed the Oliver Iron Mining Company later that same year. Oliver could grow only so far on his own, so fellow magnate Andrew Carnegie negotiated an investment of $500,000 for half of the company's stock.

In 1896, Oliver and Carnegie leased ore production from Rockefeller's mines on a royalty basis of $.25 per ton, with a guaranteed minimum of 1.25 million tons, to be carried over the Rockefeller railroads. The overwhelming combination of Rockefeller, Oliver, and Carnegie caused the price of ore to plummet from $4 per ton to just $2.50 per ton, creating havoc in the steel market. Smaller mining companies were driven off the Iron Range, and the Oliver Iron Mining Company began buying properties forced into sale.

The final scene unfolded in 1901 with an enormous consolidation which incorporated the Lake Superior Consolidated Iron Mining Company, as well as Carnegie's and Oliver's interests, into United States Steel. It was the world's first $1 billion company and represented the greatest concentration of business interests in Iron Range history. The Oliver Iron Mining Company was established as a subsidiary of United States Steel, and the company oversaw forty-one mines, roughly a thousand miles of railroad, and 112 lake vessels in northeastern Minnesota alone.[3]

Through continued acquisitions, the Oliver Iron Mining Company controlled more than seven hundred million tons of ore reservoirs in northeastern Minnesota within a year. By 1908, the first report of the Minnesota Tax Commission found the Oliver Company held nearly 80 percent of the iron ore reserves on the Range. The number of smaller mining operations was dwindling, giving way to the tycoons, even as the Mesabi Range was recognized as the greatest center of iron ore production in the world.[4]

The need for labor drove the creation of towns along the Iron Range. The establishment of Hibbing and other nearby mining communities in the 1890s would result in the unique foreign-born population that historically characterized Iron Range communities. Ultimately, significant populations from more than thirty-five countries settled in the region.[5]

Those rough mining towns developed municipal services, paved roads, and public buildings over time. Their growth came fast. By 1910, Hibbing's population was nearly 9,000 residents, larger than Rochester in the southeast and only slightly smaller than St. Cloud in central Minnesota.[6]

The Third Wave

Immigration to the Range was driven by the rapidly developing iron mining industry but also followed broader state and national patterns. The gilded age of 1877–96 and the financial panic of 1893, which led to a national depression until 1897, limited the number of immigrants, but western and northern Europeans continued to move to the United States as they had since the 1850s. By 1910, immigrants from eastern and southern Europe made up 70 percent of those entering the country and constituted Minnesota's third major wave of immigration.[7]

Minnesota's first immigration wave came in the decade prior to the Civil War, after Minnesota became a territory in 1849. Anti-slavery Yankees—the Republicans—and middle-state and southern moderates—who identified as Democrats—represented the major forces of outside influx to the state. Their differences proved so great that the two parties drafted separate state constitutions. And since neither party would ever officially sign a compromised document, Minnesota had two constitutions until a consolidation was approved by constitutional amendment in 1974.[8]

The second wave of Minnesota immigration came after the Civil War. These newcomers were predominantly from Scandinavian countries, Germany, and Ireland, and were drawn to the rich farmland and the state's growing river communities.[9]

Minnesota's third wave included miners, lumberjacks, farmers, and Jewish immigrants from eastern Europe. By 1900, Minnesota was as ethnically diverse as any state in the union. Prior to the twentieth century, the Mesabi Range consisted mostly of "Old Americans" (those of the third generation or older), western and northern Europeans, and Italians and Poles. Now, Slavic and Latin immigrants arrived in greater numbers. Slovenians and Croatians made up the two largest ethnic groups of the Slavic nations, sharing a Roman Catholic bond. The Croatians came to the Range primarily from the provinces of Slavonia, Croatia, and Dalmatia. This wave of Minnesota immigration included members of the Skrbich, Pavelich, Perpich, Klobuchar, Vukelich, and Rogich families.[10]

The Range's New Deal

By the early twentieth century, the city of Hibbing had a reputation as a center for radical union organization, with many members of the United Mine Workers (UMW) and the Industrial Workers of the World (IWW) calling the city home. Unsuccessful strikes in 1905, 1907, and 1916 were crushed by the U.S. Steel and Oliver Mining companies, which hired vigilantes and even members of the Ku Klux Klan to suppress labor organization efforts.[11]

Progressive reformers, meanwhile, pursued less-confrontational means in opposing the mining companies and their influence over the daily lives of Range residents. John Lind was elected governor of Minnesota on a reformist platform in 1899 with the support of middle-class Americans and immigrants seeking a better living. Democrat John Johnson, elected in 1904 and the state's first governor to have been born in Minnesota (and the first governor to die while in office), found similar support by championing social issues.[12]

By 1912, the year of Theodore Roosevelt's third-party presidential campaign, an increasingly adept second-generation of Hibbing residents sought to wrest control of their municipal government from the "company men" who had run the city since its founding. If the movement had a face, it resembled Victor Power, elected mayor in 1913 and a champion for the working class. The decade following Power's election would be known as the Range's New Deal—a period marked by municipalities shaking loose the hold of mining tycoons and undertaking significant (sometimes lavish) civic improvements (paid for with mining taxation).

Power, dubbed "Hibbing's fighting mayor," won notoriety at home and throughout the state as "the little giant of the north." His mayoral term transformed Hibbing into "the richest village in the world." Power fought for a host of civic improvements across the Iron Range. Streets, parks, libraries, farmers' markets, athletic facilities, and—most notably—state-of-the-art educational facilities all comprised his legacy, and all were paid for in large part with hefty taxes on the mining industry.[13]

In 1922, Hibbing completed the construction of a $4 million high school and technical college, boasting an auditorium modeled after New York's Capitol Theatre, with hand-molded ceilings and cut-glass chandeliers imported from Belgium. The facility was hailed as the "richest gem in Minnesota's educational crown," helping to earn Hibbing the reputation as an attractive place to raise a young family.

Hope had led to the mass immigration that became the population of northeastern Minnesota—hope of a new world and a new life, and it was that hope that would establish the Perpich dynasty as well.

A Father, A Fighter

Anton Perpich was born on November 22, 1899, on a small farm near Krivi Put, Croatia. He spent his childhood working on his family's seventeen acres of rock and sparse farmland. The family of eleven (seven boys and two girls) raised their own food and lived in a two-room stone house consisting of a kitchen and a bedroom.[14]

His schooling was the equivalent of kindergarten through fourth grade. It was a three-kilometer walk to school through mountain passes. The students studied math, geography, and a place called America. Their teachers said America was full of opportunity, a place everyone should want to go.

As he grew older, Anton spent most of his time away from his house working in rail yards or lumber camps for up to nine months at a time. When he returned home, the days were filled with family and church gatherings on Sundays. Their meals were hearty and practical and included walnut bread, apple strudel, and sauerkraut—always lots and lots of sauerkraut.[15]

Croatia at the time was under Austrian control, with Hungarians to the east of the country and Italians in the area near the Adriatic Sea. Serbians also constituted a large minority. All visitors were welcomed by Anton's father—whom they called *Kumstvo*, meaning "Godfather" in Serbian and Croatian—as they made their way across the region. The Austro-Hungarian army occupied Serbia beginning in 1915, the same year that Anton went into the Austrian army after six weeks of training.[16]

Anton was sent to Romania to fight the Russians on the Eastern Front of World War I. The soldiers in his unit suffered brutal conditions, often surviving on a single piece of bread per day. The war—the suffering and death all around him—and ethnic conflicts in the Balkans would shape his life.[17]

The war ended on Armistice Day, 1918, and Anton served another month and a half, ending his service three days before Christmas. He then returned to Krivi Put, where conflict had taken a toll. His father urged him and his siblings to leave their homeland and seek a new life in America. So, in December 1920, at the age of twenty-one, Anton boarded a train bound for France. From there, he traveled across the Atlantic on *The Empress France*, a ship which made its way to England and eventually St. John's, Canada. Finally, a train ride took him the final miles from Canada to the United States of America.

Anton arrived in Sault Ste. Marie, Michigan, on Christmas Day. He had no intention of staying in America. Instead, Anton planned to earn $2,000 and return home to buy a nice piece of land.

Michigan led him to Duluth and eventually to Hibbing and the Iron Range. Anton found sporadic work in the mines and took shelter in a shanty owned by the Oliver Mining Company, along with immigrants from dozens of countries. All took their meals together, just as in his father's home. The work was hard, the days were long, and the new miners slept three to a bed, but everyone had plenty to eat.[18]

During this period, Anton moved from house to house while he worked in the mines for ten hours a day and attended school at night to get his citizenship papers. He learned English and civic affairs. It was through one of these moves that Anton met George Vukelich, a leader in the local struggle for miners' rights.

George became a mentor to Anton. He had been forced from the same region of Croatia in the early 1900s. His wife, Anna, followed him to the United States in 1910. Shortly thereafter the couple had a daughter, Mary, born in Carson Lake in June 1911. Anton couldn't have predicted how their lives would intertwine.

Of Love and Loss

As a child, Mary Vukelich was a diligent student with a bright future. She was going to be a schoolteacher.

Mary idolized her father, who spoke five languages and eventually rose to the position of mine supervisor. He traveled all over the world and was influential in the early organization of union miners. Often the miners gathered at the Vukelich house during the evening to discuss their plight.

During one of these sessions, George called for a strike until their latest demands were met. It wasn't long until the mining company's superintendent arrived at the Vukelich home, demanding George return to work. But he refused. The miners, on the other hand, wavered in their resolve. They had families and needed the income; they went back to work. George could only concede, and when he returned to work, he was demoted and sent back underground. He had lost.

There was no light at the end of this tunnel. While working underground shortly thereafter, George was struck in the leg by a log thrown from the top of a trestle. He continued working, but by the next day, the leg was blue, and he was forced to stop. Without penicillin or antibiotics, his condition worsened until the infection entered his heart, and he died after a short struggle. Mary Vukelich was fifteen years old, and she was devastated.[19]

On his deathbed, George made his wife promise she would continue their daughters' education. It was a promise Anna could not keep. As the oldest child remaining at home, Mary needed to go to work to support the family. She was forced out of school while in the eighth grade. George's death was devastating for the entire family, but the loss of Mary's dreams of education and becoming a teacher made her pain doubly felt.

The tragic circumstances surrounding the death of Mary's father, Anton's idol, brought an immediacy to the budding courtship between Mary and Anton. George died in January 1927. Seven months later, when Mary was just sixteen years old, Anton and Mary were married.

Their ceremony was on Saturday, August 13, at the Blessed Sacrament Church in north Hibbing. Because it was a Saturday and all their friends and family were working, the wedding celebration took place the next day in Letonia and included a kissing dance, singing, a Croatian accordion player, and plenty of food for everyone. Following tradition, friends and family gave what they had, roughly $2,000 in total, to afford the couple a stable start.

Mary Vukelich and Anton Perpich on their wedding day. Behind the couple is Anton's brother, Rudy, with Mary's siblings, left to right, Ann, Antonia, and George. *Courtesy Minnesota Discovery Center*

CHAPTER 2

Growing Up in Carson Lake

"Everybody was broke, but everybody was happy."
—Joe Yukich, childhood neighbor of Rudy Perpich

"For us, it was feast or famine, and it wasn't much feast but a hell of a lot of famine."

—Rudy Perpich

Along a township road near Carson Lake—a mining location six miles west of Hibbing—newlyweds Anton and Mary Perpich settled into a three-room apartment on the upper floor of a home owned by Mike and Dragica Skirbich, who lived downstairs. Anton was working underground in the Utica Mine at the time. The work was hard and monotonous, setting support posts, drilling, blasting, and hauling out material—only to do it all again for hours on end.

Carson Lake was a close-knit community where residents helped one another. Neighbors talked across the backyard fence, and everyone pitched in, including the kids. Families had large gardens and most kept a cow for milk and homemade dairy products. Everything was done sparingly, whether food, clothing, or transportation.

"You did with the least you possibly could. You walked to Hibbing if you didn't have the fifteen cents for the bus," recalled Mary's younger sister, Ann. "And if you had the fifteen cents, you were afraid to spend it."[1]

Throughout the country and across the Range, the years leading up to the Great Depression were challenging—and they were especially hard for young families. Farmers were losing land, animals were dying, and the Iron Range had one of the highest rates of unemployment in the state. By 1932, unemployment rates reached nearly 30 percent statewide and 70 percent on the Iron Range. Survival fears were real.[2]

On the night of June 27, 1928, Ann was sleeping at home when she heard a rapping on the window. It was Anton. He was calling out, "Mary has a son! Mary has a son!"

Rudolph George Perpich—named after Anton's brother—was born into this hardscrabble environment. He was a good-sized but colicky child, with dark hair and big dark eyes.[3]

Shortly after, Anton and Mary moved with their one-year-old son from their rented apartment to a small, tan, three-room house they had purchased. There were two wood stoves, one in the kitchen for cooking as well as heating, another in the combined living and dining room for heating. The kitchen was sparsely furnished with a dry sink, a table with chairs, and a cabinet where dishes were stored.

Off the dining room was a small bedroom with a bed and a crib—and eventually a second bed as their family grew. A small chest of drawers with a dresser sat in the corner. There was a wooden sidewalk that led from the street to a small porch, and a stone step led into the kitchen from the side of the house. Mary would strive to make this home the center of her family's universe, a place of shelter from the economic storm that was brewing outside.[4]

On October 29, 1929, prices on the New York Stock Exchange plummeted. Investors unloaded sixteen million shares on a single day that came to be known as "Black Tuesday." The stock market crash threw the United States into financial calamity and triggered the largest economic downturn in the country's history. The Great Depression left one in four workers unemployed nationwide. Especially hard hit was northeastern Minnesota's Arrowhead region, where the mining and timber industries were rocked by falling prices, declining demand, and mechanization.

Families across the Range had their worlds turned upside down. Miners like Anton brought their lunch buckets to the mines and returned home with any leftovers—the family checking every day for scraps when the pail hit the kitchen table.

Two years after Rudy's birth, Mary and Anton had a daughter, Marian—whom the family called Bunny. Marian died in infancy of an infection following hospitalization for burns suffered in a tragic accident after she mistook scalding water for bathwater.[5]

Mary and Anton would have three additional sons, Tony (1932), George (1933), and Joseph (1941). All learned a life of hard work and believed in the promise of education. Like most in their village, the Perpiches had a huge garden and kept animals, including one particularly mean cow that Rudy was responsible for. One day, the cow pinned Rudy against the stall, between its horns, and Mary had to run with a broomstick to get him free. Rudy and his brothers slaughtered animals with their father, milked cows, churned butter, and chopped wood to prepare for the winter.

Rudy's youngest sibling, Joseph, years later would liken the period to the popular 1950s Disney cartoon: "Cinderella, Cinderella. Night and day, it's Cinderella." Money was sparse, so the family did everything they could to survive.

George, Rudy,
and Tony, ca. late
1930s. *Cour-
tesy Minnesota
Discovery Center*

They saved every loose coin toward Mary's primary goal: she was determined to ensure that all her kids would be educated.[6]

In their kitchen, a small door near the sink led to the cellar, which housed garden produce and the wine and sauerkraut they made each fall. The family canned peaches and pears, which they bought, along with blueberries and strawberries they picked amid swarms of biting mosquitoes.

A round table and chairs filled the small dining room where politics consumed discussions after dinner. They had a radio which broadcast network news commentator Hans von Kaltenborn, a respected source of news and political commentary for the Perpiches and many other families of the era.

The Carson Lake location was home to several growing families. That meant lots of kids, so along with the work, there was also fun. There was skating and sledding in the winter and biking and swimming in the summer.

One of those neighborhood kids was Frank Ongaro, who met Rudy as a youngster at Leetonia Elementary School in Carson Lake. Ongaro would become a lifelong friend and decades later served as a commissioner for the Iron Range Resource and Rehabilitation Board (IRRRB) under Perpich. The two grew up playing ball together, attending the same elementary classes, and sharing chores. They spent hours walking in the woods, just the two of them.

It's ironic, then, that Rudy's only schoolboy physical scrap was the time he punched Frank in the nose at Leetonia. Rudy's customarily nonviolent nature extended to animals as well. As a child, he had a little .22-caliber rifle, with which he shot and killed a bird. The overwhelming remorse he felt as he examined the dead creature led him to never again shoot the rifle, which he gave away. He didn't object to other people hunting, but he wouldn't do it himself.

The bonds between the immigrant children of Carson Lake instilled a loyalty within Perpich that served him his entire life—leading to accusations of cronyism by his critics. For Rudy, however, it seemed only natural to lean on others who had shared the hardships of his upbringing while he rose through the political ranks.

Plight of the Working Man

Rudy's early years were a complicated time, with great change sweeping the world. Going back to the Victor Power administration, Hibbing's working class had been cautious about joining radical political organizations because of intimidation, arrests, and even murder. Nativist groups, such as the Ku Klux Klan, posed real danger to immigrant populations.

After World War I, however, miners and the working class in Hibbing increasingly saw the positive impacts that movements such as Power's progressive party could have on their daily lives. A burgeoning relationship was forming among Power's progressivist party, the socialist party, and unionized organizations, such as the Industrial Workers of the World (IWW), leading to local support for an emerging third political party, the Nonpartisan League. In 1924 the coalition merged with the Union Labor Party of Duluth into the Farmer-Labor Party, which would become a leading voice for progressive reformers in Minnesota politics.

The Farmer-Labor Party, which would become the largest third party in the United States by the 1930s, started as a small group of reform-minded farmers on the North Dakota prairie. Their aim was to combat corporate monopolies, such as the Great Northern Railroad and the Minneapolis Grain Exchange, which they felt were unfairly reaping profits from their crops. They blamed North Dakota's Republican Party for not protecting the rights of laborers and farmers and hoped to limit the corporate excesses that both the Democratic and Republican Parties were unwilling to address.

In the early 1920s, these North Dakota farmers made a political alliance with future St. Paul mayor William Mahoney's Minnesota Association of Labor, making the Farmer Labor Coalition a formal entity. By 1924, the Nonpartisan League formally changed its name to the Farmer-Labor Party.

The group called for state ownership of grain elevators, mills, and packing-houses—as well as state-controlled banks and crop insurance. This message brought together large portions of Hibbing's ethnic populations. Hibbing's labor unions also helped in the rise of the Farmer-Labor movement, with Victor Power's progressive administration using union labor to construct major projects such as the high school and new city hall.

Statewide, however, the Farmer-Labor movement's political momentum was stunted until Floyd B. Olson announced he would run for governor under the party's banner. Olson had served as Hennepin County attorney since 1922, where he gained notoriety by indicting key leaders of the Ku Klux Klan, earning him a reputation as a hard-nosed reformer and friend of the working class.

Olson included Hibbing resident Elmer Johnson as warehouse commissioner to help galvanize Farmer-Labor support on the Range. During his 1930 campaign for governor, Olson made numerous trips to the Iron Range, and Hibbing became a major battleground between the third-party Farmer-Laborites and the Republicans.

There were union rallies and family picnic events. Olson was gaining steam across the state and achieving popularity in Hibbing and other cities on the Iron Range. When the results of the gubernatorial election were tallied in November 1930, Olson achieved an overwhelming victory in Hibbing and would go on to crush his Republican opponent by 473,154 votes to 289,000 votes. Governor Olson would reward the people of Hibbing for their support.

It was a time of integration into Minnesota's political system, with newly enfranchised women and ethnic minorities providing powerful voting blocs that influenced Range politics for decades to come. And Olson's unabashedly progressive politics would influence generations of politicians, including a young Rudy Perpich.[7]

"The income tax is the most just tax thus far devised because it is the most equitable tax; it is based on ability to pay," Olson declared in his second inaugural address. He went on to argue that "unemployment creates misery among those unemployed, adds to the burdens of the taxpayers . . . and injures business because of the lack of buying power of those unemployed."[8]

Income tax and unemployment insurance were two issues Rudy Perpich would wrestle with when he one day occupied the same office as his political hero. Meanwhile, Anton, who served as secretary of the Croatian Fraternal Order—where Rudy eventually became an active member as well—viewed the unions, Floyd B. Olson, and the populist movement of the Farmer-Labor Party (not the Democrats) as friends of working-class families like his own.[9]

The praise Rudy heard as a child for Olson's ideas to provide public works jobs through highway construction, improve unemployment benefits, and enact a progressive income tax—along with Farmer-Laborites' support for the rights of workers and the promotion of civil rights—would stay with him and echo in his proposals throughout his career.

Childhood friend George Rogich remembers this environment as the political breeding ground for the young Rudy Perpich. "We were real active," Rogich recounted. "We went door-to-door. Can you imagine [kids] going door-to-door handbilling for Floyd Olson?" Rogich and others crawled up in the rafters of the Hibbing Memorial Building and listened to the political and union conventions when they came to town. "Out of that crucible of fire that we were raised in, we got Rudy Perpich."[10]

His Mother's Dream

When Rudy started grade school, the family didn't have plumbing at home. The elementary school had huge (at least through Rudy's kindergarten eyes), tiled bathrooms with toilet tanks mounted in a line near the ceiling—all flushing automatically and simultaneously. The sound was deafening to a little kid. Rudy had never heard a toilet flush before, and the first time he did, he ran home in a panic. He was five years old, and he was scared to death.

School was a place for young mining-location children to get a meal, take a shower, and receive medical care. Most came from small houses that weren't insulated, with heat only in the kitchen, so the warmth of the schools was inviting. For Rudy, school symbolized hope for the future, a sentiment he did not associate with the mine where his father worked. He saw mining as perpetuating the same hopelessness his ancestors had known for three hundred years in Croatia.

In the Depression era of Rudy's childhood, school provided a stable environment, and education offered a passport out of poverty. The teachers were pleasant, and the kids got along because they liked being there. The saddest day of any year for Rudy was the day school was let out for summer.

Mary, motivated by her own lack of education, instilled a fierce commitment to learning in her four sons. She was interested in one thing: that her children were going to finish high school, graduate from college, and go to graduate school. She saw systems of active discrimination toward eastern

Europeans, and the way to overcome that discrimination, she believed, was to get an education. "It would be better to be dead than not to be educated," Mary would tell her boys. And she meant it.[11]

She was sending them to exceptional public schools. The Iron Range schools were mostly constructed between 1910 and 1925, largely at the tax expense of the mining industry. Mining dollars also furnished the construction of junior colleges in Hibbing, Virginia, Eveleth, and Coleraine. Because of the huge tax revenue available, schools boasted auditoriums, gymnasiums, swimming pools, greenhouses, cafeterias, and science training centers. Many, such as those in Hibbing, included medical and dental offices.[12]

Supervised recreation programs, extensive athletic offerings, public speaking clubs, band, orchestra, and student-led newspapers encouraged a well-rounded academic experience that made Iron Range schools the envy of almost all others in the state. The smaller population, in comparison to metropolitan schools, allowed greater individual involvement. Partly as a result, the number of high school graduates entering college and university from the Iron Range was as high as any in the country.[13]

To put it in numbers: during this time, spending at Hibbing High School totaled $827 per pupil, compared to the national average of $487. Teachers at Hibbing High School earned the second-highest wages in the United States, at $1,415 per year, which was 75 percent higher than the state average. Wages, along with the extravagance of the high school building itself, attracted the best and brightest teachers to Hibbing. In the 1950s, retired Harvard president James B. Conant named Hibbing High School as one of a handful of schools nationally that had done extraordinary things for kids.[14]

Despite the opulence Hibbing High School offered, Rudy seldom if ever spoke in later years about its beauty. Instead, he talked about showers, food, and warmth. Most of all, he talked about the teachers.

Rudy's brother Joseph credited the teachers for doing everything they could to create a better future for their students. Most of them were women who in a later generation might have been doctors, lawyers, or public servants. Their limited professional options in the 1930s and 1940s worked to the benefit of their students. The school system gave Rudy and others a confidence beyond the scope of an Iron Range mining town.

Young Rudy flourished. He was a voracious reader, bringing home armloads of books at a time. He would read behind the stove at night—the only warm place in the house. He read about Napoleon, Wellington, and President George Washington. He'd read social and political histories—but he never read fiction, which he viewed as wasting an opportunity to learn.[15]

Frank Ongaro and Rudy played on the basketball team together as they transitioned to Lincoln Junior High School in north Hibbing, and Rudy was a standout student. "He had those scholarship pins that you would receive," Ongaro remembered. "He had his bronze, silver, and gold pins—and he had an American Legion award for being an outstanding student athlete."

Rudy was proud and surprised by the recognition, viewing himself as a little-regarded underdog. "All of the kids from the mining locations had that inferiority complex," Ongaro said. But as Rudy continued to excel in sports and academics, his confidence grew.[16]

Rudy's fellow immigrant students were a close group, but Rudy gained notoriety. "He was a good athlete, a very good student, and extremely popular—besides, very good looking. The girls liked him," remembered classmate Norma McKanna. "Everyone knew who Rudy Perpich was. He had a stature about him even at that young age." It was a stature that served him well later in life.[17]

Norma McKanna was Serbian, and Rudy was Croatian, but shared struggles built bonds stronger than any ethnic difference among the community's kids. They felt a special obligation to do the most with their opportunities because of the uncontrollable hardships they endured at home. Rudy, as his family's oldest child, felt that sense of duty more than most. He was expected to set the example for his brothers, to establish a family tradition.

There was one main store in Carson Lake while Rudy was growing up—T. B. Hamre's grocery store—which also served as a tavern, post office, and gas station. After doing chores at home, Rudy sold groceries, pumped gas, listened to old men talk politics, and made deliveries. He listened intently. Rudy learned how to deal with people and how they behaved when trying to gain an advantage in barter or debate.[18]

One day, while making grocery deliveries, he decided to take his youngest brother, Joseph, in the company truck—a special treat for a family that didn't own a car. Toward the day's end, Rudy let the truck idle at the top of a gentle incline in front of the Perpich residence while he visited a neighbor.

Joseph, unattended, grabbed the stick and pushed the clutch, as he had watched his older brother do. Rudy came out in time to see the truck slowly roll down the hill, and he gave chase. As Rudy ran furiously behind, the vehicle picked up speed, eventually slamming into a pile of rocks. When the dust settled, Anton was furious—and so was Tom Hamre, the truck's owner. Rudy paid for the damage out of his meager salary, never letting his brother forget the incident. For the rest of Joseph's life, through all the work he would do on his brother's campaigns, he was forever paying Rudy back, but Joseph remembered those days fondly. "It was always fun. There was always excitement with him."[19]

Like his brothers, classmates saw young Rudy as a leader, partly due to his stature. People looked up to him—often literally—and Rudy relished this role.

The Perpich family at their home in Carson Lake, ca. 1940s. *Courtesy Minnesota Discovery Center*

Many location kids were shy and suffered from inferiority complexes because of their humble upbringings and unfamiliarity with English. But not Rudy. He took charge.

Mary was extremely proud of her children. "My Rudy. My Tony. My Georgie. My Joey" was how she referred to them, and nothing in her life made her prouder than their academic achievements. All four of her sons grew up to have professional degrees, with the three oldest sons earning dental degrees and the youngest becoming a doctor of psychiatry and a lawyer. Decades after her own father's death and her untimely departure from schooling, Mary accomplished her hopes through her children.

Kitchen Table Politics

Franklin D. Roosevelt had been swept into office in November 1932 on a promise of strong federal action to address the nation's woes. He offered a stark contrast to the comparatively laissez-faire administration of Republican president Herbert Hoover. FDR's New Deal contended that economic recovery required government intervention; he proposed a series of government-funded programs designed to get people back to work.

The large-scale building projects initiated by the New Deal across the country stimulated the mining and timber industries of the Iron Range and put people to work. Locally, the Chisholm Post Office and Hibbing Disposal Plant (wastewater treatment) and the Hibbing Memorial Building, which became a center of athletic, social, and educational activity, were financed by agencies of the New Deal.

The Works Progress Administration (WPA), the Public Works Administration (PWA), and the Civilian Conservation Corps (CCC) provided critical employment. Sixty-five thousand people were employed by the WPA on 1,700 projects across Minnesota in 1935 and 1936 alone. Many families pieced together a living through sporadic work from local governments and/or the WPA/PWA.[20]

For the Perpiches and many others in the Depression-era Iron Range, politics had become a way of life. Countless location children received their political education around the dining room table, watching their parents study English and learn the basics of government in their adopted homeland. Rudy's childhood friend Norma McKanna recalled fondly the evenings spent teaching her father and feeding her own growing interest in government. In the background, FDR's voice occasionally crackled through a superheterodyne radio receiver (often called "superhets") while delivering a fireside chat.

"Mama didn't care where you were, but you had better be home to listen to the president," she remembered.[21]

The Perpich family listened to "Kaltenborn Edits the News" and discussed politics at home—especially Franklin and Eleanor Roosevelt. "And they thought an awful lot about them. They really liked their politics and what they were doing with the country at a time when the country was really at a bad place," remembered Mary's sister, Ann.[22]

"So, from my father, we got the political DNA, and from my mother, we got the academic DNA," recalled Joseph Perpich. "And that informed all discussions in the house at all times. My father and mother were New Deal Democrats. Roosevelt was savior to them, and they revered him."

But the conversations went beyond America. Anton taught his children about global history and the ethnic conflicts he witnessed during his own childhood. "That is in the past," Anton would say. "It simply must be given up." And the Croatian immigrant miner practiced what he preached. He made a point of inviting his Serbian friends into the conversation—people who came from a country that Croatians had long considered their enemy. "And there was never any, ever any, kind of ethnic animosity that was permitted at our kitchen table," Joseph recalled.[23]

At Tom Hamre's tavern, the men gathered to read the newspapers, discuss the latest politics, and debate. There were newspapers in Serbian, Croatian, and Slovenian, as well as the union-published *Worker's Battle.*

Nationwide, unemployment reached 25 percent by the time Roosevelt entered office in 1933, with the United States in the worst economic crisis in the nation's history. By the middle of the decade, unemployment topped 70 percent on the Iron Range.[24]

Industries other than mining were unable to provide jobs for the unemployed, so the out-of-work were looking more and more to city councils, school boards, and county commissions for employment and public relief. It was an accepted reality that to secure this work, political influence was necessary, which led immigrant groups to vote and organize blocs. In turn, these groups backed candidates of their own ethnicity who would distribute the patronage to their own. A full-fledged spoils system was a political reality on the Range.[25]

One of the most obvious outcomes of these dire conditions was the antagonism between different groups of foreign-born individuals. Unlike in the Perpich household, ethnic animosity, race relations, and religious prejudices were prevalent across the Range during this time more than any other in the area's history.[26]

While Anton Perpich was adamantly proud that he would not take public assistance, young Rudy would see the power of government to be a force for good in people's lives—an idea he would carry with him his entire life.

Military Dealings

Rudy graduated high school in June 1946, along with his friend Frank Ongaro. Rudy was resolved to join the army, expecting a G.I. Bill college education to follow, but Frank pushed back. He was playing on two different softball teams and a baseball team and wasn't ready to enlist just yet.

By July, Rudy was growing impatient.

"When are we going to go?" Rudy pressured Frank. "I'm ready to go. If you're not going to go, I'm going to take off."

Rudy convinced Frank to give him a ride into town so he could fill out papers at the Wilson Fire Hall. Frank went upstairs to the recruiter's office and waited for Rudy. At the last minute, Frank conceded and asked if it was possible for him to enlist too. Frank was only seventeen, with his eighteenth birthday a month away, so he needed his parents' permission.

Frank found his father shopping in downtown Hibbing. After obtaining his signature, Frank hurried back to Carson Lake to tell his mother, who was left sobbing at the news. By 2:00 that same afternoon, Rudy and Frank were on a Greyhound bus bound for Fort Snelling.

Rudy's plan was simple: he'd serve twenty-four months in the military in exchange for forty-eight months of schooling under the G.I. Bill. But that first evening in the barracks, a bunkmate came back in from a wild binge, drunk and vomiting all night. Rudy told Frank the next morning that he was in for eighteen months and no more, regardless of what Frank did. He was already having enough, and the shorter stay would still fund a college degree.

The pair were sworn into the United States Army at Fort Snelling but wouldn't receive their uniforms until arriving at Fort Riley, Kansas. There, they learned they were both on the list to complete basic training at Fort Dix, New Jersey, in the same company but in different squads.

At the end of basic training, Frank was ordered to Korea. Rudy, however, stayed in America, kept from the front lines by his ability to type. Rudy's mother had insisted that he take typing in high school—something he hated because he was one of the only boys in the class. But the skill kept him stateside serving in a clerks' unit, while the buddy he convinced to join the army with him was headed overseas.[27]

Rudy had never been away from home. He wrote to his mother each week and talked about his hopes and dreams: he was going to get educated and do something to make a difference. But that resolve did not spare him from homesickness.

During that first Christmas away, Rudy longed for home. One day, he marched into his barracks, packed his bag, and announced that he was going home. The army wouldn't give him leave for Christmas, but Rudy objected. Without leave, he boarded a train for home.

In response, his squad—deciding that if Rudy could go, they could go—packed their bags as well. The entire squad was absent without leave. The penalties could have been severe. When Rudy returned, he was hauled in front of the colonel for punishment.

"Perpich, I'm going to make your life miserable," the colonel threatened.

Rudy replied, "You can do it to me, Sir, but how is it going to look on your record that the whole group under your command went AWOL?"

It was an example of his natural political instinct. The colonel, perhaps reluctantly, agreed. Instead, he punished Rudy with kitchen patrol.[28]

Eventually, in December 1947, Rudy and Frank were honorably discharged from the United States Army and headed home.[29]

College Life

During the summer following their military service, Frank and Rudy went from town to town, taking in seasonal celebrations across the Range. On the Fourth of July, Rudy and a friend visited Keewatin, which was having a street dance. Strolling down Main Street, they came to Chappelle's Sweet Shop—a drugstore with a soda fountain—and Rudy walked in. The friend Rudy was with knew the woman working behind the counter. They sat down, and Rudy was introduced to Delores Simich, who went by the nickname Lola. They talked for a while and hung around while Lola worked, returning to the counter in between waiting on customers.

Rudy asked Lola to come to the street dance after she was done with work, offering to wait for her shift to end. She did, and they danced. Later that night, Rudy told his friend, "I'm going to marry that woman."[30]

Throughout the remainder of that summer, Rudy returned to Chappelle's Sweet Shop often. Anton, pointing to the family's '36 Chevrolet Sedan, would shake his head and say "You know that car there? It can go to Keewatin by itself." From their first date forward, neither would date anyone else.[31]

"To him it was love at first sight," said Rudy's son, Rudy Perpich Jr. "For Lola, maybe second sight."[32]

Rudy would regularly bring his youngest brother—known to the family as Joey—along to Keewatin. Thirteen years younger than Rudy, Joey was crazy about Lola because she made the best malts. Being Rudy's brother, he got a bigger glass with a thicker malt than anyone. Next door to the malt shop was a theater, where the couple would take Joey to see matinees.[33]

That fall, Lola returned to Keewatin High School for her senior year, while Rudy and Frank enrolled in Hibbing Junior College, the two once again

Lola Simich, 1950. *Courtesy Minnesota Discovery Center*

together playing football and basketball in addition to their studies. Rudy was going into dentistry and Frank into education. Rudy took two years of pre-dentistry at Hibbing. Lola would join Rudy at Hibbing Junior College after graduating from high school.

Rudy honed his leadership skills and political aptitude during his time at Hibbing Junior College, which was housed at Hibbing High School. He led a student strike, calling for college students to be permitted to smoke and to have their own space within the high school—in short, to be treated as adults. His peers elected him student body president in recognition of his leadership. Ironically, Rudy didn't smoke.

Because of the low cost at Hibbing Junior College ($25 per semester including books, according to Frank Ongaro) and the fact that Rudy was able to live at home, he saved his G.I. Bill money for the four years he would spend in Wisconsin, where he enrolled in the dental school of Marquette University in Milwaukee.

After graduating from Hibbing Junior College, Lola worked for the Hanna Mining Company in its IBM processing unit and waited for Rudy to return from Marquette. She visited him occasionally and sent him care packages often.

Rudy worked constantly. He had a job in the dorms and another in the cafeteria; he worked cleaning the Eagles Club and as a line inspector at a beer bottling company in Milwaukee, where he would sit for hours watching the bottles go by.

At a girls' sorority in Marquette, his size and strength proved an asset when he was hired to do all the heavy lifting and wash the huge pots in the kitchen. In between the time when the dishes were washed and the food was served, there were some spare moments, so Rudy was assigned to work at the end of the line putting parsley on plates—just to keep him busy. One day, the sorority's leadership met, looking to cut costs, and someone stood up and said, "Get rid of that big guy that just puts parsley on plates."[34]

Rudy graduated from the Marquette School of Dentistry in the spring of 1954 and returned to Hibbing to resume his courtship of Lola Simich and start his new life. He opened a dental practice upon his return, and the young couple married on September 4, 1954.

– CHAPTER 3 –

The Senate Years

"He was always more political than he was dental."
—Norma "Nonnie" McKanna, longtime friend of Rudy Perpich

For Rudy and Lola Perpich, the first years of marriage were a mix of hope and hardships. The young couple first rented a basement apartment so full of mold that they had to move out after less than six months. They settled into a small First Avenue apartment in Hibbing. "Boy, I remember it was tough," Joseph Perpich recalled of the early years between his oldest brother and his new sister-in-law. "It started, and they worked hard."

As the couple got on their feet financially, Rudy found clever ways to show his care without breaking the bank. "I will never forget his present for Lola one Christmas: piano lessons. That was exciting, but it could be paced out in terms of payment," Joseph remembered.[1]

Rudy put everything he had into starting his new dental practice. He gained experience at the expense of friends and family while hoping word of mouth would spread.

"He practiced a lot on me and my brothers," Joseph laughed years later. "Everybody got their teeth done, whether they wanted it or not."[2]

Perpich hung a shingle at 301 East Howard Street, in downtown Hibbing, on the second floor of the Victor Power Building—a space shared with Merchants and Miners State Bank and Jack Fena's law office.[3]

The office was spartan, with a couple of small patient rooms and a waiting room that held only a few people. Perpich devoted every minute he could to establishing his fledgling practice. He worked from seven in the morning until six or seven o'clock in the evening, five days a week. On Saturdays, he would work until two in the afternoon and sometimes later, "depending on the toothaches." His work ethic, apparent early on, would become one of his defining traits.[4]

"Nobody could work harder [than] my brother. [He] did twenty-hour days all of his life," remembered Joseph. "It was just extraordinary—the stamina. And he had visions which he could communicate. He was very much a people person."[5]

Despite the apolitical nature of dentistry, young Rudy didn't avoid controversy. He entered the national fluoride controversy, which was a significant public health issue in the United States in the 1950s. Fluoride today is a common additive in toothpaste and water supplies for the purpose of preventing cavities. At the time, however, some scientists opposed the mineral additive, claiming that it caused health problems. Conspiracy theorists asserted fluoride usage was part of a Communist scheme to sabotage American health. Rudy—ahead of the curve—made sure that residents of the rural areas around Hibbing, especially children, had access to fluoride tablets.[6]

But even Rudy had to take some time away from work. Like many newlyweds in the 1950s, Rudy and Lola would get together with other young couples in a group they called the "Sewing Club." The women gathered in the living room and talked recipes and children, while the men played cards in the kitchen. Conversation often strayed toward politics, with Rudy using the group—which would become the core of his "kitchen cabinet" throughout the next four decades of his political career—as a sounding board for new ideas.

Rudy and Lola Perpich, early in their marriage. *Courtesy Minnesota Discovery Center*

One night, Rudy announced that he had decided to run for public office. "Something irritated him, which made him think he should run for the school board," remembered Norma McKanna, who, along with her husband, was a member of the Sewing Club. "Everybody said, 'You're what?!'" But Rudy had made up his mind. "No, I think I am going to do that," Rudy matter-of-factly reiterated.[7]

"He was always more political than he was dental," McKanna recalled of her longtime friend.[8]

Fateful First Steps

"Education was very important to us," Joseph Perpich remembered. "It was my mother's dream, and we owed a lot to the school system. My brother wanted to be on the board to open it up—to make sure there were opportunities for kids to see that you could go on (to college), no matter what your background was."

Perpich imagined how, through the school board, he could benefit Iron Range students and teachers alike.[9]

"And, as was typical, everyone in my family thought, 'What in the world is he doing? He has made it. He is a dentist. He is on Howard Street. What more could you ask?' My mother was very much against this. He had the political DNA from my dad."[10]

Perpich's message in his first campaign for public office was straightforward: "Elect me because I am a product of the system, and I will make sure that this system will work so more and more kids can be like me."[11]

On Friday, April 29, 1955, an ad ran in the *Hibbing Tribune* for Dr. Rudy Perpich for school board director. The ad touted Perpich as a graduate of Hibbing High School and Junior College as well as Marquette University, a veteran, and a "married and practicing dentist in Hibbing." His "program" consisted of a revision of teacher's retirement, just compensation for teachers, and state aid for junior colleges. "It's time for a change, thereby enabling the adoption of newer policies!" the ad told voters.[12]

Less than a month later, the campaign had run its course unsuccessfully. Rudy Perpich lost that first bid for elected office on May 17, 1955. Friends knew the setback would be temporary. Perseverance had defined Perpich since childhood, and second chances would ultimately come to define his political career. "I may not have made it this time," he said, "but I'm going to get in there again." It would be twenty-three years and a rise to the governorship before he experienced defeat at the polls a second time.[13]

The following year, he expanded his campaign for the nonpartisan office and touted himself as an "independent" candidate supported by labor, small business owners, farmers, and "the professions." Like Anton, Rudy Perpich

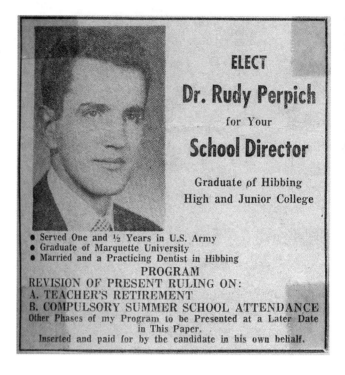

ELECT

Dr. Rudy Perpich

for Your

School Director

Graduate of Hibbing
High and Junior College

- Served One and ½ Years in U.S. Army
- Graduate of Marquette University
- Married and a Practicing Dentist in Hibbing

PROGRAM
REVISION OF PRESENT RULING ON:
A. TEACHER'S RETIREMENT
B. COMPULSORY SUMMER SCHOOL ATTENDANCE
Other Phases of my Program to be Presented at a Later Date
in This Paper.
Inserted and paid for by the candidate in his own behalf.

had been active in the Croatian Fraternal Order, so his support for labor was instinctive. However, combining small business owners, farmers, and professionals as a base of support was unusual for a candidate in Hibbing in 1956.[14]

"At the time, there was a great divide between professionals and non-professionals. If you became a professional, usually you went to a country club. You lived in a certain part of town. My father didn't accept that class divide," Rudy Jr. reflected on his father's early political career decades later. "He was a professional, but they still were friends of the people they grew up with. He didn't forget his people, [and] my mother didn't forget her people. They didn't try to become something they were not."[15]

Perpich ran with the support of teachers, custodians, and the school district's non-contract employees. "They almost drafted him to run because they weren't getting anyplace with the board members," remembered childhood friend Frank Ongaro.[16]

Another childhood friend, George Rogich, grew up beside the Perpiches in Carson Lake and would work on campaigns throughout Rudy's political career. He remembers how the work ethic, shoe-leather tactics, and appeal to everyday voters in those first school board campaigns came to embody Rudy's methods for the rest of his career.

After assessing his 1955 defeat, Perpich and his "kitchen cabinet" expanded their approach in 1956. "When he ran the second time, we beat the bushes. We went to French Township, way out to Side Lake," George Rogich remembered. Often, the response from voters was surprise. Many weren't focused on the local elections but took to the polls with a little reminder. So Perpich and his team went door-to-door to raise awareness. "We would go to Home Acres in Hibbing—where all the proletariat lived—farming country, [and] Maple Hill."[17]

The hard work paid off on Tuesday, May 14, 1956, when Rudy Perpich was elected to his first political office as a member of the Hibbing School Board. Perpich won one of two seats in a six-candidate field by fewer than 150 votes. At Kelly Lake, where many former residents of his hometown of Carson Lake had purchased residential lots (offered for $150 when the increasing size of surrounding mines required that Carson Lake be moved), Perpich collected more than 80 percent of the vote. It wouldn't be the last time that Perpich tipped a close election by drawing in voters with whom he shared an emotional connection.[18]

Later that week, he received a congratulatory letter from Charles E. Taylor, president of the First National Bank of Hibbing. "It was a pleasure to learn of your election," Taylor wrote. "The voters chose correctly, as we feel that you are well qualified to ably fulfill this important public responsibility." Taylor, along with other bankers and businessmen who had enjoyed favor with the Hibbing School Board, might soon have second thoughts.[19]

More Grift than Gift

Shortly after finishing school and returning to Hibbing, Perpich had gone to a local bank, inquiring about a $10,000 loan to set up his new dental office. The bank turned him down, knowing the young Perpich did not have any family money to fall back on if his practice faltered. Perpich instead secured funding from a Duluth firm and, in the process, developed a grudge over what he perceived as a personal slight. It was a habit he'd never fully break.

"That one bank gets all the school business. That doesn't sound fair. I think we should divide some of this business," the newly elected Perpich told Norma McKanna. "And he did. One of Rudy's favorite sayings was, 'don't get even, [get ahead].' I always chuckle when I hear it. That was one time that he did [get even]."[20]

When Perpich joined the Hibbing School Board, goods and services were acquired through an open contract process rather than competitive bidding. Perpich realized the district was overspending as a result, wasting money that could be spent on education. The first Christmas he was on the school board,

Tony, Rudy, Joe, and George during Rudy's school board years. *Courtesy Minnesota Discovery Center*

Rudy and Lola were overwhelmed by the gifts from local companies doing business with the school. Curiously, as he advocated that contracts for coal, paper, and other products should go out for bid when they came up for renewal, the flood of gifts dried up.

"It was something that had been done for years. My father came in and changed it. He was kind of an outsider," Rudy Jr. recounted. For years, a steady stream of gifts helped to keep lucrative contracts in place without a second thought to the district's spending. "My father said, 'Hey, this is not fair.' He felt they had a duty to the kids to get the best deal they could and have as much money as they could for the students."[21]

Perpich also committed himself to researching every agenda item before attending a meeting. "That guy could read and read. He stay[ed] up all night reading that stuff," Ongaro recalled. "He told how little some of the school board members knew about what was going on, and he always read everything to be sure he knew what [was] happening."[22]

Ongaro, who would work closely with Perpich throughout his entire political career, had just finished graduate school when he returned to the Iron Range looking for a teaching position. He applied to the Hibbing School District, where Perpich had influence over the hiring process.[23]

Ongaro, like many of Perpich's friends and allies, benefited from his relationship with Perpich. To Perpich, providing opportunities to those he knew was a way to return years of kindness and trust. It was his way of investing in those who had invested in him. But others would decry this pattern as nepotism and cronyism.

A Friend to Teachers

Perpich spent six years on the Hibbing School Board. He felt the teachers in the Hibbing school system—many of whom had been with the district for years—were underpaid and underappreciated.

"When he got on the school board, he was appalled to find out what very small pension and other benefits they got," McKanna recalled.

> He used to say, "How can those teachers live on that?" I think that is when he made up his mind that that was not right. Those teachers gave their whole life. Then he saw that the men teachers got more money than the lady teachers. He didn't like that. He thought that wasn't fair.
>
> I don't know if the teachers in Minnesota ever fully appreciated how he supported them. He was at that level where, when the teacher unions just were starting, he was there with full support. They knew they could count on him when push came to shove. That's why I always say, he was the best friend the schoolteachers ever had in this state.[24]

It was a time when women—not just teachers but in positions across the district—were paid much less than men doing the same work. Countless defenses and explanations were offered to justify the disparity, but the bottom line was that men made more than women. Perpich fought for pay equity for women from his first days in elected office until his last.

"He said if you are a woman, and if you are putting in your hours, you should be paid the same as a man," Rudy Perpich Jr. remembered. "Whether you are a janitor, or a teacher, or a secretary. The extraordinary thing about it is that my father was talking about this in the late 1950s, and pay equity did not become widespread until the late '80s in the United States. My father was still fighting for pay equity in the '80s."[25]

"I started working for the school in 1957," remembered Rogich. "When Rudy got on the board, we had about five different clerk-typist's salaries, we had about five different custodian's salaries. Rudy [and Hugh Harrison] got an evaluation system going, [and] evaluated the whole school. Everybody was treated and paid according to merit—not who liked you and who didn't like you."[26]

Perpich was also elected, in March 1958, as the first president of Hibbing's College Foundation—a group formed to raise funds for a Hibbing Junior College campus. The college itself wasn't new; in fact, it was one of the first junior colleges in the nation, opening in 1916. Until this time, however, the college had been housed in the Hibbing High School building. Influenced by the German university and high school systems, the Hibbing Junior College was essentially a two-year extension of the secondary school.[27]

In May 1959, Perpich was reelected to his second three-year term to the Hibbing School Board. In the uncontested, off-year election, turnout was light, with only 1,714 voters casting ballots as compared to 5,701 the previous year. Still, Perpich earned more votes than any of the three directors elected.[28]

"When he ran for school board, he never had in mind becoming governor," Rudy Jr. explained. "His progression through politics was a progression based on interest in issues. He was never interested in prestige or power. He ran for the school board because he was interested in education."[29]

A Seat in St. Paul

After six years on the school board, Perpich felt certain that the greatest positive impact for Hibbing School District teachers and students could only come through changes to the complex funding formula the state used to calculate local district aid. To make the changes required to fund education in Hibbing in a manner he considered just, Rudy Perpich would run for the Minnesota Senate.

"When Rudy was on the school board, he felt our district was not getting a fair shake and, therefore, our representatives were not doing their job," remembered McKanna. "I think that's what made him decide that was where he was going to go. He couldn't do it as a school board member, but he could do it as a legislative member."[30]

George Rogich recalled a meeting in the late 1950s at the Great Scott Town Hall, fifteen miles northeast of Hibbing on US Highway 169. All the Range legislators were there, including Senator Elmer Peterson, who represented Hibbing. The legislature was officially nonpartisan at the time, but legislators caucused as either liberals or conservatives.

"Back in those days, the conservatives [Republicans] controlled the legislature. Our legislators were all DFLers. They would come home, and they would

wring their hands. They would say, 'Oh, those conservatives. Those conservatives. We can't do anything with them,'" Rogich recalled. "They would get [the
voters] to a meeting and go, 'Rah, rah, rah,' and they would go to St. Paul and
do nothing."[31]

Perpich was frustrated that the well-liked Peterson was unable to bring
home the bacon, including funding for the Hibbing School District. Perpich
approached Peterson for assistance with a specific bill the school board sought,
but the request fell on deaf ears.

"Elmer Peterson wasn't helping him," Rudy Jr. recounted. "My father said,
'Either you get it this time, or I am running against you.'"[32]

Peterson dismissed the threat, but Perpich wasn't bluffing. Soon after the en-
counter, Perpich announced himself as a candidate for the Minnesota Senate.

Rudy and Lola faced a new challenge amid the campaign: raising a family.
During Perpich's second term on the school board, the couple welcomed their
first child, son Rudy Jr., on January 8, 1959. A year and a half later, their daughter, Mary Sue, was born.

Lola would take the young Rudy Jr. door-to-door in Hibbing, Chisholm, and
Buhl. She dressed up the three-and-a-half-year-old with the cute, fat face and
let him hand out leaflets while she talked to the people and introduced herself
and her husband to voters. Since she was from Keewatin, many voters were
meeting Lola for the first time, but "they always remembered the child."[33]

Lola had worked hard to campaign for her husband from the first race for
school board in 1955. But both she and Rudy saw his time on the Hibbing
School Board as community service, rather than a political office. With that
office, he stayed in Hibbing, was able to continue his normal hours at work,
and attended meetings a few times a month. The senate would be different. It
would cause disruptions with their home life and Rudy's dental practice, and
it would require a higher level of commitment from the entire family.

Lola supported Rudy's political career so long as there was no division or
growing apart of the family. This great adventure began, then, as a team effort. Lola would be Rudy's closest adviser—a role she played during his entire
career—and the children were included in the Perpiches' political activities
from the beginning. They wrote campaign ads, worked the phones, and engaged with voters together.

"My mother was always his closest adviser," Rudy Jr. remembered. "Even
though she didn't like politics, she understood that he loved it."[34]

Political independence was paramount to Perpich, and his only allegiance
would be to the voters of the 63rd District. Perpich made it clear to voters early
on that all financing, research, and writing for his campaign was done by him
and his family.[35]

Rudy had his family with him but the party apparatus working against him—something that became part of a pattern. To win, the Perpiches entered the race for senate with a frenetic energy that would characterize the family's entire career in public life.

Chasing Issues

In a letter to a supporter during his first campaign for state office in 1962, Perpich argued that the inequitable distribution of state aid made it a challenge for the Hibbing School District to pay teachers what they justly deserved. He also pointed out that the district's residents paid the state government far more "occupational, royalty, and income taxes" than it received back in state aid.

"A much fairer method of allocating school aids would be strictly on a per-pupil basis," Perpich wrote early in the campaign.[36]

In a speech to the Kiwanis Club, Perpich said that while funding education is a responsibility of the state, attempting to "equalize educational opportunities by complicated formulas is unworkable." He emphasized that Iron Range mines paid more than $1 million more in occupational and royalty taxes than the state's remaining 14,000 corporations paid in income tax collectively. His complex formula, with handwritten notes and calculations scribbled in the margins of his speaking text, concluded that school districts such as Bloomington and Edina received more than double the per-pupil state aid as did Range communities such as Hibbing, Chisholm, and Buhl. The speech foreshadowed the massive changes in school funding implemented a decade later through the "Minnesota Miracle."

"Rudy had a persuasiveness in him," Rogich recounted of Perpich's speeches. "He was very intelligent. He never wasted words. He could persuade. And he could persuade to the point where maybe you didn't like his persuasion, but you went along with it. He was that good."[37]

Perpich's speech touched on what would become pet topics, including expanded vocational training opportunities, increased postsecondary options for all Minnesotans (with a college in Hibbing), and reform and increased efficiency in local governments.[38]

Perpich also made jobs and unemployment a central issue of his first campaign for state office—a core priority of the Perpich platform for the next three decades. In a radio address, he told listeners that Hibbing had lost 1,300 jobs in the past three years and more than 4,000 jobs in the past decade. That figure was striking for a community whose total population was just over 17,000 people in the early 1960s.

"Of what value have the present incumbent senator's 22 years of seniority in the state legislature been to our unemployed?" Perpich asked the listeners of WMFG 1240 AM. "We in the Sixty-Third District are heading down the road to financial disaster, while Moorhead, St. Cloud, Rochester, [the] Twin Cities, and other areas are experiencing a prosperous economy."[39]

He called for reforms to the Minnesota State Act for Fair Employment Practices, which protected out-of-work individuals against age discrimination.[40]

"I suggest that the law in this state should be that if a worker is not pensionable, that he is hirable," Perpich wrote in a draft for a campaign ad. "How Tragic—Too Young to be Retired—Too Old to be Rehired."

The reference to the unemployed was part of Perpich's argument that Senate District Sixty-Three was "facing a crisis" and in a "state of chaos" under his opponent's tenure in the legislature.

"Our area has deteriorated from the richest area in the United States to one where the unemployment rate is one of the highest in the nation," Perpich argued in a typed letter to voters the week before the primary election. He cited the closure of mines, rising property taxes and declining values, and an exodus of citizens in search of jobs as reasons that "The Range Needs a Change."[41]

The Mesabi's rich iron ore deposits had fueled America's World War II effort, with more than 70 percent of the country's iron ore coming from the Iron Range, which kept the region's economy booming throughout the 1940s. But by the early 1950s, the area's high-grade iron ore was nearly depleted, leaving only low-grade taconite. As the industry's technology slowly changed to accommodate the processing of low-grade taconite, many mining companies moved on to other areas with richer concentrations of ore, leaving behind empty mines, a scarred landscape, and economically depressed cities across the Range.[42]

Unemployment was severe across the Iron Range throughout the 1950s, with the total number of jobs in the region's dominant industry dropping from 20,000 in the late 1950s to 12,000 by 1961. The economic conditions of northeastern Minnesota were in stark contrast to the rest of the state. Between 1950 and 1960, nonmanufacturing employment rose across Minnesota by as much as 60 percent in Moorhead and 27 percent in the Twin Cities, with a statewide average of 18 percent. In Hibbing, that number fell by 21 points.[43]

By 1962, while Minnesota was setting records for employment and approaching its goal of a million jobs across the state, unemployment remained a stubborn problem for Hibbing, Virginia, Chisholm, and cities throughout St. Louis County. That year, state unemployment was 3.8 percent, but in the Hibbing-Virginia area, it was more than double the state standard. It had fluctuated between two and four times the state average over the past five years.[44]

While Perpich was running for office, Iron Range union leaders reported to the Minnesota AFL-CIO executive council that the closure of as many as a dozen retail stores in Hibbing on top of several area mines was making a bad situation worse.[45]

"I seek the office of State Senate from this district because I feel the people in this area desperately need new leadership. Lack of adequate leadership in St. Paul is the contributing factor to our present conditions," Perpich told voters in a campaign speech. "Sixteen years ago, when I graduated from Hibbing High School, we were the richest area in the US, and today, we have one of the highest rates of unemployment in the nation and the highest welfare costs for the State of Minnesota."[46]

The campaign gained traction, and a Perpich victory in the nonpartisan September primary narrowed the field to Rudy and Peterson. "I propose to substitute seniority with hard work, perseverance, and ability," a defiant Perpich said in his stump speech shortly thereafter.

One of Perpich's campaign ads showed a map of Minnesota highlighting the forty-one state-sponsored colleges, vocational schools, regional treatment centers, and other institutions scattered across the state—with a line sweeping through the Iron Range where there were none. "They have institutions, we have unemployment," the flyer concluded. His promise was clear: Elect Rudy Perpich, and the Range would get its share.[47]

Perpich had learned early that in the rough-and-tumble politics of the 1950s and '60s Iron Range, the record—if not the character—of your opponent was fair game. The fifty-eight-year-old Elmer Peterson, who worked as an electrician for the Hibbing School District, had in 1940 been elected to the Minnesota House, where he served for three terms before moving to the Minnesota Senate following the 1946 election. Peterson had consistently caucused with the liberals. But the *Minneapolis Star* remarked that "the Conservative Senate leadership's high regard for Liberal Sen. Elmer Peterson is reflected in the responsibility assigned to him." Peterson was assigned to the "highly-sensitive" finance committee as well as such "wellsprings of controversy" as elections and redistricting, conservation, and public highways and universities.[48]

This might have played well in the salons of St. Paul, but it was red meat to the bare-knuckle politics of the union halls and with working-class families across the Iron Range. Those were the voters the upstart "Perpich Party" was canvassing in 1962. They would become indispensable to Minnesota Democratic-Farmer-Labor electoral politics for the next fifty years.

Peterson had been elected six times, most recently in 1958 when he defeated his opponent by more than forty-eight points. Yet he was feeling the heat from Perpich, and his nerves were beginning to show.[49]

The incumbent senator was a well-liked Scandinavian Lutheran with good connections. Perpich, meanwhile, embodied a class not represented by the status quo. Even in an area with a majority of "ich" names, he was not part of the traditional power base. Going from Peterson to Perpich would be a big deal for the Iron Range.[50]

Peterson accused Perpich of "promises spent recklessly," calling his young opponent "a picture of personal ambition." In melodramatic prose dripping with allusions to the Kennedys' Camelot, Peterson called on voters to "fire up the flame of progress under our New Future and New Range so that it will stand bright and proud before our eyes."[51]

In a draft campaign speech, Perpich categorized his opponent's twenty-two years as a time of fruitless leadership for the district with a record of "floundering ineffectiveness."[52]

Perpich touted himself as "a man with a plan" working toward a "return to full employment and prosperity" through "hard work, perseverance" and "constructive proposals." He contended that the 1962 contest was "make or break" for the future of the Iron Range.[53]

Peterson, three days before the election in a letter to voters, made a dramatic last appeal. "Tuesday, November 6th, will be the most important election day for our area in the last half-century." He would have never believed how right he was.[54]

On November 6, 1962, Perpich defeated the long-standing incumbent by 221 votes out of nearly 18,000 cast. The victory shocked Elmer Peterson and the Iron Range political establishment while simultaneously laying the foundation for Perpich's distant relationship with DFL Party insiders.[55]

A Capitol Calling

In addition to the changes the move to the senate would bring to Perpich's family life, the time spent at the capitol would mean disruptions to his growing dental practice. Perpich sent a letter to his patients detailing what his election as a state senator would mean to his business, explaining that he would be gone from Hibbing for a total of only six months during the entire four-year term—January through March of 1963 and 1965.[56]

"The short period of time that I will be away from my dental practice, my brothers, Dr. A. J. Perpich of Virginia and Dr. G. F. Perpich of Chisholm will staff my office in my absence.

"I am certain that this will not cause you any dental inconvenience, and you can rest assured that I shall work in the best interest of this area while I am in St. Paul."[57]

Perpich's dental practice was a big, happy family affair that had always been

Rudy and Lola with Rudy Jr. and Mary Sue, 1962. *Courtesy Minnesota Discovery Center*

more than a dental office—for years it was also his campaign headquarters. "The dental office was constant—it was never dull," remembered Ann Mastell, who worked as a dental assistant for Perpich starting in 1955 and remained close to the family the rest of her life. "When he came in, it was like a human tornado had walked in. Everything broke loose. The telephones, everything, went into a hurricane stage. The minute he left the office, everything died."[58]

"We would be working on a patient, and people would come [in and out of] where we were working. It was a stream of politicians, friends, whatever," Mastell said. "Dentistry was fine as far as an income and meeting people, but, in his head, it was always politics from Day One. That is all he talked about."[59]

The thirty-four-year-old Perpich took his oath of office as a state senator in January 1963 with a laser focus on legislation to benefit the voters who sent him to St. Paul. Over the next eight years, he molded the Range delegation into a legislative powerhouse that would be the envy of politicians of both parties statewide. Perpich positioned himself squarely at the heart of this political juggernaut—a group known for their loyalty to one another and ability to get things done for the Iron Range.

Early in his first session, Perpich proposed a bill to provide incentives for mining companies to process more natural ores in an attempt to maintain jobs and offset a shift to lower-grade taconite mining, which generated less production tax. By the end of his tenure in the senate, he led a tax boycott in conjunction with St. Louis County commissioner William Ojala. The two DFLers announced they would (temporarily) forgo paying their property taxes in protest of rising homeowners' taxes as the mining tax continued to decrease, and encouraged their constituents to do the same.[60]

"Perhaps a massive tax strike on the part of the Iron Range citizens will effectively point out the need for remedial action," Perpich said in a statement.[61]

Perpich called for a gasoline boycott in 1963 that oil executives branded as illegal and argued defied "economic logic." Perpich was undeterred. Two years later, he used his chairmanship of a subcommittee to hold hearings studying gas companies' discrimination against northeastern Minnesota. A study released by the group showed Range residents were paying five to eight cents more per gallon than Twin Cities motorists. By 1968, Perpich had grown tired of calling for boycotts and legislative hearings, and he personally led a group of picketers at gas stations across the Iron Range.[62]

"We're going to hang tough, but I've given up on the legislature—the lobbyists are just too influential," Perpich told reporters.[63]

He blasted Republican governor Harold LeVander and state and federal bureaucrats when he said there were "too many Pied Pipers from Washington and St. Paul" meddling in the creation of Voyageurs National Park on the Kabetogama Peninsula in northern Minnesota. Perpich contended that highways, police protection, hunting rights, and the loss of tax base should have been considered along with a multiple-use approach that would produce the highest economic impact for the area. But Perpich was equally adamant in his demands for LeVander to ban mining in the Boundary Waters Canoe Area (BWCA), urging the governor to enlist consumer watchdog Ralph Nader to lead the charge.[64]

"Teddy Roosevelt saw the need for saving the BWCA by setting aside the

Superior National Forest way back in 1909," Perpich said in his last year in the senate. "Certainly we . . . should be foresighted enough to see that saving the BWCA is an absolute necessity. There is no room for compromise."[65]

Perpich consistently advocated for highway funding for the Range, maintaining that northeastern Minnesota counties "have been neglected in road building." He opposed a penny-per-gallon increase to the gas tax by leading reporters on a tour of the Highway Department, pointing out inefficiencies along the way and arguing that payroll be reduced rather than taxes raised.[66]

"That guy must be studying traffic patterns," Perpich said sarcastically, pointing to a Highway Department employee vacantly staring out the sixth-story window while smoking a cigarette.[67]

Throughout his eight years in the senate, much like his predecessor, Perpich often found it difficult to cut through state bureaucracy and deliver results to the Iron Range. But unlike Elmer Peterson, Rudy Perpich didn't simply throw up his hands; instead, he turned to grassroots organizing and activism that was in harmony with the political currents of the 1960s. While the efforts would have mixed results influencing policy, they would endear him as a populist hero to the voters of the Iron Range.

Blood Fights

While Perpich was consolidating the power of the Iron Range delegation, the 1966 gubernatorial election exposed rifts within the DFL Party in the Eighth Congressional District. Vice President Hubert Humphrey and Governor Karl Rolvaag canceled a swing through the DFL stronghold on election day ostensibly because fog and heavy clouds prevented their plane from landing in Hibbing. But there were political storm clouds gathering over the Range as well. Humphrey referenced "blood fights" in two legislative battles, both involving Perpiches. Rudy was in a rematch with Elmer Peterson, and Tony Perpich was challenging twenty-eight-year legislative veteran state senator Thomas Vukelich.[68]

Humphrey noted that both brothers, along with labor unions from the Range, had supported state senator Sandy Keith in his primary challenge against Governor Rolvaag and had been reticent to support the incumbent governor after the interparty battle.[69]

Rolvaag, the sitting governor, lost his party's endorsement at the DFL state convention on June 19, 1966, in a twenty-ballot battle with his lieutenant governor Sandy Keith. Keith was a former state senator and had become an ally of Perpich during Keith's time as lieutenant governor when Perpich joined the senate. Perpich and Keith would develop a close relationship during their time in the legislature and the '66 campaign. The decision for Keith to challenge Rolvaag was less about policy than it was about effectiveness and aesthetics. Sandy Keith was young, handsome, and articulate in the mold of the Kennedys. Rolvaag, in contrast, was a heavy drinker and often an ineffectual communicator.[70]

"Karl Rolvaag was the incumbent. I remember Rudy saying that they were thinking about Sandy Keith running," Norma McKanna remembered Perpich telling the Sewing Club. "I was mortified. Running against an incumbent. They decided that Karl Rolvaag should no longer be the candidate of the DFL Party. So, [Rudy] got us real involved in the Keith campaign because he was so involved in it. He had us running all over the state on buses, campaigning for Sandy Keith."[71]

When Keith announced he would challenge the sitting governor, he predicted that either an infusion of young leaders or an agonizing defeat would be needed to revitalize the stagnant Minnesota DFL. His prediction proved prescient when Harold LeVander defeated Rolvaag in a lopsided election that saw Republicans win across the state and up and down the ballot, picking up thirteen seats in the Minnesota House. The press pointed out that many of the DFL survivors in 1966 were youthful and enthusiastic Keith supporters, such as state senators Wendell Anderson and Rudy Perpich. The DFL would look to these rising stars in 1970.[72]

In their 1966 rematch, thirty-eight-year-old Rudy easily defeated Elmer Peterson, while his thirty-five-year-old brother Tony defeated the incumbent Vukelich in Senate District Sixty-Two. Tony, who was quieter than his siblings, was intellectually gifted and loyal to Rudy while simultaneously maintaining an independent streak. The brothers, who practiced dentistry in neighboring communities (Tony had opened an office in Virginia), would represent adjoining districts in the Minnesota Senate, where they would sit next to one another on the senate floor.[73]

Three months into their family adventure in the legislature, the seatmates had authored—jointly or individually—more than seventy bills ranging from tax relief to statewide fluoridation of public drinking water during the 65th legislative session, which began in January 1967.[74]

"The Iron Range, its people, and its problems have been taken for granted too long," Rudy told reporters at the capitol as his brother nodded in agreement.[75]

The brothers also agreed that Republicans would never be elected on the Iron Range. However, unless politicians in St. Paul and Washington took notice of Range concern about productive land being taken for national parks and decreasing tax yields on mining companies being shifted to homeowners, they also believed there would not be support for establishment Democratic candidates from the DFL-dominated Eighth District either. Few party insiders took note, but future intraparty primaries would validate the brothers' predictions.[76]

The Vietnam War

In 1967, Vance Opperman was a young law student at the University of Minnesota, where he organized students against the Vietnam War and tried to find an anti-war candidate to run against President Lyndon B. Johnson in 1968. He organized a group called Concerned Democrats Against the War, with an office in the Loring Park neighborhood of Minneapolis. Its budget was tight, without the money to buy advertising, but it was sufficient to connect with several like-minded groups. Volunteers cobbled together card tables and chairs in the makeshift office where they organized anti-war activists to advocate for peace in the March 5, 1968, DFL caucuses. In the early summer of 1967, the group had not been able to identify a single Minnesota officeholder to oppose the war publicly.[77]

"So, this guy walked in. He said he was very interested in getting some information and he was very interested in helping at the caucuses," Opperman remembered. "So I took down the guy's name and address and asked him what he did. He said he was a state senator. I asked him what the name was. He said, 'Perpich.' He expressed how bad he thought the war was and how the American people's true views hadn't been heard. And then he walked out."[78]

Rudy Jr. was eight years old that summer and remembered walking with his father from the capitol in an anti-war march down University Avenue. He also remembered his father being booed off the stage in his hometown when he spoke against the war.[79]

"I remember kids coming up and saying that their parents had told them that my dad was supporting Eugene McCarthy. They couldn't believe that Rudy Perpich would come out for Eugene McCarthy," Rudy Jr. recalled of the opposition his father faced. "He never argued with Humphrey. However, the relationship was not as warm as it could have been, and I believe that was one of the reasons. My father would take stands which did not endear him to the party hierarchy."[80]

"He had the courage to risk something he loved so much. He was willing to constantly take these risks because he knew that they were the right thing to do."[81]

Opperman recognized Perpich as one of the first people to understand that the war in Vietnam was wrong. It was morally wrong, and what bothered him more than anything was the deceptive way the war had been prosecuted by the Johnson administration and communicated to the American people.

"He certainly was not a pacifist and would have been one of the first to fight to defend his country," Opperman explained. "[The Vietnam War] was undeclared. It was secret. It was covert. It clearly was not something that could . . .

stand the light of day. And he had an instinctive, instinctive feeling that when that was going on in government, something was wrong. And he was right."[82]

No Turning Back

In 1969—his last legislative session as a senator—Rudy Perpich voted against what he saw as a pay raise masked as a per diem increase and then refused to take the additional money when it passed despite his objection. He also rejected an advantageous legislative pension plan in favor of the option made available to rank-and-file state employees.[83]

Those moves were consistent with Perpich's thinking about money and politics, ideas that had been evident from the start of his political career.

"I never accepted one cent in financial donations," Perpich said, referring to the self-financing of his school board and senate campaigns. "It's the money that's coming in that controls after it's all over."[84]

Asked what he did other than politics and dentistry, Perpich twirled his glasses and then responded. "You know, I hadn't thought about it, but that's all I do. Politics and dentistry. I don't remember doing anything else."[85]

Rudy Perpich cared about people and believed in government. Dentistry had provided a living for his family; politics gave him the opportunity to exercise his core values of empathy and compassion by improving people's lives.

"He said to the people, 'I will work for you.' They believed him, and he knew what government could do for people," Rudy Jr. asserted. "If Elmer Peterson had done that, my father never would have been state senator. They left that gap for him to fill. The Democratic Party in northern Minnesota left that gap for Rudy Perpich to fill."[86]

And once he was given an opening, there was no stopping him. "He loved it. He found his life's love, which was politics," his son explained. "After that, there wasn't any going back. At the school board, I don't know if he really considered himself in politics. Once he got to the senate and caught the political fever, there wasn't any going back."[87]

CHAPTER 4

Statewide Office

"I think that Rudy always wanted to be governor. When he walked into that lieutenant governor's office for the first time, he knew exactly what he wanted to do."

—*Gary Lamppa, chief of staff to*
Lieutenant Governor Rudy Perpich

From his early time as a Minnesota state senator, those closest to Rudy Perpich knew he had a larger goal in mind.

"When we are thinking about yesterday and today, he's thinking five and ten years down the road," said lifelong friend Norma McKanna. "I can just hear him saying, 'You know, I can be governor someday.'"

Rudy knew that the key to reaching his political goals was to develop a base of power on the Iron Range. Although the area had been heavily DFL since the Democratic and Farmer-Labor movements merged in 1944, a small group of people controlled the DFL precinct caucuses that wielded real political power. Few in Hibbing, Keewatin, or across the Range knew the caucus system existed, and even fewer showed up at caucuses to vote.

Rudy understood that he needed delegate support to gain the power he wanted, and that meant he had to turn out voters at precinct caucus meetings. Together, he and Lola paged through Range area phone books, dialing one number after the next, persuading Iron Rangers to show up at caucus meetings on February 24, 1970, and cast their votes.[1]

Throughout the late 1960s, after Rudy was established as a state senator and Tony had been elected to represent Virginia in the neighboring 63rd Senate District, the Perpiches leveraged the caucus system toward Rudy's next goal: becoming lieutenant governor in the 1970 election. With any luck, the support of delegates elected at caucuses would translate to support at the DFL state convention that summer.

Unlike today, gubernatorial and lieutenant gubernatorial candidates in 1970 ran separate races, with the responsibilities of the lieutenant governor largely confined to presiding over the state senate in a nonvoting role. The benefits of joining the two positions into a single electoral ticket had been long discussed in Minnesota's political circles.

Perpich was a leading proponent of the proposal. In a campaign interview, he cited the unnecessary cost of separate campaigns along with the inevitable strife of a mixed-party executive branch. He envisioned the lieutenant governor as a liaison between the executive and legislative branches, as the point of contact with key interest groups regarding legislation, and—perhaps with his ultimate political goal in mind—as a statewide envoy to "muster grassroots support."[2]

To win a position of statewide importance, it would take more than a strong showing on the Iron Range. Rudy and Lola traveled the state, hitting every DFL Party event they could—picnics, labor rallies, wherever people gathered. Rudy didn't have the money to advertise, but what he did have was a drive few other political candidates could match. He would work at his dental practice during the day, then he and Lola would load the campaign car. Lola would drive, Rudy would sleep. Rudy would speak, shake hands, and then Lola would drive back to Hibbing. And then they would do it all again.

With two young children at the time, it took tremendous dedication and balance to keep the family, the dental practice, and the campaign going, but Rudy's hardworking, family-man image proved an asset to the campaign.[3]

Against All Odds

"We were approaching the convention center," remembered Rudy Jr. "My dad was saying to my mother, 'Do you think I've got the votes?' "[4]

Minnesota's 1970 state DFL convention took place in Duluth during the last week of June. The convention was a mixture of optimism and uncertainty, with popular former vice president Hubert H. Humphrey at the top of the ticket running again for the US Senate after his failed presidential campaign two years earlier. But down ballot, a largely unknown and untested slate of candidates vied for spots.

Among them was unpredictable Minneapolis businessman Robert Short, campaigning for governor. Short stormed out of the convention after failing to capture the endorsement, vowing to run anyway in the September 15 primary election. This provocation would fall flat but foreshadowed a similar threat which would doom Democrats later that decade.

Rudy Perpich, meanwhile, had all his support lined up behind gubernatorial candidate Nick Coleman, as did Tony Perpich in his senate district. Both Rudy and Coleman had been elected to the senate in 1962 and were among the young senators who had supported Sandy Keith's 1966 insurgent campaign. They became friends and allies through their time in the senate.

"I can still picture Rudy up at the top of the DECC in Duluth sitting on a seat way up at the top," remembered Frank Ongaro, Rudy's floor manager for the convention. Ongaro would run up and down the steps, relaying the orders from Perpich above to his team below—hold tight for Coleman, don't back down.

It wasn't enough.

A charismatic, thirty-seven-year-old St. Paul legislator and former Olympic hockey player named Wendell Anderson gained the endorsement, besting Coleman and University of Minnesota law professor David L. Graven. Coleman and Graven, fearing a repeat of the twenty-ballot fiasco that divided the party in 1966, conceded on the sixth ballot, with Coleman requesting the convention make a unanimous endorsement of Anderson. By Saturday's end, Humphrey and Anderson had secured the two top slots on the party ticket.

While Coleman failed to win the endorsement, Perpich's loyalty would pay off the next day. Because of Coleman's support on the Iron Range, Anderson had hoped to persuade his former opponent to campaign as lieutenant governor. "No way," Coleman replied. "[Rudy] worked hard for it." Coleman threw his support behind Perpich.[5]

The next morning, Rudy's supporters showed up early at the convention. By the time the delegates arrived, every seat had a "Perpich for Lt. Governor" flyer attached.

Both Humphrey and Anderson pushed Coleman and Graven to accept the number two slot, but both turned them down, leaving top DFL power brokers concerned over the viability of their remaining candidates. Perpich was running against former St. Paul mayor Thomas Byrne and Jon Wefald of St. Peter. Wefald was the grandson of former Minnesota congressman Knud Wefald and had gained considerable strength from rural delegates when Dennis Peterson of Moorhead dropped from the race.

On the other side of the political line, the GOP selection of Duluth mayor Ben Boo one week earlier in St. Paul as the Republican-endorsed candidate for lieutenant governor proved favorable for Perpich's candidacy. The DFL needed Rudy's Eighth District backing to counter the Duluth mayor's supporters.

The first ballot returned 603 votes for Perpich to Wefald's 301 and Byrne's 286, prompting Byrne to withdraw. Before the second round of voting, Humphrey, Mondale, and Anderson gathered in a suite overlooking the convention floor. Rudy's floor manager knocked on the suite door, asking why they didn't just end this by endorsing Rudy. Anderson was incensed by the suggestion, but Mondale was silent, cautious. The gregarious Humphrey burst out laughing. Like Rudy, he saw politics as a great game.

Even without their support, Perpich collected 802 votes on the second ballot, considerably more than the 731 needed for the endorsement. Perpich had

DFL gubernatorial candidate Wendell Anderson files for office as Hubert H. Humphrey (US Senate), Rudy Perpich (lieutenant governor), Warren Spannaus (attorney general), and Elmer Childress (secretary of state) wait their turn, July 1970. *Photo by Skip Heine, Minneapolis and St. Paul Newspaper Negatives Collection, MNHS*

now become one of the first Iron Rangers in state history to win a statewide endorsement.[6]

"Well, good for him, he is on the ticket," Humphrey exclaimed.[7]

In addition to Humphrey, Anderson, and Perpich, the DFL endorsed Warren Spannaus for attorney general, Jon Wefald for state auditor, and Elmer Childress, a Minneapolis labor official and the first African American endorsed for statewide office by a major party in Minnesota history, for secretary of state.

Road Dogs

Rudy hit the campaign trail with typical zeal. Shortly after the convention, he was endorsed by a group of three hundred New Democratic Coalition members who broke free from the DFL and endorsed civil rights activist Earl Craig Jr. for the US Senate because of Humphrey's association with the Johnson administration's Vietnam position. Once Perpich had made it through the convention and the DFL establishment, his prior record on Vietnam helped him bridge the divisions within the DFL, where he had already established his credibility with activists as someone willing to challenge party orthodoxy.

The DFL ticket made stops in Moorhead, Alexandria, and Duluth. Perpich campaigned on the inability of small and poor communities to take advantage of government programs, calling for experts in outstate areas to help navigate the "mass jumble" of applications and contracts.[8]

In Mankato, Perpich promoted a constitutional amendment to accelerate highway construction in rural areas, stating, "Minnesota's highway construction has always been one left over from horse and buggy days." He described the existing system as one of "crisis proportions."[9]

That August, Perpich—along with Anderson and Humphrey—was endorsed by the United Labor Committee. He spoke to the League of Women Voters in Crystal, New Hope, Robbinsdale, and Brooklyn Park. At an old-fashioned rally at the Winona Senior High School, he campaigned in front of five hundred people while bands played and cheering sections paraded about to the sounds of bells and gongs.

In Plummer, a little town in Red Lake County with a population of fewer than three hundred people, Rudy was the first statewide candidate to visit in support of Roger Moe, who was in his first campaign for the Minnesota Senate. By paying attention to races such as Moe's, Perpich was forging important political alliances with up-and-coming legislators. "I remember he and Lola drove over," Moe recalled. "Wasn't a big crowd at all, but he came over and was just nice to everybody."[10]

In Stearns County, he spoke alongside Senator Walter Mondale at a DFL bean-and-burger fundraiser at a National Guard armory and was endorsed and spoke at a state convention of the National Farmers Organization at the St. Cloud State College. Alongside Wendell Anderson, Perpich attended a church smorgasbord in Coon Rapids. At each stop, Perpich spoke to issues relevant to the local audience.

Minnesota Republicans had endorsed Attorney General Douglas Head for governor, who led Anderson by 5 percentage points in statewide polling by midsummer. Yet, political insiders from both parties believed these results favored the DFL. Head's lead was minimal, they argued, for a candidate with the name recognition gained through serving three years as Minnesota's attorney general. In the lieutenant governor race, Boo led Perpich by a similar margin according to the same poll.[11]

Rudy promised to campaign for his party's legislative candidates, in addition to himself, decrying the conservative-controlled legislature as beholden to lobbyists and special interests. At a fundraiser in St. Cloud, he called for strict legislation requiring registration and financial disclosure by lobbyists.

"If a legislator is a drinking man, he can stay drunk the entire session and never have to spend a penny," Perpich said, referring to lobbyist favors. "They take you to a play and tell your wife how beautiful she is and send her a dozen roses."[12]

Campaign advertisements touted Perpich's "rare selfless political courage" in his fight against "the special interests and influence peddlers of Minnesota when they were picking the pockets of Minnesota's taxpayers."[13]

At a press conference in Moorhead, Perpich challenged Boo to disclose all candidate and committee campaign contributions fully. He further proposed a gross earnings tax as a replacement for real estate and personal property taxes, which he claimed had grown by 53 percent over the previous three years. Property taxes had become a significant source of resentment among rural voters.[14]

Perpich proposed a 2 percent tax on business and industry as well as high-earning professionals but spared wages, salaries, and retirement income. When Rolland Hatfield, who was running as the GOP state auditor candidate and had been appointed to head a property tax study for Republican governor Harold LeVander, called the plan a "cruel hoax," Perpich fired back. "Is it not cruel that homeowners, pensioners, farmers, and small business owners have experienced a 53 percent rise in property tax in the last three years?" he responded.[15]

Tax reform was the central issue in state government in 1970—and the big issue in the governor's race. The DFL staked out a position favoring progressive taxation that sprang from Floyd Olson and its Farmer-Labor roots. The position defined the DFL for decades but was one with which a future Perpich would wrestle.

Perpich would also propose a state department of senior citizens as a remedy to the "bureaucratic mix-ups, red tape, and lack of information" in areas such as health care, housing, transportation, and tax relief.[16]

That September, the Americans for Democratic Action released a ranking of Minnesota legislators based on bills of "public interest" voted on during the 1969 session. Members were rated in several categories, including electoral reform, education, civil liberties, and criminal reform. Votes were scored on bills to increase the taconite production tax, which Rudy and his brother Tony had championed, along with increased sentences for felonies committed with firearms, and the outlawing of hunting wild game with the aid of snowmobiles, among others. Perpich and Anderson fared well, both scoring above the liberal caucus average.[17]

Frozen Food, Fresh Opposition

With only weeks to go before the election, Rudy Perpich had a fighting chance. Unfortunately, his upstart campaign had drawn the ire of Duluth frozen pizza magnate and maverick millionaire Luigino "Jeno" Paulucci. Paulucci had supported fellow businessman Robert Short at the June convention and threatened to back a Republican governor if Short wasn't endorsed. Instead, he funded ninety billboards statewide supporting a split ticket of DFLer Anderson for governor and Republican Ben Boo for lieutenant governor. He urged Minnesotans to "be an independent" and "vote the man."[18]

The week before the election, the Paulucci-Perpich political feud reached a fever pitch, with the food mogul purchasing a half hour of TV airtime for an election-eve special for Humphrey and Anderson. The caveat was that Perpich was not allowed to appear on the show.[19]

"Paulucci must have gotten tired of running around Florida and drinking champagne," Rudy retorted. "He's playing games. Jeno sees himself as an impresario. He does that sort of stuff in Minnesota politics. I still like the guy, you understand, but this is his recreation."[20]

The unpredictable millionaire, who had once proposed using bubbles to keep Lake Superior open year-round and building a canal between Duluth and the Twin Cities, differed with Perpich on the taconite production tax, calling for an increase to 50 cents per ton in stages (Rudy and his brother Tony had authored legislation to increase the tax to 11.5 cents per ton).[21]

"Wouldn't you know it. We're both from Hibbing," Perpich lamented. "One time the Iron Range has the chance to get a man in state office and the guy from across the street tries to knock it in the head. You don't think we've had trouble getting into the Capitol? I understand it wasn't many years ago when the sergeant-at-arms used to ask the Iron Range legislators to point out their interpreter."[22]

The state's largest newspaper also endorsed Boo over Perpich, although it wasn't splitting its ticket. The editorial boards of both the *Minneapolis Star* and the *Minneapolis Tribune* endorsed Douglas Head for governor and Ben Boo for lieutenant governor but did give Perpich credit, with the *Star* calling him "able and congenial" and the *Tribune* recognizing him as an "honest, hard-working, and effective legislator" but emphasizing his lack of a "broad grasp of issues from the statewide viewpoint."[23]

Even Perpich's hometown newspaper, the *Hibbing Tribune*, supported his opponent. "Many disagree with some of Perpich's philosophies and programs, but everybody who closely watches politics has nothing but admiration for his ability to develop a strong following," the paper opined.

But in the end, Perpich rode a Democratic wave to victory on Tuesday, November 3, 1970, besting his GOP opponent 671,749 to 654,486. His margin of victory was considerably smaller than that of the two DFLers higher up the ticket. In what had been predicted to be a toss-up, Anderson beat Head by more than 116,000 votes.[24]

"We were led by the best vote-getter and best public official we've ever produced, Hubert Humphrey," Anderson, with his two-and-a-half-year-old daughter seated between him and the senator-elect, said at a press conference the next morning. Humphrey had won his sixth straight race for statewide office by more than 200,000 votes.[25]

"The DFL blitzed the Republicans and switched the tone of politics in the state," wrote the editor of the *Fairmont Sentinel*.[26]

The election would have far-reaching effects on the politics of Minnesota over the coming decade and farther-reaching implications for a lieutenant governor–elect with higher aspirations.

"My God. He won. Can you believe it?" Joseph Perpich asked his family as they watched the election results roll in.

Anton beamed, proud of his oldest son. But Mary wasn't so sure. "I don't know about this," she said. "I think he should have been a dentist. Stayed here. What is he doing?"[27]

Always the Outsider

While preparing for his higher-profile position, lieutenant governor–elect Perpich made it clear he planned to make the most of his opportunity. In early December, he told the *Hibbing Tribune* that he would push for campaign finance reform of statewide campaigns.

"If we don't change, only the very rich will have a chance to get elected," Perpich said. "Every candidate on (the DFL) ticket ended up broke." The Perpich campaign reported spending $16,380 on the election, with $11,677 coming from Perpich personally, the largest personal expenditure of any of the statewide candidates.[28]

Additionally, Perpich wanted the Iron Range to benefit from his ascension to statewide office. He proposed moving the Minnesota Department of Lands, Minerals, and Waters from St. Paul to Hibbing as well as relocating the University of Minnesota's mineral research to the university's Duluth campus. Naturally, he felt the Iron Range Resource and Rehabilitation Department should be headquartered on the Range.[29]

Rudy's relationship with Anderson and the DFL establishment, however, remained as rocky as ever. At his first press conference since the election, Governor-elect Wendell Anderson announced the appointment of Thomas Kelm as his executive secretary. "If the governor is out of the state or out of the cities," Anderson said, "I think he's the man who's in charge."[30]

The next morning's headline was like the twisting of a knife: "Anderson Appoints Kelm Top Aide, Indicates He'll Be State's No. 2 Man."[31]

Any effort to diminish Rudy's role in the capitol was bound to fail, however, as Perpich was about to take center stage in one of the most dramatic political showdowns in state history, which was set to unfold in the Minnesota Senate.

The Democrat-aligned liberals had picked up fifteen seats in the Minnesota House in the 1970 election, but the conservatives still held a majority in the chamber, 70–65. In the senate, the DFL made even greater gains, picking up ten seats and pulling to a 33–33 tie with one independent, Richard Palmer, who defeated incumbent DFLer Francis "Frenchy" La Brosse in Duluth's 59th District.[32]

Palmer indicated during his campaign that he would caucus with the majority. With an even split, whomever the Proctor independent sided with would have control of the senate. There was a further wrinkle, though, as Palmer had been charged with unfair campaign practices by his opponent. The allegations stemmed from a front-page editorial published in the *Duluth Budgeteer*, a newspaper for which Palmer sat on the editorial board and which was published by Palmer's father.[33]

As the new session of the legislature approached, Palmer declared he would caucus with the conservatives. The Democrats refused to take this lying down and devised a plan to take control of the senate—for the first time in state history.

On the first day of the session, the new lieutenant governor and presiding officer ruled that Palmer could not be seated until the senate adjudicated charges against him later in the session. When Perpich ordered that Palmer not be given the oath of office, Chief Justice Oscar Knutson, who was there to administer the oath to all members, objected to what he saw as political gamesmanship.

"If you do not wish me to give it to all, you can get someone else to administer the oath," Knutson remarked as he walked out of the chamber.

Perpich did.

State representative Jack Fena, of Hibbing, who qualified as a notary public, administered the oath to all members, including Palmer, despite Perpich's order. Subverted but undeterred, Perpich ignored Palmer when he attempted to participate in the organization of the senate.[34]

Perpich then made his second unprecedented ruling, by breaking a 33–33 tie on the election of a senate secretary, giving the DFL-aligned liberals control of the Minnesota Senate for the first time in state history.

Roger Moe, a twenty-six-year-old freshman senator—who had never been inside the capitol prior to his election—had a front-row seat.

"It was great theater. It was really bare-fist politics and Rudy was at the epicenter of it all," Moe recalls. "Nick Coleman was a master political strategist and a man with great flair. But, let me tell you, in Rudy Perpich, he found a very willing accomplice."[35]

At this point, Grove City conservative majority leader Stanley Holmquist led the Republicans out of the chamber, adding to the chaos of Perpich's first five hours as presiding officer. The Democrats remained in session, electing officers and appointing DFL chairs for sixteen committees.

The high drama continued over the next seven days. Each day, the conservatives would open the session by moving for adjournment. When Perpich continued to ignore Palmer and rule the vote a tie, Holmquist would get up, remove his glasses, and say, "Mr. President, I distinctly heard 34 votes for the [Conservatives]." At that point, Holmquist and his caucus would leave.[36]

Finally, on January 13, the Minnesota Supreme Court ruled 6–1 in favor of the conservatives, with five justices siding with Chief Justice Knutson. Palmer took his seat the following day and the Republicans maintained a slim majority for the rest of the session.

Moe, who would serve in the senate for the next thirty-two years, twenty-two of them as DFL majority leader, said it was a chapter like no other. "It was unbelievable. Nothing near as exciting has happened ever since then. I can assure you."[37]

But to Perpich, it was part of a larger plan. He knew that the episode would hurt Palmer in his district, making the Duluth district susceptible to a DFL pickup—which would be critical to their efforts toward taking control of the chamber in the next election. The incident also made clear to Perpich that changes in the structure of Minnesota's executive branch, including increased powers for the lieutenant governor, were needed.

In February, just five weeks into his term, Perpich supported a constitutional amendment to abolish his own office.

Making History

With thirty-eight-year-old Anderson well entrenched in the governor's office, Perpich saw risks to his political future unless major changes to his office were made. "Until you get into the office itself, you aren't aware of the limitations," Perpich explained before a shocked House Appropriations Committee while requesting a reduction in the budget for his office.[38]

Perpich said he would support the legislation proposed by DFL senator Jack Davies of Minneapolis to abolish the office of lieutenant governor. Simultaneously, Perpich's brother George, who had won Rudy's District Sixty-Three senate seat in the 1970 election, authored a bill for a constitutional amendment that would have partisan candidates for governor and lieutenant governor run as a team and put the office of lieutenant governor in the executive branch with expanded duties.[39]

The measure was ultimately approved by the legislature and sent to voters in the 1972 general election. They likewise approved it, providing for the joint election of the state's top two posts and removing the lieutenant governor as presiding officer of the senate. The role of lieutenant governor now rested firmly in the executive branch.

History books highlight the 1971 legislative session for the set of government finance proposals that became known as the "Minnesota Miracle." On November 1, the day after the governor signed the legislation—ending the most extended session in state history—the *Minneapolis Star* referred to it as a "palatable compromise" resulting from a "mysterious blending of people, ideas and events . . . left to simmer a long time and put under public pressure."[40]

The state's system of financing education and local government was spiraling into a tailspin during the late 1960s, with rapidly rising property taxes coupled with growing inequities in local school funding. During the 1970 campaign, Anderson hammered on the fact that Republicans, when they addressed property tax reform in the 1967 legislative session, had provided permanent tax relief for businesses but only temporary relief for homeowners.[41]

"There was a consensus among many Minnesotans, including the influential Citizens League, that property taxes were out of control," said Tom Berg, then a thirty-year-old attorney from Minneapolis running for a state house seat against a five-term conservative incumbent.[42]

The Citizens League, a nonpartisan organization dedicated to solving state and local policy problems, consisted primarily of corporate and business bosses, but also included labor, civic, and academic leaders. In early September 1970, the league released a report calling for the state to play a "central role" in determining the amount of taxing capacity that existed at local levels of government and calling for a reduction of local property taxes through the replacement of these taxes with state-collected income and sales taxes.[43]

Soon thereafter, Anderson announced his support for the league's proposal at a candidate forum, while his Republican opponent said the plan would significantly raise taxes and erode local control.[44]

"The election of Wendy Anderson in 1970 set up a showdown between the DFL governor and the conservative-controlled legislature," explained Berg, who also ran a successful campaign in 1970 and would go on to serve eight years in the house.[45]

The governor's staff put the plan in legislative language called the "Fair School Finance Plan," which was presented to the legislature in January. The complicated proposal, which went further than the Citizens League recommendations, included increasing state revenues by 37 percent, raising taxes by $762 million.

Not surprisingly, the legislation faced immediate and staunch opposition from most conservatives in both the house and the senate. But among con-servatives, there were also a handful of independent thinkers who had the potential to be dealmakers—or so Anderson hoped.[46]

While everyone agreed that something needed to be done, each chamber's majority developed its own counterproposal to the governor's plan. In the senate, a bill was introduced by Wayne Popham, a conservative representing Hennepin County, that paralleled many of the league's recommendations. At one point, there were six competing proposals in the house, which ultimately passed a largely status quo bill offered by longtime representative and dairy farmer Harvey Sathre of Adams, a small town five miles north of the Iowa border.

As the stalemate over how to finance local schools and governments—along with the broader tax implications—ground on, Anderson kept up his relentless advocacy for the need to reduce property taxes and eliminate the disparities between cities and school districts with limited taxation and spending capaci-ties and those with higher property tax bases.

The governor's message was striking a chord. In April, a flood of angry homeowners and farmers converged on the capitol during a joint House and Senate Tax Committee hearing. The crowd was so large that the hearing was forced to move from the capitol to the state armory.[47]

As the constitutionally mandated end to the session approached, there was no agreement in sight, and the legislature adjourned in May without settling the issue and without passing a broader tax bill.

Unlikely Allies

Rudy's brother Tony, now in his second term representing Virginia and the 62nd District, and George, elected to fill Rudy's 63rd District seat, focused their energy during the 1971 session on increasing the taconite production tax to provide much-needed property tax relief to the Range and to fund environ-mental cleanup of the mess left by decades of heavy mining and lax regulatory measures.

In April, the lieutenant governor also put aside his differences with Jeno Paulucci to support antipollution activities outlined in a report by Ralph Nad-er's crusading Center for Responsive Law. The group accused Reserve Mining Company of Silver Bay of dumping 67,000 tons of taconite tailings into Lake Superior per day, while federal water quality officials looked the other way.[48]

The frozen-pizza magnate then teamed up with the Perpiches, testifying at the legislature in favor of increasing the taconite production tax from 11.5 cents to 50 cents per ton, while establishing a northeastern Minnesota environmental and development fund. Wayzata conservative Salisbury Adams voiced support for a Stanford University study—which had been commissioned by Paulucci—confirming the mining industry's ability to pay the additional taxes.

But when Salisbury stopped short of supporting the full increase, Paulucci erupted.

"You're killing my study with kindness," Paulucci shouted from the gallery.

"You're a very difficult man to agree with," Adams responded without raising his voice.[49]

The senate ultimately approved the measure, but it faced the same fate as other tax provisions, as the legislature ended the regular session without a broader tax agreement.[50]

With the regular session complete, Rudy Perpich and his two younger brothers hit the road on a barnstorming tour across the state to ensure that their taconite proposal would be part of any final agreement in the special session. During one week in June, the brothers traveled together to Rochester, Austin, Albert Lea, Mankato, Winona, Faribault, St. Peter, Alexandria, Moorhead, East Grand Forks, Fergus Falls, Crookston, Bemidji, Grand Rapids, Hibbing, Virginia, and Duluth.

In Winona, the lieutenant governor blamed the "powerful special interest lobbying forces for the 1971 Legislature's failure to deal with the problems of pollution and unfair taxation."[51]

Perpich told a gathering in Fergus Falls that the taconite industry paid the equivalent of 29 mills (the tax rate applied to the assessed value used to determine property taxes) while other corporations, such as 3M, Honeywell, and Dayton's, paid an average of 335 mills.[52]

At a stop in Faribault toward the end of the tour, perhaps affected by their travels, the brothers took turns escalating their criticisms against conservatives in the legislature. Rudy again denounced the Republicans for "protecting special interests." Tony called the GOP-proposed tax break to taconite companies "an attempt to cheat the people of Minnesota." But George went the furthest, saying his opponents would be willing "to sell the Virgin Mary into prostitution if it would create full time jobs."[53]

Stanley Holmquist

Agreement finally came in October 1971 after the longest special session in state history. The special session called by Anderson was so unpopular with rank-and-file legislators that freshman representative Tom Berg inquired about the resignation process and Senator Florian Chmielewski of Sturgeon Lake staged a "polka protest" in response to the lack of compromise. Armed with his accordion, Chmielewski played "Please Release Me" on the steps of the capitol for much of the day. He got his wish, after a fashion: the special session recessed between July 31 and October 12, allowing all but the negotiating legislators to go home.[54]

Governor Anderson held his course and vetoed the conservatives' first attempt at a tax bill. Throughout the 157-day ordeal, he never lost sight of his larger goal. Patience paid off, and by the end of October he managed a compromise that would raise state taxes by $580 million and increase the state's share of school operating costs to 65 percent.[55]

Conservatives got a one-cent increase to the sales tax. Liberals secured increases to income taxes and agreed to local levy limits and changes in the formula for the distribution of municipal aid to cities. Ultimately, all parties made concessions. The legislation increased state revenues by 23 percent but lowered property taxes throughout Minnesota. The state distributed the new revenues back to school districts and local governments, reducing disparities between wealthy and poor areas of the state.[56]

The Minnesota Miracle, as it became known, sought to increase state help to local governments, reduce property taxes, limit spending, reduce disparities in education funding, and shift Minnesota's tax structure to a more progressive system. Mark Dayton, who by the late 1970s served as an aide to the Perpich administration, described the legislation as "one of the most momentous bipartisan agreements in our state's history." Tom Berg credited that bipartisanship to "Wendy's ability to bridge gaps and make friends across partisan lines."[57]

Often overlooked—but critical to the legislature's eventual success—was the relationship between Governor Anderson and conservative senate majority leader Stanley Holmquist of Grove City. Holmquist, a business owner and former school principal and superintendent, shared Anderson's progressive view of government and had authored the state's first sales tax legislation in 1967.

"From the day he was in the legislature, until the Minnesota Miracle passed, his big goal was to level the playing field in funding for education. So the kid from Edina got the same education as a kid from Grove City," recalled Holmquist's son, Charlie. "My father was a progressive. The Minnesota Miracle leveled spending on education, and my father always said the most regressive tax in history is the property tax because it penalizes people for ownership, and that he was very much opposed to."[58]

"You are elected to lead, never to follow," Stanley Holmquist would often say.[59]

"His service to the public was more important to him than membership in a party," said Representative Dean Urdahl, who was elected to the house in 2002, considered Holmquist his political mentor, and delivered a eulogy to Holmquist on the house floor in 2003.[60]

Holmquist was able to convince enough of his conservative colleagues to support the compromise, which passed on October 27 and was signed by Anderson on October 30. The legislature adjourned. The federal Advisory Commission on Intergovernmental Relations said the legislation "made Minnesota a model for other states to follow."[61]

The Minnesota Miracle strengthened the hand of state government, making it a driving force in funding everyday services critical to Minnesotans, such as education, public safety, and local infrastructure. It strengthened the importance of state taxes relative to local ones for cities, counties, and school boards across the state. And it made the governor a more important figure in Minnesotans' lives.

The Perpich brothers' statewide tour had also been successful, with a more than doubling of the taconite production tax included in the final omnibus tax bill. Next, the three turned their attention to statewide support of DFL candidates in the 1972 election, with control of the legislature on the line.

For Rudy Perpich, 1971 was a pivotal year. He had stood on the state's largest stage and proved he belonged. He had shown Minnesota the underdog spirit and tenacity that had carried him to the top of the bare-fisted Iron Range political world.

CHAPTER 5

Rivals, Reelection, and the Scandal-Fueled Recession of the Republican Party

> "We had control. We were young. We had ideas. It was a
> very exciting time to be in public life. The conservatives had
> control for too long. They had bottled everything up."
>
> —*Senator Roger Moe*

With narrowly divided majorities in both the house and senate during the 1971 legislative session, each side recognized the significance of the following year's election. Both Democrats and Republicans began recruiting candidates and raising money before the conclusion of the historic 67th legislative session— more than a year ahead of the 1972 election. With no serious challengers to US senator Walter Mondale's reelection bid, the focus of both parties was squarely on the state legislature.[1]

The DFL had gained twenty-five seats in the 1970 election and needed to flip just one seat in the senate and three in the house to take total control of state government in 1972. The GOP, meanwhile, entrusted Dave Durenberger—a future US senator who had served as former governor Harold LeVander's chief of staff—to coordinate the Republican effort to retain control.[2]

Perpich told the *Minneapolis Tribune* that he planned to campaign full-time and travel to every legislative district in the state, hoping to bring attention to the lobbying and special interests he saw as impeding his party's progressive agenda for Minnesota. In the coming year, Rudy, George, and Tony—the "Perpich Party," as they were becoming known—would be instrumental to the Democrats' efforts.[3]

Like any good team, each brother brought his own strengths. Rudy considered Tony to be the most articulate of the three and credited him with authoring most of the arguments in favor of the trio's Iron Range liberalism. George was the most colorful, figured Rudy, who predicted George would one day be the best known. That left Rudy, described by his former chief of staff Gary Lamppa as the consummate politician.[4]

"George would get up on the floor and bellow. Rudy would do the politics," Lamppa remembered. "And Tony would be in the office, writing the bill."[5]

Joseph Perpich, the youngest brother and only non-dentist of the bunch (graduating instead from the University of Minnesota Medical School as well as Georgetown Law School), saw it as a historic time. "I think it could be a Broadway play," Joseph said in an interview years later. "These characters. These dentists. These funny names. They spoke a little funny with clipped accents."[6]

Rudy made the most of his statewide campaign, promoting Democratic candidates while simultaneously leveraging his platform to protest the Vietnam War. At an anti-war rally at the University of Minnesota in April, Perpich urged elected officials in Washington to disrupt the status quo.

"It's time for Congress to say, 'Until we're out of Vietnam, the business of Congress stops,'" Perpich said, before turning his attacks to presidential politics and Republican Richard Nixon. Calling out what he perceived as hypocrisy, Perpich alleged that if the president were to mistreat his dogs at the White House "he would be finished politically. But the same president can give orders to bomb millions of people and he's given a good chance at reelection."[7]

The next month, Perpich announced before a crowd at Edina High School that he was on a "semi-fast" until the war ended. He would drink only water and forego all desserts. He was also limiting himself to two meals a day—what he dubbed his "peace-meal." He urged the students in attendance to stop buying soda and candy as a means of protest.[8]

"If we are successful in getting large numbers to participate, we could then move on and consider organizing against the purchase of other commodities such as stereo record albums," Perpich proposed. He hoped the combined tactics might persuade manufacturers to apply pressure on Nixon to end the war.[9]

Throughout his career Perpich would exhibit this pattern—uttering top-of-mind ideas for political action or policy change without either first vetting them with others or following up later to build support. His ideas were many times good—brilliant, even—but often half-baked and led to a reputation for impulsiveness that would dog him later in his career.

Drawing Lines

In early June, a constitutionally mandated redistricting that had slogged on for more than a year was finally over. A three-judge federal panel announced new districts for that fall's campaign after Governor Anderson and state legislators failed to reach an agreement during the special session. The panel initially reduced the size of the legislature from 202 members to 140—making headlines even in the *New York Times*—before the US Supreme Court ruled the panel had overstepped its authority.

The new districts pitted a number of incumbents against one another, including Minneapolis conservative house members Arne Carlson and F. Gordon Wright. But one competition in particular drew the attention of political observers across the state—and offered the Perpich brothers a chance at revenge.[10]

The newly drawn Senate District Six extended from the Canadian border to the Duluth suburbs and included portions of Richard Palmer's 59th as well as Tony Perpich's 62nd districts. Tony, along with the entire Perpich Party, "relished" the opportunity to run against the one member of the senate who had blocked their chance at DFL control during the '71 session.

"I look forward to being in the Duluth area," Tony told the *Associated Press* the day the new maps were released.[11]

Palmer, however, wasn't so sure.

"My reaction at this point is that I haven't made up my mind whether I'll run again," Palmer told the same reporter.[12]

On Wednesday, June 28, Palmer announced he would not seek reelection. He believed he had been vindictively targeted and that the politically motivated maps were drawn by a panel led by Judge Gerald Heaney, a former Democratic national committeeman from Duluth who remained "quite active in local politics."[13]

The Perpich brothers organized campaigns for their new districts while simultaneously fanning out across the state in support of other Democratic candidates. The DFL coordinated a campaign around the conservative caucus's unanimous opposition to liberal proposals to record votes, tape hearings, and require stricter financial campaign disclosures during the 1971 session.

"Open state government to the people," "no secrecy in government," and "let the sunshine in" were common DFL slogans that year.[14]

In July, Perpich underwent what was described as "minor" proctology surgery and spent four days at Methodist Hospital in Rochester. The *Minneapolis Tribune* reported that Perpich would rest at his home in Hibbing for three weeks before campaigning throughout the state for Democratic candidates. But Rudy had a hard time sitting still.[15]

"In the summer of '72 I had a fundraiser in Crookston. He and Lola drove all the way across the state from Hibbing," recalled Roger Moe, a freshman senator who was in the heat of his first reelection campaign. "Miserable. Low turnout. But he was gregarious to everybody. Nice to everybody. Then they would turn around and drive back. He would do that all the time. He was just there for you."[16]

A Historic Election

On Election Day, November 7, 1972, DFL officials and candidates gathered in downtown Minneapolis to await returns at the Leamington Hotel while election workers tallied results at polling stations across the state. Nixon would win Minnesota's presidential vote by 5.5 percent—the last time that century the North Star State cast its electoral college votes for the GOP. It was clear early in the evening that DFL US senator Walter Mondale would also win reelection.

With the two top-of-the-ticket races decided, all attention turned to legislative races. It would be a historic election. Six women—four liberals and two conservatives—were elected to the legislature—as were the first two African Americans of the twentieth century. Minnesota's voter turnout was again among the highest in the nation at more than 70 percent, and the recently adopted Twenty-Sixth Amendment to the US Constitution, which allowed eighteen- to twenty-year-olds to vote for the first time, helped contribute to a "major generational shift" in the Minnesota Legislature. Thirty newcomers were elected to the Minnesota House, including four liberals who were college students in their early twenties and had defeated incumbent conservatives.[17]

The liberals won control of the house 77–57 and the senate 37–30. In addition to giving the DFL total control of Minnesota's government for the first time in state history, the voters also approved four amendments to the state constitution: bonus pay for Vietnam veterans, a reorganization of Minnesota's judicial system allowing for the appointment of clerks to district court and the removal of judges for disciplinary reasons, flexible legislative sessions (allowing for the legislature to meet annually rather than biennially), and the joint election of the governor and lieutenant governor—all agreed to overwhelmingly by voters.[18]

The changes also removed the lieutenant governor as presiding officer of the senate. The position now belonged to the executive branch, and would bring with it a set of administrative responsibilities.

Savoring the Democratic victories and eagerly anticipating an increase in his official duties, Perpich announced that he would be moving his family from the Iron Range to the Twin Cities.

"I'm going to be full-time," Perpich said. "I'm going to be working twenty hours a day." Anyone who knew him knew he meant every word.

A Full Partner

Legislation was needed before the voter-approved changes could go into effect, and anticipation mounted as Minnesota's 68th legislature prepared to convene at noon on January 2.

Rudy and Lola, along with thirteen-year-old Rudy Jr. and twelve-year-old Mary Sue, set out early from their home on Sixth Avenue in Hibbing to their new residence in St. Paul. Shortly before 9:00, blinded by the sun reflecting off freshly laid snow on Highway 73, Rudy drove the family car into a ditch seven miles north of Moose Lake. After a tow truck failed to break the vehicle free, Perpich, via a car radio connected to the State Highway Patrol, asked officers to alert the capitol that he might not make the opening.

When soon-to-be majority leader Nick Coleman learned of the situation, he hurried together plans for a helicopter to transport Perpich to the capitol. But the plans were scrapped when a passing snowplow happened upon the stranded Perpich family and broke their vehicle free from the snow. Rudy and his family drove the remaining 115 miles in their freshly dented car, arriving only minutes late. Perpich strode into the chambers and opened the session. His calm demeanor masked the chaos of the day's earlier mishap.[19]

One of the first items of business was an executive order from the governor designating full-time responsibilities to his lieutenant governor and calling him a "full partner" in the state government's executive branch. The order gave Perpich more than twenty specific duties, including representing the governor on the State Arts Council, Indian Affairs Commission, and Capitol Area Architectural and Planning Commission. Perpich would also serve as coordinator on environmental affairs, as overseer of the state's human services programs, and as coordinator of a "systematic state program to preserve and enhance the aesthetic environment in Minnesota."[20]

Perpich started his work enhancing the aesthetic environment and beautification of Minnesota during his time as lieutenant governor, and it remained a priority throughout the remainder of his political career. The duties at the time included regulating highway billboards, cleaning up junkyards and roadside restrooms, removing dilapidated buildings, and reclaiming mine lands across the Iron Range.[21]

"I couldn't be happier," Perpich told reporters. "I will be a partner and this is what I wanted."[22]

The 68th Minnesota legislature would go down in history as one of the most productive and consequential in state history—remaining the standard by which others are measured more than a half century later.

"We had control. We were young. We had ideas. It was a very exciting time to be in public life," recalled former senator Roger Moe. "The conservatives had control for too long. They had bottled everything up."[23]

The list of successful legislation would become extensive. Bills addressing the environment, consumer affairs, the Equal Rights Amendment, minimum wage, political party designation for state legislators, public employee bargaining, same-day voter registration, mass transit, ethics, and campaign finance reform flowed out of committee, through each chamber, and on to the governor's office on the way to becoming law.[24]

From Moe's perspective, the groundwork that Rudy Perpich, Nick Coleman, Martin Sabo, and countless others had laid over the previous decade was finally paying off. The research, legislative hearings, investigations, and proposed bills that had died in committee under conservative gavels were now a runaway freight train of progressive legislation.

"We made changes in tax policy and education policy and social services. We changed labor laws and consumer protections. Environmental efforts were hot. It was just a grand, grand time."[25]

When the dust settled on the 68th legislative session, a combined total of 7,315 bills had been introduced and 1,366 passed into law.[26]

Core Convictions

Even with his increased responsibilities as lieutenant governor, Rudy made time to travel and speak about issues he prioritized. He was relentless in his attacks on President Nixon's continued support of the war in Vietnam. In July 1973, when Congress authorized another month of bombing in Cambodia, Perpich decried it as "airborne barbarism" and labeled the president's request for the action "among the most frightening and certainly the most callous of decisions ever made by an American chief executive."[27]

Months later, Perpich again targeted Nixon during a speaking event in Eveleth. Oil prices had quadrupled following an embargo against the United States in retaliation for aid provided to Israel during the Yom Kippur War. Perpich maintained that the crisis was manufactured and recommended a "trip to the woodshed" for the oil companies involved. He challenged the federal government to take antitrust action and review tax breaks benefiting the oil industry, saying that "the only person who pays less taxes than the oil companies is President Nixon."[28]

But while Perpich could be reflexive and hyper-partisan on national issues, he continued his lifelong pursuit of equitable and sustainable policies for the Iron Range and beyond—often through his new role as coordinator of the state's environmental and aesthetic affairs. In particular, Perpich was willing to take on powerful mining interests in a way few politicians dared.

"Environmental protection was, for my father, a fight with the mining companies. They were polluting, both aesthetically and environmentally," Rudy Jr. remembered. "Mine land reclamation started with my father. If you went to a mining location before this program started, you would see mine shops left [behind]. The garages for trucks were left. Concrete slabs were left. Anything that wasn't valuable was left to rust. The streets of the town were just left there."[29]

By 1974, Kelly Lake, where Rudy and his friends would swim as kids, was an "old smelly lake" after its natural flow was rerouted and then shut off by the closure of a nearby mine. When township officials settled for $45,000 from Picklands Mather Mining Company instead of demanding the natural flow be restored, the money was quickly exhausted on legal and engineering fees for two wells that failed to produce enough water to remedy the green slime covering the lake, leaving one exasperated town supervisor to summarize, "we got the shaft."[30]

"We can't just let that lake go," declared the lieutenant governor, vowing to use the new powers of his office to bring the lake back to life.[31]

Speaking to a group of mining executives in Duluth, Perpich warned that the Reserve Mining Company was ruining the reputation of the entire industry and that opposition to reasonable environmental legislation was damaging to the "community welfare of the Range and to the public interest of the state." As high-grade iron ore deposits were depleted across the Iron Range, companies like Reserve shifted to extracting ore from a gray sedimentary rock called taconite, which contained only about 25 percent iron ore. The Reserve Mining Company had built a plant in Silver Bay, along the North Shore, to process the taconite but dumped the leftover waste material—known as tailings—into Lake Superior. By the late 1960s, these were becoming an environmental concern, along with human exposure to carcinogenic materials and air pollution from the company's exhaust stacks.[32]

To those closest to Rudy Perpich, his political drive, compassion, and commitment to his core principles were matched only by his devotion to family. Lynn Anderson, who met Perpich as lieutenant governor and would stay on his staff for nearly two decades, described Rudy's dedication to family as "grounded in great love and respect, (and) he lived it. Every single day."[33]

Perpich's commitment would be tested in February 1974 when Eighth District congressman John Blatnik abruptly announced his retirement after twenty-seven years in Washington. For years, Perpich had been expected to run for the seat once the dean of Minnesota's congressional delegation stepped aside.

"I Never Expected Him to Do It"

On the day Blatnik's announcement went public, Perpich told the reporters flocking to his office that he "very definitely" would consider getting into the congressional race.[34]

The news of Blatnik's retirement surprised political insiders, including Perpich himself, who only learned of it when his phone began ringing that morning. Blatnik, who had suffered a heart attack in 1971, said the decision was based on advice from his doctors and a desire to spend more time with his family. Many suspected the timing was to force Perpich's political hand.[35]

Perpich and Blatnik had a feud dating back to 1962. Blatnik had supported state senator Elmer Peterson when Rudy challenged Peterson in his first bid for senate.[36]

"I never expected him to do it," Perpich said of Blatnik's retirement. The poor timing would force Perpich to choose between running for reelection as lieutenant governor, as he had planned, or running for Congress. But the timing meant more than politics alone.[37]

"I've been moving my family back and forth," he lamented the same day. He had hoped by June to have his family fully established in the Eighth District. Perpich said the lake home near Biwabik that he and Lola had begun extensively remodeling was to be their home away from Washington—a clear indication his sights had been set on the congressional seat. Still, he said of his family, "I made a commitment to them you wouldn't believe. I'll know by the end of the week. I do have a problem there, I really do."[38]

Perpich knew in his heart that the decision was already made. His family meant more than his ambition. After talking the matter over with Lola and their two children that night, he announced at a press conference the next morning that he would not be a candidate for the congressional seat.

"These are critical years in the life of my children," he said, his family at his side. "Running for Congress would involve another tough campaign with much time away."[39]

Still fielding calls urging him to run later that morning, a testy Rudy Perpich told reporters in his capitol office, "They're not for it, all right." One caller, Richard Nordvold, worked in the radio industry and had first met Perpich during his time on the Hibbing School Board.[40]

"I couldn't believe it. I was absolutely dumbfounded," recalled Nordvold. "I called his office and got him on the phone: 'Rudy, what are you doing? You have been wanting that!'" Nordvold insisted. "No, no. Not this time. It is not the right time," came the reply.[41]

In his office, the newly bifocaled Perpich ran his hand across his face as he sank into his chair. "It's like winning a lot of battles, and then you walk away and somebody else takes the sword," he told the gathered reporters. "You win the battles and lose the war. It's not easy.

"I'm not dead politically. I get along very well with the governor, and I'm happy," Rudy said, adding that his becoming governor was "very possible."

Rudy Jr., Rudy, Lola, and Mary Sue in the lieutenant governor's office. *Courtesy Minnesota Discovery Center*

As for his longtime rival, Blatnik? "At least he can retire laughing," Perpich mused.[42]

With Rudy out, the *Minneapolis Tribune* handicapped the contest as "wide open" and predicted "the Eighth District DFL would have a blood bath." Two candidates emerged as clear front-runners: James Oberstar, who had served twelve years as an aide to Blatnik and was the hand-chosen successor, and the "No. 2 man in the Perpich Party," Tony Perpich.[43]

Oberstar was born and raised in Chisholm, just down the road from Hibbing, and had attended St. Thomas College, graduating with a degree in French and political science. He studied economics and international relations in Belgium before earning a PhD from Georgetown in international studies. He also spent time teaching foreign languages abroad before a chance meeting with Blatnik set him on a course to a political career.[44]

The matchup set up a showdown for supremacy of the northeastern Minnesota DFL machine. Many, including Rudy Perpich, thought Oberstar's years in Washington would be a detriment with voters. But Oberstar saw it differently.

"I thought about how I had put twelve years into this position. I know the district. I know the people. I know the needs," Oberstar remembered years later. "I could serve in Congress. So, I announced my candidacy."[45]

Al Zdon was a freshman reporter for the *Hibbing Tribune* during this period and remembered the contest as "one of the great political races of all time on the Range."[46]

The marathon DFL Eighth District convention carried over from Saturday night into Sunday and was a battle between the followers of Blatnik, who had ruled the Eighth District for twenty-eight years, and the Perpich brothers. Tony Perpich eventually prevailed on the thirtieth ballot, which was believed to be a record for a state or district convention. The results were a blow to Blatnik, who left the convention and returned to Washington when convention leaders refused to let him address the floor.[47]

When the victorious Perpich went to the platform to accept the nomination, Oberstar was the only other of the seven candidates not to join him on the stage. Tony was ready to put the Blatnik-Perpich feud to rest, noting that "I understand the Congressman considers me the white sheep in the family." Yet Oberstar wouldn't concede, noting "great pressure" from his supporters to challenge Perpich in the primary.[48]

"In the aftermath, a number of groups said that thirty ballots didn't constitute an endorsement. They said 'even though you said you would abide by the endorsement process, that was really an indecisive and inconclusive outcome,'" Oberstar recalls. "Many of those I had worked with over the years, such as veterans groups, mayors, county commissioners, township officers, small business people, labor interests, all said I should run. Twenty-five thousand people signed petitions to encourage me to run."[49]

Meanwhile, in the Perpich camp: "There was a whole group of people telling Tony to let it go. Don't push for the endorsement. There was another group that said we should get the endorsement. It proved to be one of the biggest mistakes, I think, that Tony made," remembers longtime Perpich Party lieutenant Gary Lamppa. "Oberstar came out the next day with 'Let the People Decide.' How do you argue with that?"[50]

And the people did decide, for Oberstar. The future congressman won the primary handily, defeating Tony Perpich by more than 20,000 votes in the six-person DFL primary. The deciding factor may have been Oberstar's attractiveness to GOP voters in Duluth, a characteristic of his old boss that fed the Perpiches' distrust of the Blatnik shop.[51]

"Tony Perpich—no, I'd say the Perpiches—are not particularly popular in Duluth," noted one Republican businessman from the Zenith City the day after the primary. "And Jim Oberstar is a physically and conversationally attractive fellow who, like John Blatnik, has a lot of support in the Republican segment."[52]

Rudy Perpich refused to endorse Oberstar in the general election, where the DFL candidate was almost guaranteed victory in the overwhelmingly Democratic Eighth District. Sounding bitter and resentful, he told the *Associated Press* that "Republicans spent so much [on] Oberstar's behalf that the St. Louis County GOP went broke."[53]

The incident provoked a rare public statement from Lola Perpich, defending her husband's actions as more than brotherly disappointment. "Congressman Blatnik broke the rules because he wants a congressman from the Eighth Congressional District who will continue his policy of being silent on the Reserve [Mining] case and support the mining interests in their efforts to exploit the Boundary Waters Canoe Area," she wrote in an awkward and defensive reference to the controversy surrounding the Reserve Mining Company's dumping of taconite tailings.[54]

Oberstar won the general election by more than 60,000 votes and would go on to represent the Eighth District for the next thirty-six years. The episode opened a wide rift between Oberstar and the Perpiches that would take several years and another primary election—this time with Rudy at the center—to heal.[55]

Reelection

Rudy Perpich had his own reelection bid in 1974, as Governor Wendell Anderson's running mate in the first election in state history where the governor and lieutenant governor would run as a team. If there was a silver lining in the Perpich Party's Eighth District loss, it was the support that state DFL leadership—many of whom Rudy had regarded as adversaries or potential challengers—had expressed for the lieutenant governor throughout the ordeal.

Governor Anderson, meanwhile, was increasingly mentioned as a potential candidate for the second spot on the 1976 Democratic national ticket. Alternatively, some predicted Anderson moving to the US Senate if either of Minnesota's senators, Walter Mondale or Hubert H. Humphrey, earned one of the two top spots. It was understood that Perpich would move to the governor's office in either event.

The relationship between Perpich and Anderson appeared to be in good order. While Anderson had indicated he would support Perpich running for Blatnik's seat, the day Rudy announced his decision to stay in his current position the governor said he was "very satisfied" with the job Perpich had done as his lieutenant and "comfortable" with him on the upcoming ticket.[56]

But there was gossip to the contrary.

For much of the previous year, the political rumor mill had been abuzz with speculation that Anderson would prefer to dump Perpich. The *St. Cloud*

Times alleged that Anderson was considering someone "more mature" and more closely aligned with his political ideology. St. Cloud mayor Al Loehr might fit that bill.[57]

But six weeks before the 1974 DFL state convention, Anderson announced his reelection campaign with Perpich as his running mate. Any doubts had been erased.[58]

The DFL, meanwhile, hoped to add to their control of both legislative chambers and the governor's office by sweeping all six statewide offices for the first time since Republicans had accomplished the feat in 1952, with then Governor C. Elmer Anderson heading the GOP ticket.[59]

The 1972 platform had been seen as extreme, and the party's desire in 1974 was a platform that would not make headlines.

Gathered at the Minneapolis Auditorium, the DFL convention was a tense affair. Key issues—including abortion, the legalization of marijuana, expanded legal rights for homosexuals, and amnesty for draft dodgers—threatened to splinter the party before the fall campaign. Minnesota's elder statesman, Hubert Humphrey, urged caution, imploring his fellow Democrats to "reject those who would lead us down the path of dissension and disruption—those who believe in sensationalism rather than common sense."[60]

The delegates followed his advice, with no controversial issues making their way into the party platform. The convention did, however, nominate Joan Growe as secretary of state, making her the first female to run for statewide office on a major party ticket in eight years. (Betty Hayenga ran for state auditor in 1966 but was defeated in the DFL primary.)[61]

The delegates gave the new ticket a warm send-off on the last night of the convention. Governor Anderson took an unusually sharp partisan tone, tying the Minnesota GOP to their disgraced national party in the wake of the Watergate scandal.

"The goal of the Republican Party in Minnesota is the same as the goal of the national Republican Party," he told the cheering crowd. "To do as little as possible for as few as possible for as long as possible. They commend Mr. Nixon and are extremely critical of us."[62]

The election was a landslide. The DFL swept the fall elections, winning all six statewide offices, picking up twenty-six seats in the Minnesota House, and gaining one congressional seat. Anderson and Perpich won by one of the largest margins in state history, besting their Republican opponents, state representative John W. Johnson and Moorhead mayor Dwaine Hoberg, in all eighty-seven counties and by more than a two-to-one statewide margin. The winning pair managed a near-record 63 percent of votes in a field of eight candidates.[63]

The margin of victory intensified speculation about Anderson's future on the national stage, yet many cautioned against DFL hubris, believing the results were as much the fallout of poor Republican turnout in the wake of Watergate as support for Democrats. Less than half of eligible voters cast ballots in 1974 in comparison with nearly 60 percent voting in 1970. In addition to Republicans failing to show up at the polls, models showed defection by Republicans to Anderson and other DFL candidates. Anderson had received 25 percent higher vote totals in some strong Republican precincts.[64]

The Republican candidate for governor summarized what many were thinking: "Our defeat started in Washington, and it demoralized our people," Johnson told reporters the day after the election. "And from the demoralization came apathy."

CHAPTER 6

Party Planning and the Hubris of Wendell Anderson

"Wendy Anderson was already being mentioned as presidential timber, certainly destined for a higher office. And Rudy being the politician that he was, I think he saw that as an opportunity, an excuse to go into every little Podunk town in Minnesota and cut ribbons, stand there with the mayor, and hand out a plaque."

—Gary Lamppa, chief of staff to Lieutenant Governor Rudy Perpich

"In the next four years you'll see me speaking out a lot more on issues," Perpich told reporters one week after the 1974 elections. To help, he had added radio and television broadcaster Robert Aronson to his staff. Perpich planned to travel and speak extensively throughout the state in an effort to develop a political image that was independent of Governor Anderson.[1]

Perpich saw an opportunity. Regardless of what national events transpired and how they might affect the Minnesota executive branch, he was determined to use his second term as lieutenant governor to his future advantage.

It began with a month-long tour of state hospitals for the handicapped in January, emphasizing improving medical care for the disabled and institutionalized. In Faribault, Perpich proposed that local communities should have more flexibility to develop local programs that met patients' needs. In Bemidji, he proposed local "one-stop human resource centers" throughout the state.[2]

"The emphasis would be on treating the individual as an entity," he said.

Perpich believed local programs could offer more personalized and effective care than one-size-fits-all state systems. It was the same critique of large-scale government programs that propelled the federal revenue-sharing system President Richard Nixon had championed in the late 1960s. Perpich was starting to demonstrate his appreciation for wide-ranging policy ideas, regardless of their partisan pedigree, that would define his political career.

Soon, Rudy Perpich was everywhere. He spoke to resort operators in Pequot Lakes and to the Red River Basin Planning Commission in Grand Forks. He addressed students from Winona, Lewiston, and Lanesboro—and dedicated the first medical center on the Vermilion Lake Indian Reservation. If there was a crowd, Perpich was there.

"I can't imagine how many miles he must have logged on his car," recalls former senator Roger Moe.[3]

A National Event

In June 1972, an executive order by Governor Wendell Anderson created Minnesota's Bicentennial Commission in preparation for the country's 200th birthday. He appointed his lieutenant governor as its chair. Anderson couldn't have known at the time, but the commission would become Perpich's most effective vehicle for reaching voters and establishing his political future. The commission's work was in full swing by early 1974, and Perpich didn't hide from the press that he saw his appointment as chair as a tool to be used at a time when Anderson was enjoying national attention.

"Sure I'm building a name," he told reporters in February, noting that he had visited eighteen communities the previous month alone. "Here's the way I look at it; If [Anderson's ascension to higher office] does happen in 1976, I have to be more visible and establish a track record. People won't have to ask, 'Who is this guy and what is he all about?' "[4]

"It was the perfect vehicle because he got to go into the community," Rudy Perpich Jr. recalled. At community celebrations "he would meet a lot of people—the mayors, the officials, but also the voters. [He'd] present a plaque, congratulate the town, make a general speech. He would interview on radio and TV—a great deal of noncontroversial coverage simply to get his name out. 'Perpich,' which a lot of people could not pronounce."[5]

"Purr like a kitten and pitch like a ball," Perpich told his press assistant, Barbara Rhode, who added, "You would drive into these small towns with him. Even if he didn't know one person, by the time you left, everyone ended up loving him. Sometimes we would do two or three communities in a day."[6]

"A new spirit of '76, let it begin with me" was the national slogan for bicentennial events, and communities were encouraged to undertake projects falling into three categories:

1. "Heritage '76" projects, such as the restorations of the courthouse in Grant County, the town hall in Lanesboro, and a hand-operated railroad turntable in Currie, population 368. Under the same rubric were a Finnish farmstead serving as a summer language camp in

New York Mills and a logging museum on the Leech Lake Indian Reservation. All were aimed at fostering "a time to remember."[7]

2. "Festival USA" projects, such as parades, concerts, and folk dances. Ice cream socials, smorgasbords, and beer gardens. Softball games, more parades, and more folk dances. In Cass Lake, a high school band presented original compositions by four students, and at the College of St. Benedict, maestro Stanislaw Skrowaczewski of the Minnesota Orchestra wrote a piece performed by the college's regional choral group. The Festival USA theme was "a time to celebrate."[8]

3. "Horizons '76" projects ranged from the dedication of a city park in Eden Valley, to installation of street signs and house numbers in Rothsay, to the building of a community center in Deer Creek. Millions of trees were planted across the state in cities such as Fergus Falls and Preston, where Perpich encouraged students to take action that would mean something in fifteen or twenty years. It was "a time to shape tomorrow."[9]

At the outset of the bicentennial project, administrators hoped to engage two hundred communities. In the end, more than 350 Minnesota towns and cities were involved in the celebration.[10]

The process of becoming a Minnesota Bicentennial City was straightforward, allowing towns large and small to participate. Once an application was received, a letter was sent to local officials and media, informing them that Perpich was recognizing their community as an official Minnesota Bicentennial Community and that their application would be forwarded by Perpich to dignitaries in Washington, DC. A presentation of the official flag by Perpich was typically announced along with a citizen chairperson and the projects the local commission would sponsor.

A full year ahead of July 4, 1976, patriotic fever was causing a shortage of flags. Bicentennial officials announced that "the commission is running out of flags for Lt. Governor Rudy Perpich to hand out during ceremonies."

Communities across the state went all out for America's 200th birthday party. Heidelberg in Le Sueur County may have been uncommonly small, with a population of seventy-two, but the scene there was typical. Cars lined the main street outside the tavern, the church, the city hall, and most of the town's thirty houses. Inside the tavern, red-faced revelers chugged Grain Belt beer, listened to speeches, and danced to accordion music. One of the speeches was, of course, delivered by Perpich, who rode into town in a Ford Model T. After presenting the ceremonial flag, Perpich dealt the first hand of a two-hundred-hour euchre marathon card tournament.[11]

Lieutenant Governor Perpich outside the capitol, June 1975. *Photo by Roy Swan, Minneapolis and St. Paul Newspaper Negatives Collection, MNHS*

In mid-April, an estimated 6,000 people lined the streets leading into Lake City as the mayor and the Lincoln High School marching band led a parade welcoming the Bicentennial Wagon Train on its way from St. Paul to Valley Forge, Pennsylvania. Four official wagons sponsored by Minnesota's Bicentennial Commission joined sixteen others along with fifty outriders as they reversed the path of many early Minnesota settlers. There was music, food, and Lieutenant Governor Perpich at a gathering at camp Hok-Si-La, where he presented a flag and a plaque and spoke to the crowd before the caravan headed east.[12]

"Wendy Anderson was already being mentioned as presidential timber, certainly destined for a higher office," remembered Gary Lamppa. "And Rudy being the politician that he was, I think he saw that as an opportunity, an excuse to go into every little Podunk town in Minnesota and cut ribbons, stand there with the mayor, and hand out a plaque." It was that rare sort of political publicity that is almost devoid of partisanship or controversy.[13]

"From a political point of view, it was pure gold," recalled Roger Moe.[14]

Barbara Rohde, who was with Perpich on the endless hours of travel across the state, saw that to him, the trips were more than politics. It meant something to communities to be included in a state and national celebration, and it meant something to individuals to meet the lieutenant governor. That's what made them valuable to Rudy.

"The bicentennial engendered so many good ideas, so much goodwill amongst communities," she recalls. Perpich knew this national sense of unity was temporary. "He kept saying, 'We should capture this.' I never ever once thought of him as thinking of how he could use this [politically]. Never. It was how this would help Minnesota, what was best for the state."[15]

And in some cases Perpich went to unlikely extremes to make a positive impression. A nurse relayed the story of a man Rudy had met at a coffee shop who was later hospitalized and awaiting an amputation. "He had no family, and he was scared," she recalled, saying the patient refused to go into surgery without speaking to the lieutenant governor. "For some reason, this old man felt that Rudy Perpich should be there."

The hospital called the lieutenant governor's office. Perpich came to the hospital to talk. Then he stayed all night until the man woke—for one final chat.

"That was Rudy Perpich. He could be tough as nails, but when somebody had been hurt by this world, he would do anything in his power to turn that person's life around," recalled Eldon Brustuen, who was related to the lieutenant governor through marriage and would be a staple in future Perpich campaigns and administrations. "He had a compassion. He had a heart that was incredible."[16]

Higher Aspirations

Speculation surrounding Wendell Anderson's political future had been a topic of capitol conversation since he took office as governor in January 1971. After his overwhelming reelection in 1974, the gossip had become a favorite pastime for St. Paul politicos and average Minnesotans alike. Through much of 1975, most of the rumors centered around whether Senator Hubert H. Humphrey would make another run at the presidency and the political ripples such a move would create.

Humphrey had made it clear that were he to undertake a sincere run for president, he would vacate his senate seat to do so. Many believed Anderson would seek to fill Humphrey's seat. Fourteen months before the '76 election, Anderson continued to deny he had any larger political aspirations, but observers noted his increasing attention to national and international affairs.

Early analysis of a potential contest for a vacant senate seat anticipated Anderson and Attorney General Warren Spannaus as the leading DFL candidates. Spannaus was more liberal and closer to the party organization than Anderson, whom many DFLers saw as clannish and arrogant. According to the *St. Cloud Times*, Spannaus informed the governor in late 1975 that if Anderson could guarantee him the DFL's endorsement for the governor's seat in 1978,

Spannaus would not contest an Anderson move to the Senate. There was, of course, one major omission in this arrangement—Rudy Perpich.[17]

Republicans, meanwhile, preferred contests against either Anderson or Spannaus to the venerable Humphrey. Retail lumber magnate Rudy Boschwitz and congressmen Bill Frenzel, Al Quie, and Tom Hagedorn were offered as potential candidates.[18]

If Perpich were to become governor as part of any reordering, "there would be a dozen Republicans itching to take a shot at Rudy in 1978," Frenzel said. "We could hardly wait."[19]

There was another alternative. Rudy saw the vice presidency rather than the Senate as Anderson's most likely vehicle to the national stage. He predicted that unless Humphrey were to enter at least a few of the upcoming year's primary contests, he would not be the Democrats' presidential candidate in 1976. In that case, Perpich believed the party's chosen nominee would want Wendell Anderson in the number two spot, a move that would secure Humphrey's support.

"It happens often in politics that maybe you can't do it for yourself, but you can for someone else," Perpich told reporters. "Minnesota is really respected for its state government and the people that come from Minnesota. Wendy Anderson would be acceptable to whoever is on the top of the ticket."[20]

Anderson downplayed the speculation, saying only that he was "at a loss to know" who might ultimately be selected as VP.[21]

As the 1976 primary season wore on, it became increasingly apparent that Humphrey would not be the Democrats' nominee. Minnesota's other senator, Walter Mondale, was gaining attention as a likely contender in the "veepstakes" should Georgian Jimmy Carter remain the front-runner for the presidential nomination. Mondale capitalized on politics' greatest intangible—being in the right spot at the right time.[22]

In 1960, Mondale, a thirty-two-year-old Minneapolis attorney with strong ties to the DFL Party, was appointed as Minnesota's attorney general by Governor Orville Freeman. Mondale won election in 1962 with 60 percent of the vote. He served until 1964, when he was again appointed—this time by Governor Karl Rolvaag—to the US Senate at the same time that Hubert H. Humphrey was selected to be President Johnson's running mate at the 1964 Democratic National Convention.[23]

During his time as a US senator, Mondale maintained a close relationship with Humphrey and together they worked to help secure the passage of landmark civil rights legislation. Mondale also had been an early presidential candidate in 1975, only to drop out well in advance of the primary season. The Minnesota senator offered geographic balance to the Carter ticket.

Carter made the selection of Mondale official on July 15, sending Minnesota's political prognosticators into a frenzy and giving Minnesota's Independent-Republican Party—which had officially become the name of Minnesota's Republican Party in 1975 in an attempt to distance it from the national GOP in the wake of the Watergate scandal—hope that a rebound to relevance was possible for the party that had been completely shut out of power since 1974.

"From a political standpoint, we have our tongues out on the sidewalk a foot long," said Republican Frenzel. "To us, unjamming that Democratic phalanx is like finding money on the street."[24]

If the Carter and Mondale ticket were to win that November, "the politics of the state would be turned upside down more on the Democratic side because they have so many horses that are teething at the starting line, waiting to get going," added Rudy Boschwitz.[25]

Perpich, with his increased visibility following statewide work on the bicentennial, was exactly where he wanted to be—squarely in the middle of the action. He made it clear he would do his part if Mondale were elected vice president and Anderson chose to fill his seat in the Senate.

For this to be accomplished, Anderson would need to resign his position as governor, leaving the new governor, his lieutenant, Rudy Perpich, to fill the Senate seat by appointing Anderson. If Perpich harbored any private reservations about how this backroom arrangement would appear to voters, publicly he was adamant that Anderson was the best person to fill the seat.

"Anderson would make an outstanding US senator," Perpich told reporters a week after Carter selected Mondale. "I really don't see anyone else who can match his qualifications."[26]

Perpich dismissed the idea of anyone, including himself, acting as a "caretaker" for the seat until Anderson could run in 1978, avoiding potential backlash from the public over Anderson having himself appointed to the position. He called the idea a "disservice to the people of Minnesota," making it clear he wanted no part of any such process.[27]

In New York for the Democratic National Convention, Perpich and Anderson talked strategy on the day of Carter's announcement. Anderson said he would consult his family about moving to Washington and that he wouldn't rush the decision. It seems Anderson had genuinely not made up his mind. Despite that, Perpich publicly committed in late July that he would make Anderson's appointment if the governor chose to seek the Senate vacancy.[28]

Anderson said he would make his decision after the voters had made theirs. "I honestly do not lie awake thinking what I might do if Jimmy Carter and Walter Mondale win the election," he said.[29]

Suddenly, Rudy Perpich was the most talked-about person among the capitol press corp. What kind of governor would the dentist from Hibbing make?

Forecasts ranged from a disaster that might sink the entire 1978 DFL ticket to a "refreshingly open, honest, and surprisingly able administration." Journalists predicted Perpich would appoint greater numbers of women to top state positions and support bold new environmental initiatives, and that Lola, introduced to the readers of one paper as "extremely bright," would remain his closest adviser.

DFL detractors characterized Rudy as an erratic and antibusiness Iron Ranger who would be an easy target for Republicans in 1978. Other Minnesota Democrats saw an honorable and decent man of compassion, someone who was "absolutely clean—there's no way you could buy him."[30]

A Vote for Perpich

"I don't think Carter is going to make it," Perpich told reporters in late September. Perpich saw the Carter campaign as collapsing, but his honesty before the press caused tension within the DFL Party. These moments revealed Perpich's "bedrock of unscared independence," according to *Minneapolis Star* columnist Jim Klobuchar, a fellow Iron Ranger who evinced an instinctive understanding of Perpich's style. Speaking to Klobuchar, Perpich described a local newspaper cartoonist as a "dishonest son of a bitch" for portraying the lieutenant governor as a backstabber for his remarks about Carter's faltering presidential run.

"What I said was nothing more or less than the truth," Perpich insisted. "Did the fact that I belong to the same political party make it less true?"[31]

Perpich, still traveling extensively throughout Minnesota in conjunction with the bicentennial, also shared his thoughts on the state of the Independent-Republican Party, adding "there's nothing left of the Republican Party in northern Minnesota." The fact that Democratic US representative Jim Oberstar was running unopposed in his first reelection campaign seemed to prove his point.[32]

By October, a group of Perpich supporters had buttons made with a simple message: "A vote for Jimmy Carter is a vote for Rudy Perpich." The buttons were soon followed by letters such as one written to the editor of the *Minneapolis Tribune* on October 11 that read: "Just a reminder of things that may come; Remember that a vote for Jimmy Carter is a vote for Rudy Perpich for governor."[33]

In this case, the letter's author neglected to clarify whether they considered this a favorable outcome.

Less than three weeks after predicting Carter's defeat, Perpich changed his mind. After visiting nearly two dozen communities, Perpich felt a "new groundswell of enthusiasm" for the Democratic ticket. He cited comments made by President Gerald Ford at the second presidential debate he deemed offensive to "eastern ethnic" voters, a Canadian TV report on Carter's support among

African Americans, and his perception that labor was "moving solidly behind Carter" as factors swinging the election in Carter and Mondale's favor.[34]

"If it does happen, I'll be a good governor," Perpich said a week before election day. But he didn't stop there, adding that he took exception to multiple polls showing voters did not want Anderson to take the Senate position. "I know this state and this government as well as anyone in Minnesota," adding that he resented his portrayal as a "dumb hunky" from the Iron Range.[35]

On November 2, 1976, Jimmy Carter and Walter Mondale received just over 50 percent of the popular vote, defeating Gerald Ford and Bob Dole 297 to 240 in the electoral college.[36]

Hopes and Hubris

In Minnesota, Carter and Mondale won in a landslide. Anderson's closest advisers urged the governor to move to the Senate and to make the announcement as soon as possible. Minnesota House speaker Martin Sabo, one of Anderson's most trusted associates in the legislature, summed up what many in the governor's inner circle were feeling: "He's the logical person to go," the speaker said the day following the election. "He likes public life. Clearly, he could be elected in two years. It all points to him."[37]

Perpich and Anderson were contemporaries in age and shared hardscrabble backgrounds, but they were never close. Part of their distance was political—Anderson belonged to the establishment wing of the DFL Party, and his decisions were calculated based on their effect on his future within that organization. Perpich had supported Nick Coleman over Anderson at the 1970 DFL state convention and was closer to the progressive, working-class issues of the party's liberal wing. Anderson viewed Perpich as an undisciplined maverick whose greatest value was his command of Iron Range voters.

Perpich, while not in Anderson's inner circle, shared Sabo's sentiment. "Absolutely not," Perpich responded when questioned whether such a decision by Anderson would carry political risks. "He's very, very popular."[38]

It was a rare instance of Perpich's political instincts failing him. His forecast of voters' reaction to the arrangement was badly off the mark. Others, including Hubert Humphrey, disagreed, citing historic examples of governors around the country who had made similar decisions and subsequently faced the wrath of voters. Some might perceive such a maneuver as circumventing the election process.[39]

Everyone, it seemed, had an opinion. The editorial board of the *Minneapolis Star* opined that an Anderson-contrived self-appointment would be a "shame" and urged a special election to fill the soon-to-be vacant seat. The Nicollet County DFL Central Committee passed a resolution requesting Anderson call a special session to change the law (which required the governor to fill the vacancy), allowing a special election. Conversely, a majority of rank-and-file members of the AFL-CIO supported Anderson taking the seat. Most conceded that Anderson would win a special election if one were to take place.[40]

Waiting for Anderson's decision, Perpich became restless. When the young editor of the *Hibbing Daily Tribune*, Al Zdon, caught wind that Anderson would inform Perpich of his decision that day, he hurried to the Perpich's residence on Sixth Street in Hibbing, a quaint white house with black shutters. Zdon knocked at the front door, and Lola answered.

"Is Rudy here?" he asked.

"Yes, out in the garage," Lola replied.

Knowing that Perpich was never handy, a genuinely curious Zdon asked, "What is he doing?"

"Painting the studs in the garage," Lola explained. "He has got to do something because he has all of this nervous energy and nothing he can do but wait for Wendell."

Word came a few hours later. Anderson was choosing to resign his position as governor to assume the position within the Senate. He told Perpich he would make his decision public the following day.

Rudy summoned Zdon along with Mike Barrett, the editor of the Virginia paper, to accompany Frank Ongaro and himself to the former Carson Lake site where Perpich and Ongaro had grown up. All the houses had been destroyed or moved, and everything was overgrown. Wandering aimlessly through the underbrush, they searched unsuccessfully for the Perpich homestead until Ongaro said, "it is over here."

All that was left of Perpich's childhood home was the front stoop. Rudy climbed on the steps.

"I wish I had had a tape recorder," remembered Zdon. "He hadn't been inaugurated yet, but it was basically his first speech as governor. He stood on the stoop and talked about growing up in Carson Lake. We were furiously taking notes. Then we all hopped back in Frank's car and drove back to Hibbing."[41]

On the eve of becoming Minnesota's first governor from the Iron Range and standing amid the now-vacant site of his childhood home, the place and people that had been so instrumental in shaping Rudy Perpich were with him as he made his way to St. Paul.

On Wednesday, November 10, at a capitol press conference, Anderson publicly announced his plans to resign as governor and accept an appointment to the US Senate. He acknowledged he had considered a special session to change the law but reasoned that it would take too long.

"It is my hope and prayer that the quality of my work will earn [the voters'] support and justify my election to a full term in 1978," he told a cheering crowd in the governor's reception room at the state capitol. "I will leave the office of governor in good and experienced hands. Rudy Perpich has twenty solid years of service as a school board member, state senator, and lieutenant governor. He is bright and honest and dedicated to the people of this state."[42]

After Anderson finished, Perpich stepped to the podium, his elation barely contained beneath a dark pinstriped suit, white shirt, and black-and-white polka-dot tie.

"At this moment I'm the happiest person on earth," he told the gathering of reporters and supporters as Lola, Rudy Jr., and Mary Sue smiled at his side. "By this time next week, both my feet will be back on the ground."[43]

After the press conference, the Perpich family returned to their home on the Iron Range. Barbara Rohde accompanied the family on the journey to Hibbing, where Rudy—soon to be the first Iron Range governor—spotted a newspaper's headline. "Instead of 'Perpich to Become Governor' it said 'Anderson to Step Down,'" recalled Rohde. "His reaction was, 'I can't believe this,' but he just laughed."[44]

The media immediately seized upon the story. The day after Anderson's announcement, a front-page headline in the *St. Cloud Times* blazed "Perpich Rises with 'Firsts,'" noting that the governor-designate would be the first Catholic, Iron Ranger, dentist, and ethnic Yugoslavian in Minnesota's top office. Emphasizing his rags-to-riches rise from poverty, some suggested that a "mild paranoia" might arise during a Perpich administration. Conventional wisdom, however, was that the new governor would be straightforward and express his opinions "openly and honestly."[45]

Republicans weren't as charitable.

"We don't want to be smug or underrate the future Governor Perpich," GOP chairman Chuck Slocum told the *Associated Press*, "but he does look to be vulnerable."[46]

Perpich wanted to set the tone of his new administration early. He clearly had been thinking about his new duties for some time. His first major announcement, reported in the *Minneapolis Star* on November 18, was that he sought to appoint a woman to lead the Minnesota Pollution Control Agency—succeeding Peter Gove, who was resigning to accompany Anderson to Washington. With more than a hundred appointments to make, Perpich intended to fill half with women and minorities. He revealed his intentions to create the position of "citizens advocate" and that the new post would go to Bettye Bates, a longtime state employee who served as assistant commissioner of administration.[47]

He unveiled a long list of priorities once sworn in, including increasing the number of low-income housing starts, an "all-inclusive" resolution to the Reserve Mining pollution problem, the development of a major health research center in conjunction with the University of Minnesota, increased funding for the arts (particularly in areas outside of the Twin Cities), the preservation of historic properties, limiting class sizes in public schools, and restricting commercial activities in the Boundary Waters Canoe Area. Many of these priorities had a decided focus on rural areas of the state.[48]

The same man who once expressed doubts about whether he would ever run for governor was brimming with confidence in interviews with the press by late November. Before he had been sworn in, Perpich announced he would seek the DFL endorsement for governor in 1978—assuming his performance met with "a reasonable reception" from voters. His hesitation was his antipathy for raising money.

Perpich had run his three campaigns for Hibbing School Board and two for the Minnesota Senate without soliciting any outside funds. During his 1970 campaign, however, he had only secured about 25 percent of the $43,000 he spent and had mortgaged his house to make it through.[49]

"The political process is the one in which I am the happiest," he said a few days after Thanksgiving. "Raising money is the only thing I don't like about politics—that and riding in parades. I refuse to ride in parades."[50]

Rudy hated parades because he was an intensely private person—often even bashful. When he did participate in parades out of political necessity, he did so in a nontraditional way. He didn't bring the entourage of an organized political campaign event—handing out stickers or political literature. Instead, he preferred the simple company of his family and a more informal interaction with voters.[51]

Inauguration

Perpich, feeling there were too many other priorities at the time, announced in early December that he would forego the typical inaugural festivities. Instead, after a modest swearing-in ceremony, he planned an open house in the capitol.

"Anybody who wants to come and meet the governor can do so, from noon to midnight," he said.[52]

Perpich had a knack for spotting political talent. He began to assemble his political team with rising and ambitious young leaders. He tapped Terry Montgomery, a moderate DFLer and unsuccessful 1970 DFL congressional candidate in the Sixth District, to be the top aide in his administration. The move caused consternation among many in the liberal faction of the party, but Montgomery explained that both he and Perpich believed his connection to "the more traditional elements of the party will provide a good balance" to Perpich's liberalism.[53]

It wouldn't be his last controversial decision. A week before Christmas,

Perpich made good on his earlier promise by naming twenty-nine-year-old Sandra Gardebring as executive director of the Minnesota Pollution Control Agency. Perpich lauded Gardebring as a hardworking and articulate spokesperson with a "genuine concern for the environment."[54]

"I was not a very likely candidate," recalled Gardebring. "I was inexperienced, utterly inexperienced." A young lawyer, Gardebring had driven through a snowstorm to turn in her résumé at the urging of a friend at the last possible minute. After a series of interviews, five candidates remained, including Gardebring. All were invited to a dinner at the governor's residence, where each sat at a table with members of the search committee. Rudy went from table to table, talking to the candidates.

After a week passed without word, Rudy called out of the blue and invited Gardebring out for an ice cream soda. In person, Perpich told her, "I have decided to appoint you commissioner of the PCA. Bob Aronson will drive you to the capitol because I have told the press corps that the new commissioner was going to be arriving—but I didn't tell them who it was."

Gardebring asked if it would be all right to call her family. Rudy laughed and said, "They can just hear it on television."

"I don't know what it was. I think Lola liked me," Gardebring muses. "I didn't have any political background. I wasn't a Democrat particularly; I wasn't an activist in the party. I believe there was personal chemistry, and I've always believed that involved Lola."[55]

Gardebring would go on to become one of Perpich's most trusted advisers, serving in a sequence of high-profile positions within future administrations, including as chair of the Met Council, as commissioner of the Department of Human Services, and ultimately as a justice on Minnesota's highest court.[56]

Perpich spent Christmas with his family in Hibbing. Then, he turned his attention forward, leaving early one morning for St. Paul, along with Richard Nordvold, Frank Ongaro, and Bob Aronson—all of whom had been tasked to assist with the inaugural.

"It was snowing and his car pulled into the driveway," recalls Nordvold. "Rudy, from the time we left my driveway to the time we got to the capitol, reminisced on his life. As we got closer and closer to the Cities, it was almost as if he was becoming governor, getting himself ready—psychologically prepared—for the days ahead."[57]

Wendell Anderson resigned his office on December 29, 1976, after serving as governor for more than six years without falling below 51 percent in approval polls. He had done so largely by avoiding controversy and maintaining an above-the-fray approach while his top aides bore the brunt of daily political skirmishes. The feeling among capitol observers was that a Perpich administration would take a different approach—one less guarded, less calculated, and more spontaneous. Perpich's leadership would be less pretentious and engage more directly with the people of Minnesota.[58]

Perpich made this change in governing style clear with a down-to-earth inaugural that shunned traditional pomp and circumstance in favor of a simple ceremony paying homage to his Iron Range roots. Where Anderson's first inaugural included a performance by the Minnesota Orchestra, Perpich invited the Hibbing High School Band. There would be no inaugural ball; rather, Perpich began the day with a simple "polka mass" at St. Paul's Church of the Assumption, with Eveleth priest Frank Perkovich celebrating the rites.

The one-thousand-seat church was overflowing as Perkovich, who referred to Perpich as "Rudy" throughout the ceremony, called on the new governor to be a peacemaker, community builder, and "father of the people of Minnesota." There would be no engraved invitations or formalities of a black-tie dinner; instead, Perpich delivered an open meet-and-greet invitation and vowed to stay as long as it took to shake the hands of the thousands of everyday Minnesotans who flooded the capitol to meet their new governor.

"That kind of explains his background and personality; he doesn't like a lot

Mary, Anton, Lola, Rudy, Mary Sue, and Rudy Perpich Jr. listen to the Polka Mass-ters Orchestra as part of an inaugural service at the Church of the Assumption, December 1976. *Photo by Charles Bjorgen, Minneapolis and St. Paul Newspaper Negatives Collection, MNHS*

of fanfare and pomp," explained George Perpich, Rudy's cousin, one of dozens of relatives in town for the occasion.[59]

The service complete, Perpich moved with his family to the capitol to take his oath. He delivered a seven-paragraph tribute to family, education, and the immigrant struggle. Then, he confidently raised his right hand, placed his left hand on the Bible that Lola held, and—with their children at his side—Rudy Perpich became the 34th governor of Minnesota.[60]

Surrounded by family, Rudy Perpich is sworn in as Minnesota's 34th governor. *Photo by Mike Zerby, Minneapolis and St. Paul Newspaper Negatives Collection, MNHS*

CHAPTER 7

Governor Perpich

"I'm proud to be the governor, and I'm not going
to be hangdog about how I got there."
—*Governor Rudy Perpich, 1976*

Rudy Perpich may have assumed Minnesota's highest office by chance, but he
was very intentional about using the opportunity to help others. He would re-
define, at least for a time, the role of governor. Indicative of the changes ahead,
Perpich planned a down-to-earth inaugural—swapping the traditional black-
tie dinner with the political upper crust for cookies and punch with everyday
Minnesotans.

"His entire time as governor was based on compassion for people," remembered Lynn Anderson, who served as assistant to the governor starting in December 1976. Perpich held to "his belief that people cared about him as he was
growing up, that they never lost hope in him, that they encouraged him and
pushed him and looked out for him. He felt a tremendous obligation to do that
for other people."

Anderson witnessed that compassion on inauguration day as her new boss
stood shaking hands for twelve hours.

"His compassion to make sure that people had water, that they had a place
to sit—that everybody felt they had enough time," she recalled. "It didn't matter
if you were eighty years old or eight, he made you feel like you were an important individual."[1]

One of those standing in line was thirty-year-old Mark Dayton, the son of
Bruce Dayton, one of the five brothers who headed the state's leading retail
enterprise. Dayton had spent the past ten years away from Minnesota, most
recently working in Washington, DC, for Senator Walter Mondale. He had
moved back to his home state earlier that month and reached out to Perpich's
soon-to-be chief of staff, Terry Montgomery, about a job in the new administration. Dayton stood in line for two and a half hours in the capitol rotunda for
a chance to introduce himself to Rudy and Lola. It was the first time Perpich

and Dayton had met, and it was the beginning of a friendship that would last for the next fourteen years.

About a week later, Dayton was invited to a meeting at the governor's residence.

"As was typical with Rudy, one meeting led to another meeting," remembered Dayton. "He was in the habit of inviting people who were part of one meeting to stay on for a next meeting even if it was on a very different topic. I think that was part of his genius. He was able to draw people from different backgrounds and different perspectives to offer their input into a whole variety of issues."

Dayton stayed on for a second and then a third meeting. As midnight approached, with business coming to a close, Perpich reached across the table, picked up a plate of cookies and a couple drinking glasses, and headed for the kitchen. Dayton figured that if his new boss, the governor of Minnesota, was taking out the dishes, he should follow suit.

"There he was, standing at the sink, sleeves rolled up, washing the dishes. I thought to myself, 'That's a good example to follow.' I rolled up my sleeves, and we stood, side by side, doing the dishes. Right away, I understood that this was a very different politician from the ones that I had read about or been around in the past."[2]

Throwing Away the Rule Book

"I'm going to surprise a lot of people," Perpich had told a reporter on the eve of his inauguration. Within weeks of taking the oath of office, the *Associated Press* reported that the new governor had "not only rewritten the political rule book—he's thrown it away."

In his first forty days in office, Perpich opened nearly all his meetings—including those on sensitive topics—to the public and press; instructed agency heads to join him on unscripted weekly 6:00 A.M. press calls; and bewildered the same media along with his staff and security by vanishing from St. Paul, only to appear unannounced on the doorsteps of farmers dealing with an escalating power line dispute.

Perpich also personally cracked down on speeders, honking his horn at offenders and even instructing the driver of his governor's black Ford State Patrol One to trail culprits until a state trooper could pull them over and issue a ticket. On January 18, during a nationwide energy crisis, the new governor declared a state of emergency and took to the phone lines himself, calling random households and asking if they had "dialed down" their thermostats to sixty-five degrees.[3]

In keeping with his desire for an open administration, Perpich went so far as to take his office door off its hinges—though his staff later convinced him that this wasn't practical, and he put it back.[4]

"He really believed that, by opening the doors, he assured a cleaner, better-run government," recalled Montgomery, his new chief of staff. "He believed that by inviting the press to see how everything worked, they would report that to the people [who] would understand better what was going on."[5]

Rudy Perpich required little sleep and thrived off the energy of others. He had promised that his administration would be hardworking, but no one expected the extent to which Perpich would make good on that promise. One day in early February, the *Minneapolis Star* reported that Perpich's final meeting the day before had concluded at 3:10 A.M. after an agenda of more than forty appointments with legislators, state officials, and private citizens ran three hours behind schedule.

"I'm one of those people who only needs four or five hours of sleep," Perpich explained to reporters. "If I go to bed at 8:00, I'm up at 2:30. What good does that do? If I was bowling, I would be tired in 10 minutes—or golfing, I'd get tired right away. But I love this job. I'm like a teenager in love."[6]

Perpich was determined to make the most of every moment he had as governor, feeling that time was short and he now bore a great responsibility.

"I would like to get in six years as governor, I really would," Perpich said at the end of a nineteen-hour day early in his term. "But I feel it might not happen. That's why I'm crowding things in a little. When my picture is hanging up there on the capitol walls, I want people to say that Rudy Perpich really did a good job." As Frank Ongaro recalled, "Boy, that guy never stopped. He would always say, 'We have got to get these projects done. You don't know what is going to happen in '78.'"[7]

Minnesotans loved the exuberance of their new governor, with the exception of some grumbling over Rudy's crackdown on speeders. "The people love it. He can't miss," observed state senator Mike Menning, then a DFLer who represented the southwestern corner of the state. "They talk about him over their coffee cups."[8]

A Populist Approach

Early in his administration, Perpich announced that he would open his office once a week to anyone who wanted to visit him from noon to midnight, vowing to resist the "insulation syndrome" that plagued elected officials. The press, however, questioned whether Perpich's frenetic and accessible style was a calculated contrast to his predecessor. "Hell no," Rudy shot back. "I've been doing this for six years, but nobody paid any attention."[9]

While the public appreciated the personal attention Perpich paid them, the press challenged the effectiveness of such an unorthodox style. In early March, an obviously irritated Perpich cut off a reporter who referred to a recently published account of fellow DFLers who were critical of his governing. "That's not true," Perpich snapped, before launching into a long defense of his handling of issues, including the power line controversy, the Reserve Mining Company case, and the energy crisis plaguing the nascent administration.

After putting more than 170,000 miles on his car during his travels as lieutenant governor, Perpich asserted, "I know this state. And I have a whole drawerful of things I want to get done."[10]

"I think that he felt that he really needed to hear from the people. He had his finger on the pulse of the state as lieutenant governor" and wanted to maintain that sense of connection, Lynn Anderson believed, even though doing so made great demands on his staff.

"We had almost no time. We were thinking on our feet constantly. We never took a breath, we just went from one issue to another," she recalled. "Every day there was something we were preparing for."[11]

Perpich delivered his first State of the State address to the legislature exactly one week after assuming the governorship. He set a populist tone for his administration, announcing a $2 million temporary program to provide jobs for farm families affected by drought, along with a commitment that members from both the house and senate would hold hearings within two weeks on the mounting power line controversy. Additionally, he pledged no increases in state taxes and a freeze on hiring state employees—although he did promise more women and minorities in "major policy positions in state government." He also committed to improving state services for Native Americans.[12]

With an emphasis on standards over specifics, Perpich set forth the "most comprehensive energy-saving program ever considered by any state." He made clear his vision for creating jobs and protecting the environment were not mutually exclusive. "There is no need to abuse the environment to protect jobs," he affirmed by pledging to work toward a compromise to stop the dumping of taconite tailings into Lake Superior while preserving the jobs of 3,000 Reserve Mining Company workers.

Perpich called for "a healthy environment, healthy people, and a healthy economy."[13]

The Reserve Mining issue put Perpich in a particularly tough position. "He was a very, very strong environmentalist," recalled Montgomery. "On the other hand, Reserve Mining was very important to the job economy of the very part of the state he came from."[14]

The message was short on details and high on nervous energy. "He must have had about a forty-minute speech which he gave in about twenty minutes," remembered Senator Roger Moe. "I think it was the first time we had a signer [for the deaf]. That poor woman was just worn out by the time she got done with that speech."[15]

Perpich established at the outset that he would not present a comprehensive legislative proposal, saving the details for his budget message later in the month. "Today, I simply want to tell you how I feel about Minnesota, our government, and our people," he told the 70th session of the legislature.

Perpich saw the ideals that aided his rise to Minnesota's highest office expressed in the spirit of everyday people. "The people of this state are an inexhaustible resource of faith and optimism, pride and high expectations," he asserted in rapid-fire staccato. "They try hard. They work hard. They look forward to better lives for themselves and their children, and better lives for those who haven't been so fortunate."[16]

He ended with a familiar championing of self-improvement and a dose of Minnesota modesty. "Our people are committed to education and opportunity. They believe you can succeed if you work at it. They know Minnesota is not perfect. But they think we can do better than just about anybody else."[17]

Above all, Perpich vowed to listen to, and talk with, the people. Following the speech, he again opened his office to all comers.[18]

"That was one of the first things that people of Minnesota found out about Rudy Perpich," remembered Montgomery. "He was going to do things in a very personal way, which had not been the tradition for many, many years."[19]

The Power Line Controversy

In the early 1970s, regional power utilities recognized the need for more diverse sources of electricity to meet the requirements of their electric cooperative customers—which make up roughly two-thirds of power customers in the state. The United Power Association of Elk River and Cooperative Power Association of Edina set in motion what would become one of the greatest challenges of Perpich's first administration when they proposed to build a 440-kilowatt high-voltage transmission line from North Dakota across 170 miles of Minnesota to connect their grid to a new coal power plant near the Missouri River, between Underwood and Washburn, North Dakota.[20]

Farmers in the affected areas felt the line would damage their property and the environment. Construction was scheduled to begin in late spring of 1977, but angry landowners had halted work for two months in some areas.

With mounting tensions, Pope County Attorney David Nelson said "the sheriff feels he's unable to get sufficient deputies and it's almost a certainty he's unable to control the crowd." The day before the State of the State speech, Pope County officials indicated they would ask Perpich to call out the National

Guard to protect project workers from protesting farmers. Work on the line was halted until the county could ensure the safety of the surveyors.[21]

Perpich, who seemed sympathetic to the plight of the farmers but who also realized the train had left the station, remained optimistic that he would be able to bring the sides together and that an agreement could be reached. After announcing legislative hearings on the issue, he told reporters "I feel it in my bones that we are going to resolve that issue. That's really saying a lot, isn't it? But I'm going to try. If we can resolve things on the Iron Range, why can't we resolve this?"[22]

He would need more than his intuition. A week after pledging to listen to the people, Perpich did just that. Returning from a Seventh District DFL convention in Moorhead, he made an unannounced and unaccompanied appearance at the local bar in Lowry, Minnesota, looking for directions to the Dennis Rutledge farm. Rutledge, who was active in local DFL politics, was involved in the protest movement.

"It was a Sunday night. I was home early from the Reserves because of a snowstorm," Rutledge recounted. "Jerry from the bar calls me and says, 'There is a guy all dressed up in a suit who is asking for directions to the Dennis Rutledge farm. What do you want me to do?' I said, 'Ask who it is.' He came back to the phone and said, 'He says, "I'm Governor Perpich."' I said, 'I don't know who is playing a joke but send him out so I can see who this joker is.' Pretty soon there is a knock at our door."[23]

When Dennis Rutledge's wife, Nina, answered the door, Perpich "just came right in." He spent three hours talking with the Rutledges and their neighbors before getting into his car for the two-hour drive back to St. Paul around 10:00 P.M.[24]

"He did not consult anybody. He just showed up in a farmer's yard," recalled Montgomery. "We in the governor's office did not know he was there. Nobody else knew he was there except the farmers. We all found out about it about the time the reporters found out about it. He got a lot of criticism, but I think he also got some support from people who felt that he was being genuine, straightforward—that he was not doing it the traditional, political way."[25]

Returning to the governor's residence after midnight, Perpich woke early the same morning to return to Pope County, visiting with farmers in Villard, Starbuck, and Glenwood. He went without staff, without security, and without reporters—without any notice. The people, of course, loved it. "It shows an openness in government that I haven't experienced in my lifetime," said Harold Hagan, president of Counties United for a Rural Environment (CURE).

"People are just thrilled that this man would come to them on a one-to-one basis," Nina Rutledge told reporters the day after the governor's visit. "With Governor Anderson, all we ever got was an aide. It's such a contrast."

Public opinion polls showed that Minnesotans liked what they saw in

Governor Perpich takes calls from WCCO listeners, May 1977. *Photo by William Seaman, Minneapolis and St. Paul Newspaper Negatives Collection, MNHS*

Perpich. "They liked the openness, the candor," Montgomery remembered. "He had tremendous charisma. They hadn't seen anybody like him in Minnesota since Floyd B. Olson or Harold Stassen. He had great public interest and great public appeal."[26]

In the power line affair, Perpich believed fault ultimately lay with the power companies for a lack of communication. He believed they acted arrogantly and that the problem could have been avoided if they had involved those affected from the beginning. Still, the line had progressed far enough by the time he took office that he couldn't simply reverse course. He believed his visit helped cool the escalating tempers, allowing the legislative hearing process to play out. The only path to a solution would require public input and support.[27]

"It's really going to be a toughie," Perpich said, appraising the situation and his involvement. "I still think the chances of getting this resolved are a hell of a lot better if I get in it myself."[28]

After spending all day Monday visiting with farmers and listening to groups including Save our Countryside (SOC) and Families Are Concerned Too (FACT), Perpich took the Rutledges out to dinner at the Minnewaska House near Glenwood before driving himself back to the governor's mansion.[29]

"Rudy Perpich was higher than a kite after his first visit out to western Minnesota," recalled special assistant Ronnie Brooks. "He felt he could solve anything."[30]

Perpich related to the plight of the protestors, calling the power line opposition a grassroots effort grounded in a sense of universal morality—often with women more involved than men. "It's like the peace movement, the civil rights movement, the women's movement. It's a family effort," he told reporters.[31]

"I think he knew he was doing the right thing if he could sit in that farmhouse in central Minnesota and have a conversation with those people in a way that they felt that they could say anything they wanted and they were safe in their convictions and their views," recalled Anderson.[32]

Opening Doors

Hoping that his personal involvement had calmed the power line controversy, Perpich turned his attention to diversifying state government. Before members of the DFL Feminist Caucus on January 15, he vowed to open the appointment process for all major state positions to all applicants, specifically encouraging women and minorities to apply.

"We want your talents. We want your recommendations. We want to encourage women from rural and outstate Minnesota to serve in state government along with those from the metropolitan area," he told the caucus, pledging that a new commission established to make recommendations would be "broadly representative" of the economic, cultural, and geographic diversity of the state.

Perpich tapped fifty-one-year-old feminist Gloria Griffin of Tonka Bay to chair the Governor's Appointments Commission. She had run unsuccessfully for Congress in Minnesota's Second District in the previous November's election. After her defeat, Griffin had approached governor-to-be Perpich to find positions within his administration for her campaign staffers—a common practice for defeated congressional candidates.[33]

"I don't do plums," Perpich told her. But he did have something else in mind. He and Lola had watched Griffin during the 1976 congressional election and admired the way she carried herself. He asked her to lead the effort that ultimately selected Sandra Gardebring to lead the Pollution Control Agency. So began a long partnership between Perpich and Griffin. Under Griffin's leadership, half of all state appointments during Perpich's trailblazing first year were either women or minorities.[34]

"His philosophy was very simple: the people that live in the state ought to be represented," remembered Ray Bohn, special assistant to the governor.[35]

In his budget message to lawmakers that month, Perpich proposed a sevenfold increase in funding for University of Minnesota women's athletics, calling it an "important first step" toward the equal treatment of women at the university.[36]

During his speech to the DFL Feminist Caucus, Perpich cited a study by the one-year-old Council on the Economic Status of Women that noted women in state government with twenty years of experience earned the same as the average starting wage for men. Harkening back to his days on the Hibbing School Board, he told his audience that he had demanded a complete review of "what and why" state employees are paid.[37]

"This administration pledges that it will make a determined effort to promote women to all levels of state government," he told his audience. "Not because it is the political thing to do, but because it is the right thing to do."[38]

And Perpich went beyond what nearly anyone expected when he promised the crowd that he would appoint a woman to Minnesota's highest court if a vacancy arose. While the audience erupted in applause, many remained skeptical. It was a vow wholly uncharacteristic of typical male politicians. The doubters did not yet recognize that Rudy was not a typical politician.[39]

Her Honor

Perpich would have the chance to make good on his promise only a few short months later, in May 1977, when President Jimmy Carter nominated Minnesota Supreme Court associate justice Harry MacLaughlin to succeed retiring US District Court judge Earl Larson. MacLaughlin was a former law firm partner and remained a close friend of Vice President Walter Mondale. With the US Senate controlled by Democrats, MacLaughlin's confirmation was all but assured, leaving Perpich with a vacancy on Minnesota's highest court.[40]

Perpich's appointment staff sprang into high gear. A state-level meeting of the National Women's Conference was scheduled to take place in St. Cloud in early June, and his team agreed it would be the time and place for a historic announcement. The only problem was that Perpich—trying as ever to balance his family and political lives—was scheduled to give the Hibbing High School commencement address at nearly the same time. His son, Rudy Jr., was a graduating senior.

Perpich devised a plan: he would make the announcement part of his speech in Hibbing; immediately thereafter, his friend and Secretary of State Joan Growe, also chair of the Women's Conference, would announce the news to the thousands of women expected in St. Cloud.[41]

This left little more than two weeks for the ad hoc judicial selection committee to bring a slate of candidates to the governor. Interestingly, the three-member committee did not include Gloria Griffin, but it did include Perpich adviser and University of Minnesota history professor Hyman Berman, along with William Kennedy, lead Hennepin County public defender, and Joseph Summers, a district county judge in Ramsey County. Regardless of the group's gender makeup, their charge from Perpich was clear: find the most qualified female candidates—and do it quickly.

Despite the short turnaround, the selection process would be remembered as one of the most transparent in state history. As the committee began its task, the five-year-old Minnesota Women Lawyers group circulated a letter among feminist and politically active women's groups recommending the names of seven women. The letter lauded the seven's credentials, acknowledging that "the appointment of a woman will be more closely scrutinized than that of a man."[42]

Perpich's panel brought back a list of six candidates that, while not identical, closely resembled the Minnesota Women Lawyers' list.

Soon the six were culled to three. None of the finalists were prosecutors or sitting judges—traditionally a cultivator for judicial appointments—and that is exactly how Perpich wanted it. According to Berman, gender was not the only norm on the bench the governor hoped to change. Rudy was looking for humanity and compassion. Notably, he also did not seek the counsel of the Minnesota Bar Association, customarily at the center of such an important appointment.

"He didn't want some cigar-smoking, fat-cat corporate lawyer telling him who to appoint," remembered Berman.[43]

The day before his announcement, Perpich summoned fifty-two-year-old Rosalie Wahl to his office for a final interview. Wahl was an associate professor at her alma mater, William Mitchell College of Law. She had served for six years as an assistant state public defender, which was experience Perpich had sought in the top candidates, as all the sitting justices had corporate or prose-cutorial training. Wahl was well regarded within the feminist movement as a champion of the disadvantaged and had a record of supporting human rights. The divorced mother of five had put herself through law school while juggling the responsibilities of motherhood.

"I had spent a lot of time sitting outside the doors of board rooms where men were sitting inside making decisions," she said. "Law was one key to the door."[44]

It was part of a compelling life story that began in "a little town [in Kansas] that no longer exists." Wahl attended a one-room rural schoolhouse and was required to live with relatives "in town" to attend high school. Her story not only resembled Perpich's, but he believed it would resonate with Minnesota voters as well. This last point was crucial, as the appointee would have to stand for statewide election in 1978.[45]

"We had heard many, many good things about Rosalie Wahl," remembered Ray Bohn, who worked on the appointment. "She wasn't the longest in terms of legal experience or, perhaps, expertise. But she had that life experience that Rudy wanted. He said to me many times that she was the perfect person for that."[46]

Perpich asked Wahl about two issues specifically: her views on the death penalty and abortion. Wahl told the governor she was against corporal punishment. He was as well. Wahl also said she supported the Supreme Court's

Roe v. Wade decision. While Perpich was personally against abortion, Wahl remembered him on the issue as "understand[ing] how women felt. He was for the downtrodden." He made it clear that any differences on abortion would not be a factor in his decision.[47]

On the night of the announcement, Friday, June 3, Secretary of State Joan Growe sat backstage at the Minnesota Women's Meeting, anticipating word from Hibbing. Waiting in the wings of Halenbeck Hall on the campus of St. Cloud State University with Growe was the next supreme court associate justice of Minnesota, Rosalie Wahl, along with her daughters Sara and Jenny.

Shortly after 8:30 P.M., word reached St. Cloud that the governor had made his announcement in Hibbing. Growe and Wahl took the stage moments later.

"We've heard a lot of talk this weekend about women striving for equality," Growe told an attentive audience. "I'm terribly pleased and terribly privileged to make the following announcement: The new associate justice to the Minnesota Supreme Court is Rosalie Wahl."[48]

The crowd erupted. The auditorium was filled with tears of joy and shouts of approval—recognizing the moment as a long-overdue victory toward the equal treatment of women in Minnesota.

Wahl understood the impact of her appointment, as did the man who appointed her. She "just happened to be standing in the right place at the right time in history," she would say afterward. "I think he wants somebody on the court to bring the perspective I've got. I've looked at the system from the bottom up, and you see things differently from there."[49]

To those gathered in St. Cloud, Wahl offered these words:

Men are not the enemy. Men are our brothers, our husbands, our sons, our fathers, our friends. The enemy is fear—fear that by being all of what we are, by realizing our full potential, we will somehow jeopardize what little security we have attained for ourselves and our children.

A good many years ago, when my then-four children were in school and I had gone with some trepidation to law school to prepare myself to help share the economic burden of supporting those children, a poem came to me which expressed my feeling at that time of what it meant to be a woman:

Foot in nest,
Wing in sky;
Bound by each,
Hover I.

Now I know it is not necessary to hover. Now I know it is possible to soar, to know the vastness of the sky and then come back, fully, to the nest, enriched by the vision of the whole and by the exercise.

Now I know it is possible to extend the nest to include our children wherever they are—in the factories, at the switchboards, in the mines, the shops, the halls of finance and commerce and government—and nourish there the values which were sprouted by the hearth—a sense that every individual in the human family is a unique and precious being, a sense of justice and fair play, a sense of compassion where justice ends or fails.

I pledge to you and ask your pledge that wherever we are, we will never cease to work for these goals.[50]

Commenting on the appointment to reporters, Wahl said, "You're going to please some people and displease others. I hope I please the ones rooting for me. The only concern I have is not to fail the people who share my concern."[51]

Wahl went on to win reelection after reelection, eventually retiring in 1994 after having authored 549 opinions. She remained active as a speaker and social justice advocate for many years after her retirement before passing away in July 2013 at the age of eighty-eight.[52]

An Ongoing Controversy

Not long after returning from his initial visit to western Minnesota, Perpich began to realize that the power line issue wouldn't be easily resolved. He did little to persuade the farmers to flatly accept the power line as inevitable, as he believed his involvement could ultimately result in an acceptable solution. Still, he underestimated how deeply all parties were entrenched.

Perpich personally invited professional mediator Joseph "Josh" Stulberg to Minnesota to bridge the growing divide. Things seemed encouraging when the New York lawyer was first greeted by hundreds of farmers at a town hall in Lowry, population 257. But when Stulberg returned for a final time a month later to meet with both sides in St. Cloud, things quickly turned sour. Farmers complained that they felt Stulberg was unwilling to hear their arguments and that they'd be better off foregoing the meetings and continuing to protest. Furthermore, they felt the mere presence of a mediator suggested the State had already taken a side with the power companies. Stulberg, meanwhile, described the mood in western Minnesota as "potentially dangerous."[53]

Five hundred farmers attended a special legislative hearing at the St. Cloud Armory, demanding lawmakers make changes to siting regulations, consider alternate routes, overhaul state permitting agencies, encourage conservation efforts, and, above all, institute a moratorium on construction of the line until health and safety concerns were met. Power company officials countered that a lawful siting and permitting process had been undertaken, that proposed alternate routes were not feasible, and that the project was moving forward. The only point they were willing to reconsider was the amount farmers would be paid for easements required to build the line.

The 1977 legislature ultimately passed a series of reforms to change the way future projects were permitted but sidestepped any action on the current line.

The farmers were infuriated. As Perpich's efforts at mediation ended without agreement, and the legislature declined to act on the line currently under construction, the power line opposition turned to the courts.

In early March, the Minnesota Supreme Court considered seven separate cases brought by various groups opposed to the line and combined them into a single suit to be considered by a three-judge panel. For an establishment known for its protracted and methodic approach, the courts moved quickly. The panel of district court judges convened three weeks later in Glenwood and promptly ordered a cessation of work on the line until they delivered a final ruling. But in July, they handed down a unanimous decision dismissing all the farmers' suits. In September, the supreme court upheld the ruling. Anger and cynicism grew among the protesters.[54]

The governor made another unannounced visit to west-central Minnesota a few days after the supreme court ruling, this time showing up at the Virgil and Jane Fuchs farm in Stearns County. He brought with him a proposal to establish a "science court" to study health and safety considerations raised by the line's opponents. It was an idea Perpich had been advocating since early in his involvement, and the concept followed a model that had been developed the previous year by a physicist leading a White House task force.

The plan would consider public health and safety concerns to be decided by impartial scientist-"judges," leaving political, social, and ethical considerations for other entities to decide. In the end, the "science court" faced a similar fate as legal and legislative approaches—a series of fits and starts that seemed promising, only to ultimately tilt toward the power companies and end with intractable differences.[55]

As Governor Perpich approached the end of his first year in office, he found himself in a difficult position. He had dedicated more of his administration's energy and political capital to the power line than any other issue, yet, despite his personal commitment, the situation was more volatile than ever. As the new year approached, he faced a no-win situation: either call for a moratorium on the line (which was certain to be contested by the power companies), or call out state troopers or the National Guard when the farmers inevitably took matters into their own hands.[56]

Either plan risked political suicide.

Escalation

When survey crews returned to the fields in early January 1978, they were immediately met by protesters. On January 3, eight were arrested, including fifty-nine-year-old Alice Tripp, who was dragged across a field to a waiting squad car when she refused to comply.

"An old lady treated like an animal," as the angry farmers described it.

Public sentiment was on the side of the farmers, and the entire state was watching to see what Perpich would do. The governor gave a short and direct message to the people of west-central Minnesota on Alexandria television station KCMT, insisting that his administration had "gone the extra mile," before announcing the largest utilization of state troopers in Minnesota history. Nearly half of the state's patrolmen were headed to Pope County.[57]

The following Monday, the national press was focused on Lowry, Minnesota. On a bitterly cold day, two hundred protesters waved flags and homemade signs as they headed west of town to a tower assembly yard guarded by the state patrol. When the line reached the troopers, protesters offered the officers plastic flowers, hot coffee, and homemade cookies. There would be no violence that day.

The national media, not impressed by Minnesota hospitality, quickly lost interest in the story.[58]

Still, the protests continued to grow, with up to a thousand people taking to

Power line protesters clash with state patrol officers, January 1978. *Photo by Jim McTaggart, Minneapolis and St. Paul Newspaper Negatives Collection, MNHS*

the fields daily. Hoping to build on the momentum, several thousand protest-ers journeyed to the capitol, demanding a moratorium. Glenwood, the county seat of Pope County, let schools out early so students and teachers could travel to St. Paul. In the State of the State address the following day, Perpich acknowl-edged the escalating tension and urged against violence.

"In our democracy, there is a system of law to resolve disputes. If democracy is to endure, our respect for law must endure," Perpich declared. He assured everyone that "the parties to this dispute have had the fullest access to our entire political system."[59]

Despite Perpich's urgings, resistance in the fields continued to escalate. In mid-February, farmers unleashed a manure spreader along with anhydrous am-monia on a line of state troopers protecting survey crews in Stearns County. On another bitterly cold day in early March, thousands of people from around the state demonstrated solidarity with the farmers in a "March for Justice." They marched behind a monstrous red tractor, a coffin with "Justice" inscribed on the top, and a papier-mâché "Corporate Giant" for a nine-mile journey from Lowry to Glenwood. It was a high point for the protest against the power line.[60]

One week later, a security guard was injured by shattered windshield frag-ments when his truck was shot while he stood guard over an assembly yard in Villard. The violence in Stearns and Pope Counties exacerbated the dilemma that faced Perpich. In addition to the growing unrest—and danger to the well-being of those on both sides—having the state patrol, under his com-mand, face off against Minnesota farmers was a political predicament of the worst order.[61]

"There was nothing politically, socially, or economically we wanted to get rid of faster in the governor's administration than this particular dispute," re-membered Ronnie Brooks.[62]

Perpich made one final push toward securing a science court to arbitrate health and safety concerns. The farmers insisted again that the scope of the hearings be broadened and that the governor himself mediate the sessions. But in the end, as much as Perpich pushed for it, the science court was not meant to be. For all the appeal of focusing on technical and scientific questions, the power line struggle, at its core, was a political problem.[63]

That political problem manifested itself when Pope County DFLers met to send delegates to the state convention. They looked for someone to oppose Perpich, and they found that person in Alice Tripp. Her now-famous run-ins with law enforcement while protesting and her demonstrated leadership during gatherings at the Lowry Town Hall made the former English teacher and current farmer a natural choice to challenge the governor's election bid. She was a favorite among local and statewide media and was recognized across Minnesota.[64]

In early June, at the DFL state convention in St. Paul, Paul Wellstone, a thirty-three-year-old college professor at Carlton College who had spent time with the protestors, made a fiery nominating speech for Tripp. She surprised many by winning 17 percent of the first-ballot vote and decided to challenge Perpich in the September primary.

Wellstone's Carlton colleague and coauthor of a forthcoming book on the power line, Mike Casper, became Tripp's running mate. The campaign was a low-budget, old-fashioned affair—with guitars, singing, a solar-powered sound system in the back of a 1972 Ford pickup truck, and a repurposed giant papier-mâché puppet named "Corporate Giant." A sign on the truck's tailgate read, "Our truck powered by gasohol! Our loudspeakers powered by the sun! Our campaign powered by the people."[65]

On Tuesday, September 12, Alice Tripp startled many political observers when she received 20 percent of the votes against Perpich in the state's DFL primary. The results were a telltale sign of the toll the power line issue had taken on Perpich's popularity as governor, and a harbinger of things to come in the general election.[66]

"The first time I actually came to know Rudy Perpich, it wasn't adversarial, but it was different," remembered Wellstone years later. "He didn't know me, but I had a chance to observe him at a variety of different meetings, at a variety of different critical points of decision during this struggle—which was really the most volatile, turbulent struggle in Minnesota history since the days of the Depression." He continued,

Perpich was so different. Most of the people in politics just ran away from [difficult issues]. Whether you agree or disagree with some of the final decisions he made, he went out to meet with farmers. . . . I think he was with the farmers. I don't think he felt the co-ops or the power companies had dealt with them, had been straightforward with them. I think he felt they were getting the short end of the stick. But it was also difficult for him as governor to directly side with them. But I at least could see him as opposed to just running away from the issue and running away from the people, he was trying. He was trying.[67]

– CHAPTER 8 –

The Minnesota Massacre

"We were good and getting better, then we were gone."
—*Lynn Anderson, assistant to Governor Perpich*

The DFL had been increasing its stranglehold over the state capitol since taking control of the house, senate, and governorship for the first time in state history in '72. The party's power reached its zenith following the 1976 election, when Democrats controlled all statewide offices, both US Senate seats, three-quarters of the state legislature, and five of eight congressional seats.

Only two years later, the DFL would suffer a precipitous fall in an election that came to be known as the "Minnesota Massacre."

State Republicans had sensed opportunity since President Jimmy Carter chose Minnesota senator Walter Mondale to be his running mate. The state's Independent-Republican chairman, Chuck Slocum, predicted that, "If Mondale is elected and the Senate seat opens up, the situation in the DFL would border on civil war." Slocum's prediction came true shortly after the 1976 Democratic National Convention, months before Perpich became governor. Already then, he classified Perpich as "extremely vulnerable."[1]

"We would like to take on Gov. Perpich. He'd be a great target," Slocum added.[2]

After the Carter and Mondale victory, months of speculation ended with Governor Wendell Anderson's resignation, and Republicans wasted no time announcing that the Anderson appointment would be a top campaign issue in the 1978 midterm election.

Perpich's abbreviated term forced him to spend his entire time in office with one eye toward the 1978 election. He was hounded about whether his trips across the state—to ribbon cuttings, county fairs, and coffee shops—were campaign stops or official business of the governor's office. During his first summer as governor, Perpich zigzagged the state, once telling a crowd at the Winona County Fair in St. Charles, "I think as long as I touch base with the people, I'll be okay."

Governor Perpich winds up at the Cannon Valley Fair, Cannon Falls, Minnesota,
July 1977. *Photo by Richard Olsenius, Minneapolis and St. Paul Newspaper Negatives
Collection, MNHS*

The remark capped a day spent touring a junkyard, crowning an eighty-five-
year-old pageant queen, and conducting multiple TV, radio, and newspaper
interviews.[3]

"When I start campaigning, you'll know it," Perpich retorted when questioned whether the trip was truly state business. He defended the Winona trip,
saying, "I learned three things in my first twenty minutes here that I wouldn't
have known if I'd stayed in St. Paul."[4]

When, toward the end of his first year, aides tried to convince him to work
on his image and accept professional coaching in advance of the approaching
campaign, Perpich dismissed the notion, saying "I'm not a fancy Dan."[5]

A Legendary Loss

In the first weeks of 1978, Minnesota and the nation were rocked by the death
of Hubert H. Humphrey, following years of cancer treatments and a sudden
coma. Services were held in Washington and St. Paul, where, amid freezing
temperatures, thousands offered their respects to the venerable mayor, US
senator, and vice president. Humphrey had been a liberal luminary since urging the Democratic Party to "get out of the shadow of states' rights and to walk

forthrightly into the bright sunshine of human rights," at the 1948 Democratic National Convention.[6]

Tributes for Humphrey poured in from around the country, including those from Presidents Ford, Nixon, and Carter. Vice President Mondale called the loss "one of the saddest moments of my life," saying the late senator had been like a father to him since the passing of his own father in 1948.

As the election was yet months away, Perpich was tasked with appointing a replacement—stirring, for many, still-raw memories of Wendell Anderson's self-engineered Senate appointment. Perpich chose Muriel Humphrey, the late senator's widow, who became Minnesota's first female US senator on February 6, with Mondale conducting the swearing-in ceremony.[7]

It was assumed that Muriel Humphrey would not seek election in the fall. Liberal Minneapolis congressman Don Fraser made his intentions clear that he would seek the seat, as did senate majority leader Nick Coleman, congressman and Perpich-rival Jim Oberstar, and "flamboyant Minneapolis entrepreneur" Bob Short. Short planned to forgo the DFL endorsing process and proceed directly to the September primary.[8]

Republicans wasted no time in response. Dave Durenberger, former chief of staff to Governor Harold LeVander, and Al Quie, a dairy farmer and longtime congressman from Minnesota's agricultural First District, both announced they would run against Perpich. Former Minneapolis city council president and current state house member Arne Carlson made a bid for state auditor, while colorful lumber retail and remodeling mogul Rudy Boschwitz pledged his "best shot all the time" in a campaign for Anderson's senate seat.[9]

Even early on, cracks were visible in the DFL Party—especially in the contest between Fraser and Short for Humphrey's seat. A rural-urban divide was widening. Durenberger, recognizing the opportunity and accepting that Quie was likely to be his party's choice for governor, shifted his campaign toward Humphrey's seat as well.[10]

Meanwhile, on the Iron Range, DFLers assembled in International Falls for the Eighth Congressional District convention in early May. On topics like abortion and protection of the Boundary Waters Canoe Area (BWCA), it became clear that DFLers in Perpich's home region were as far removed politically as they were geographically from party leaders in St. Paul.

The week before the district convention, Perpich predicted that the BWCA would hurt the DFL if common ground wasn't found, saying, "If it goes into the fall, very obviously it's going to be detrimental."

The issue was over logging, mining, and the use of motorboats and snowmobiles in the federally protected wilderness area. Like the power line issue, Perpich recognized the line in the sand drawn by the opposing sides and believed he could bridge that gap. He believed he could find a middle ground that recognized the concerns of both Twin Cities environmentalists and Iron Range residents worried about the economic impacts to tourism. Perpich had long supported a compromise that would allow motorboats on some peripheral lakes and snowmobiles on designated routes, while opposing logging and mining in the area.[11]

At the Eighth District convention, party members attempted to halt Fraser's endorsement by instead putting forward a "Draft Doug" resolution—supporting state senator Doug Johnson. The anti-Fraser sentiment stemmed from his support for abortion and for restricting motorized vehicles in the BWCA. Delegates hoped the move would send a clear message to state party leaders that "they didn't have the Eighth District in their hip pocket."[12]

The convention closed with delegates chanting "We want Johnson!" Doug Johnson was a longtime member of the Perpich Party. "Dougie was with the Perpich team from day one, way back," remembered Joe Begich, an eighteen-year veteran of the Minnesota House from Eveleth. "In fact, Rudy is the one who encouraged Dougie to run for the house."[13]

Busloads of Iron Range DFLers made the trek to the state's capital city to deliver their resolution in person at the DFL state convention and to oppose Fraser's endorsement. They drowned out Fraser's attempts to address the convention with "wilderness whistles" until Congressman Jim Oberstar intervened and pleaded with his fellow delegates to let Fraser speak.[14]

On the first night of the convention in St. Paul, Perpich brushed aside a challenge from anti–power line activist Alice Tripp at a rate of four-to-one. But Rudy wasn't around to savor the victory. Instead, the Perpich family was in Hibbing for daughter Mary Sue's high school graduation. Perpich delivered the commencement address and became visibly emotional when a group of students presented a birthday cake and sang "Happy Birthday" ahead of his fiftieth birthday later that month.[15]

"The governor, during '77 and '78, was also a father and a husband. His children were still young and in high school. His family was split much of the time," Lynn Anderson remembered of the hectic period. "He was at the governor's residence a lot by himself because Lola and the children were up north. It was very important to him that they graduate with their Hibbing High School classes. I remember making many, many road trips to Duluth or to Hibbing so he wouldn't miss that period of time. We'd use the drive time to work in the car, to process paperwork, and to make sure appointments were being handled. He was a full-time governor and a full-time parent."[16]

Wendell Anderson was endorsed on the first ballot. But Fraser, who had predicted an early endorsement, failed twice before prevailing on the third ballot. It was indicative of troubles to come—for Fraser in the primary and his party in the general election. Ahead of the primary, the internal DFL battles over abortion, guns, and the BWCA that had been developing since the early days of the caucuses were now in full public view.

Perpich returned to St. Paul for the closing night of the convention and was himself questioned by the Endorsement Committee over his ability to run a campaign for the state's top job. He warned the party faithful that dividing over single issues could cost them in the fall. "If we really split up, we're going to lose not only a Senate seat but the first governor from the Iron Range, too."[17]

Later that month, the Independent-Republican state convention in downtown Minneapolis endorsed Quie, Durenberger, Carlson, and Boschwitz without drama.

Too Big to Fail

Having complete control of the state government, along with a Democrat in the White House, Minnesota's DFL candidates were seen by the public as bearing at least some responsibility for major national economic issues—including rising inflation and gas and oil prices. Carter's presidency was likewise under scrutiny, with Vice President Mondale remarking that "skepticism and distrust had taken root among Americans."[18]

Betty Wilson, writing for the *Minneapolis Star*, summed up the party's predicament, saying the primary results would be "the first test this year of the future of the troubled DFL Party."

Absent the guidance and charisma of Humphrey, and amid deepening divisions at county conventions across the state, party leaders seemed beset and adrift. They felt mounting pressure from a national taxpayer revolt and a swelling anti-government conservative movement—even in traditionally liberal Minnesota. Finally, the primary would be a referendum on the state's caucus and convention endorsement process, which had been championed by DFLers as a grassroots, effective way to choose candidates, but was faulted as elitist and insufficiently democratic.[19]

For the DFL Party, primary election night started strong. Perpich swept Tripp shortly after the polls closed, taking 80 percent of the vote, and Wendell Anderson prevailed in his contest over St. Paul attorney John Connolly. The Fraser-Short battle, conversely, wouldn't be decided until well into the following morning. At midnight, Fraser led by 30,000 votes, but the Iron Range had yet to be counted. Hours later, Short emerged with a narrow 3,451-vote victory out of more than half a million votes cast. It was a blow to the DFL establishment and a clear indicator of how divided the party was heading into November's general election.[20]

Perpich appeared undaunted. Despite tightening polls showing he and Quie were neck and neck, he predicted a 58 percent win. He traveled the state in his signature whirlwind fashion, exuding confidence. One such day found Perpich hosting several early morning meetings at the governor's residence, including negotiations with the White House over an upcoming visit by President Carter, before leading reporters to the Brown County Fair in New Ulm. When rain made that trip unfeasible, Perpich stopped at a coffee shop before detouring to the state prison for women in Shakopee, where he dropped in unannounced. After touring the facility and speaking with inmates, Perpich lamented the horrid conditions and lack of recreational opportunities, telling officials he would return with the state corrections commissioner to advocate for improvements.[21]

Quie tried to portray Perpich as ineffective and eccentric, claiming his kinetic motion was a political act. Perpich maintained that his approach favored putting people first and that he went where the problems were.

"I just get in the car and go," he said.

Privately, some DFL legislators complained that Perpich was unpredictable and reclusive. They saw little logic to his frantic, dash-around style, leaving the "ship of state afloat but drifting."[22]

Perpich's unconventional methods rankled politicians of both parties and often landed him at the center of controversy—from power lines to coffeepots (which would be a future battle; see page 112). DFL Party chair Rick Scott remarked that, "No one in politics is totally comfortable with anyone as unpredictable as Rudy Perpich. People in the party want to be supportive, but they never know which way to lean."[23]

Usually, the fastest way to learn Perpich's position on an issue was to check the newspapers, as Rudy kept capitol reporters better informed than his party cohorts. Such was the case when Perpich advocated cutting income taxes as the centerpiece of his 1978 legislative priorities, a proposal that ran counter to the DFL legislature's stated aims.

"The trouble with Perpich is he won't listen to anyone who tries to tell him he's wrong," a disgruntled DFL legislator told one reporter.[24]

While Perpich could be impulsive, his attitude toward taxes, particularly income taxes, changed gradually, representing his growing appreciation of the correlation between taxes and the economy. During his time in the state senate, Perpich had voted along with his liberal caucus and DFL roots on significant tax policies of the 1960s, including joining his colleagues in voting against the 1967 tax bill that established a state sales tax in exchange for lowering property taxes.

But as he matured politically, tension grew between his native polka populism and his belief in Minnesota's potential as a national and global business leader. As early as his first term as governor, Rudy Perpich began exhibiting independence on the issue of the state's system of taxation. Perpich thought the DFL had gone too far in its reliance on income taxes to pay for basic government services.

Perpich was willing to let property and sales taxes rise to keep income taxes down, which departed from Floyd B. Olson's insistence that taxes should be based on the ability to pay. Increasingly, Perpich would challenge his political hero's philosophy and his party's dogma. It was part of Perpich's growing political independence and central to his vision of Minnesota becoming a global leader in business and trade.

In the 1970s, DFL orthodoxy considered a progressive income tax the cornerstone of state tax policy. It was the foundation of the Minnesota Miracle, enacted in 1971, which would keep property taxes down while sales and income taxes grew to finance schools and local governments. By the time he was governor in 1977, Perpich believed the tax system was out of balance and corrections were needed.

Perpich was not opposed to using the progressive income tax to balance the regressive sales and property taxes, which affected lower-income Minnesotans disproportionately. Still, he simultaneously saw Minnesota's reputation as a high-tax state with complicated compliance as increasingly detrimental to the state's ability to attract new business. He proposed a $100 million cut to income taxes in 1977, just weeks after being sworn in as governor. Instead, the DFL legislature sent him a bill establishing a new and even higher top income tax bracket for Minnesota's uppermost earners while reducing property taxes by $163 million. Perpich considered calling a special session but ultimately signed the bill.[25]

As the confrontation between the governor and the legislature intensified, East Grand Forks legislator and house Tax Committee chair Bill Kelly articulated the DFL position in a November 1977 op-ed in the *Star Tribune*. He argued that Minnesota had established a stable tax system insulated from service disruptions due to deficits. Furthermore, he claimed the system was fair because it relied on those most able to pay through an emphasis on a progressive income tax.

Perpich countered that the DFL policy was bad for business.

"Minnesotans are eighth per capita nationally in state and local taxes paid. We are fourth in the income tax, 24th in the property tax, 36th in sales tax, and sixth in corporate income tax," Perpich wrote in an op-ed published later the same month in the *Star Tribune*. "Our income tax has become inequitable in certain categories. There are brackets where we are the highest in the nation. . . . It's not good policy to have the highest income tax in any categories because people begin to think we are the highest, period! This attitude creates a bad tax climate that can become detrimental to the state."[26]

Perpich lost his first ideological skirmish with his party over taxes in 1977, but many more battles would come throughout his time as governor.

Perpich hadn't become governor to please his party. If he believed a tax cut was best for Minnesotans, he would support it regardless of party dogma. The cold shoulder offered by some within his party was more than balanced by "the acceptance of the people—the warm feeling I get . . . when I travel around the state."[27]

"I certainly don't want to be political head of the DFL Party in Minnesota," Perpich explained, adding that he couldn't imagine building a state party machinery in his image.[28]

"I don't know what it was about the party, but he never felt the party had done much for him," remembered Tom Triplett, head of the governor's policy office during Perpich's first term. "It was controlled by the Twin Cities Democrats. He thought a lot like [them] on gut-level issues, but [he] was never comfortable with them."[29]

Though his style sometimes rankled other elected officials, Perpich wouldn't stop being himself. When criticized for substituting a polka dance with a waitress for an after-dinner speech, Rudy brushed off his critics, saying, "I'm not going to act any differently than I did before I became governor. When I was lieutenant governor and went out on Bicentennial trips I used to dance the polka and have a good time. I can't see why I can't enjoy myself while being governor."[30]

And while Perpich's tax-cutting proposals annoyed DFLers, his plan to fund a portion of the cut through slashing government inefficiencies infuriated and alienated state employees. He ordered coffeepots unplugged in state offices and cut back on the use of air conditioning, telephones, and state cars. He ordered a sale of the buildup of unnecessary surplus items such as desks, chairs, and typewriters, which he saw as "a wasteful and intolerable situation." Perpich maintained there was $50 million in wasteful spending to be saved.

"We have to do a better job of managing the public's resources," he said.[31]

Perpich understood that his waste-cutting measures would rankle public employees, a traditionally reliable DFL voting bloc, but he refused to pander.

"Sure, I know they're unhappy," he said, noting that he had stayed in $16-a-night motels during his travels around the state as a way to save money. "If for twenty years you can do whatever you want and somebody suddenly says no, you know what your reaction is going to be."[32]

"He was trying to cut back on the bureaucratic nightmare that people told him they were constantly dealing with," Lynn Anderson recalled of Perpich during his first term. "A lot of those initiatives were started in '77–'78 and they were, I think, a lot of times misunderstood and portrayed in a way that was more negative than what the intent was. The intent really was, I think, that you didn't need fifty copies of something on file with the state. As he would say, 'Trees fall for the amount of paperwork that we process in state government.' "[33]

Regardless of Perpich's intent, his decision to make the daily workings of state employees into the subject of statewide media coverage would come at a high price.

"He created a commission on waste and mismanagement in government—a classic example of how the name is what people remember," recalled Roger Moe, then chair of the state senate Finance Committee. "That commission looked at all kinds of things [and delivered an] excellent set of recommendations. But it was called 'The Blue Ribbon Task Force on Waste and Mismanagement in Government,' which meant every public employee was wasteful and mismanaged. And that's what they remembered."[34]

"It unfortunately eroded tremendous support from the public employees in Minnesota, who tended to be DFL, and who were, I think, at the outset strong supporters of Perpich," remembered Terry Montgomery. "They got the impression that he was holding them accountable for the problems of state government, and that became kind of a personal matter. As a result, they voted against him, many of them, in the election."[35]

"It just wasn't handled well," remembered Tom Triplett, who said the entire process left the state's 15,000 employees and their unions feeling furious and alienated. "It just didn't work. But he learned a good lesson that served him well later: the only way you can make change is with the support of the people most affected."[36]

Just Folks

In October 1978, Perpich brought his polka populism to Gotvald's Corner, on the back roads of Benton County, to present a plaque to high school students from Hillman who had broken a world record by playing volleyball for forty-three hours while raising $2,400 for muscular dystrophy. To his campaign aides, it was all part of the "down home, just folks" image they hoped to capitalize on. To Perpich, it was simply who he was.

"It's just like the Iron Range. I feel at home here," he said while making his way through the crowd of 150, shaking hands and posing for pictures—noticeably gaining energy as he went. Perpich delivered a version of his stump speech, telling the crowd, "This is what makes Minnesota such a great state: People with this kind of spirit." He dubbed Minnesota the greatest state in the union, to an eruption of applause.

Meanwhile, Perpich labeled his opponent, not mentioning Quie by name, an outsider who didn't recognize that spirit.

"If my opponent wasn't in Washington for twenty years, he'd know how great it is and how we work together."[37]

Perpich rattled off his accomplishments as governor, including a $110 million tax cut, 175,000 new jobs since taking office, one of the lowest unemployment rates in the country (4 percent), a booming construction market, his work in keeping Reserve Mining Company and its employees in Minnesota despite threats to leave, and a $50 million savings through reduced government waste. But Perpich said his greatest satisfaction was his administration being the most open of any in the country.

"We have brought into the decision-making process more women, minority members, senior citizens, rural persons, [and] groups in our society who have never been included before," he told the crowd. "I've worked hard for the people of Minnesota. I'll work even harder if I'm elected."[38]

Between campaign stops, Rudy assured Lola that he had a good feeling about his chances in November.[39]

The Bucket Treatment

That same month, a BWCA compromise bill authored by Wendell Anderson and supported by Perpich passed the US Senate. The bill would limit the use of motorboats to 24 percent of the water surface by the year 2000, but also outlawed mining and logging and increased the protected wilderness area by 45,000 acres. Days later, representatives of two dozen citizen groups, including BWCA and power line protesters, joined forces in Duluth to tell the world they were "mad as hell and not going to take it anymore."[40]

Perpich and Anderson were the targets of much of the group's ire, along with "government land grabbers," people from the metropolitan areas, and the "big city press." The leader of one of the groups, Minnesotans for Equitable Government, claimed Perpich had displayed "a lack of leadership and sensitivity" in his handling of the power line and BWCA controversies.[41]

"I don't think they caught him by surprise," his chief of staff recalled, "[but] I think he was surprised by the bitterness and the intensity that he encountered. I think he was disappointed, to a great degree, on how quickly they turned on him if he didn't accept exactly what they wanted."[42]

Perpich, apparently as confident as ever, seemed unfazed by the criticism and unaware of the disparate forces that were coalescing against Democrats. "I tell you how I feel," he said to reporters in mid-October. "I'm the best governor in the United States right now."[43]

Perpich wasn't the only one who felt he was doing a good job. The *Minneapolis Star* described him as a congenial, direct, and effervescent leader "who has accomplished more in his two years as governor for the cause of openness in government than any of his predecessors." He had also done more to bring women into government than any governor in state history while holding down costs and showing a willingness to tackle tough issues, the editorial board said in their endorsement, making the case that Perpich could bridge the growing rural-urban divide better than any other statewide leader.[44]

But the fissures within the DFL were on full display when President Carter visited Minnesota two weeks before election day. At a campaign rally for the state's Democratic candidates, held at the Minneapolis Auditorium, the president received a warm welcome when he advocated backing Anderson, but was summarily booed when he urged similar support for Robert Short.[45]

It all seemed to exist in another world from Perpich, who remained "very, very, optimistic." One aide said Rudy was on such a high that "he could take on Kennedy, Carter, Quie, and Durenberger all on the same day."[46]

Part of Perpich's confidence came from his feeling that the Quie campaign had begun to panic.

"He's starting the bucket treatment now," Perpich said, claiming that the Quie team was beginning to dump anything and everything they could in a last-ditch effort. But such tactics would not prevail, Perpich believed, because "I know the people, and they know me."[47]

Quie went on the attack in a televised debate, referring to Perpich as "Rubber Stamp Rudy," questioning Perpich's role in the "deal" that sent Wendell Anderson to the US Senate, and referencing a recent *Newsweek* headline that summed up the Minnesota gubernatorial race as "Crazy Rudy vs. Stolid Al."[48]

"Rudy is doing a lot of things, but he doesn't seem to have any direction," Quie remarked. "I hear from people that there is a great deal of tension among state employees—they are demoralized. Rudy does too many things spur of the moment."[49]

Perpich brushed off the criticism as more "garbage pail tactics."

"I haven't been subjected to those types of tactics—name calling—since I was on the Iron Range. I was hoping he would stick to the issues," Perpich said.[50]

Campaign ads played up Quie as a Lutheran dairy farmer and a family man beyond moral reproach who offered "dignity Minnesota hasn't seen in the governor's office for quite some time." Many of Quie's campaign staff and volunteers talked openly of being born-again Christians and of their work on his campaign as part of a "Christian commitment."[51]

"I pray that I might do the Lord's will. I pray that I will be filled with the Spirit. I pray for all the other people's struggles," Quie said during the campaign, making it clear that this intention included Perpich. Quie saw no problem praying for Perpich and then attacking him, saying, "I believe it would be wrong if I said anything about him that wasn't true."[52]

Perpich became increasingly annoyed by what he saw as "gutter politics" from his Republican opponent. "When my opponent started in with this crazy

Rudy stuff during the debates, his campaign went downhill," Perpich said in the final week of the contest. "People don't go for that stuff in Minnesota."[53]

Quie's high moral standard was ultimately tested by the actions of his campaign staff. The incident would forever estrange Perpich and Quie.

"Everything looks like I'm going down the tubes," Quie told his campaign staff two weeks before the election. "I say to you right now, you're free. You do what you believe. . . . You be yourselves. Just go for it. You don't have to check with Bob [Andringa, Quie's campaign manager] or anyone else."[54]

On the Sunday before the election, Quie's ethically liberated campaign staff placed leaflets on the windshields of cars parked outside metro-area churches falsely claiming the pro-life Perpich was pro-choice.

Two days later, on November 7, 1978, Al Quie defeated Rudy Perpich, 52.3 percent to 45.7 percent.

Sweeping Changes

Perpich's 6.6 percent loss seemed small in the larger view of what happened that night. Rudy Boschwitz defeated Wendell Anderson by 16 points, and Dave Durenberger bested Robert Short by nearly 27. Arne Carlson won his state auditor race, giving the Republicans four statewide offices.

In the legislature, Republicans picked up 32 seats, turning a 64-seat deficit into a 67–67 tie.

Democrats across the state were dumbfounded, and Perpich was devastated, likening the defeat to "falling off a cliff." The results in his home district were especially painful—even though Perpich won the Eighth Congressional District with 57 percent of the vote, it was considerably less than the nearly 64 percent that Carter and Mondale tallied two years prior.[55]

DFL attorney general Warren Spannaus was a bright spot for Democrats, carrying 62 percent of the statewide vote, and becoming the DFL's most popular vote-getter for the second time.[56]

Opinions differ as to the causes of the Minnesota Massacre, and partisan affiliation often influences analysis. Republican explanations include the arrogance of the DFL, questionable appointments, and out-of-control state spending under Democratic leadership. Democrats blame Republican mischaracterization of their positions combined with national dissatisfaction and their own growing complacency. There is merit in both accounts, but neither tells the complete story.

Several elements contributed to the lopsided Republican victory in 1978, though Wendell Anderson's appointment to the Senate was a leading factor. Likewise, the heavily Democratic legislature's vote to raise their own salary and pension during the '77–'78 sessions supported Republican claims that the

DFL was out of touch amid rising inflation, energy shortages, and an energetic "tax revolt."[57]

The divide within the DFL over the BWCA and abortion helped Republicans. State employees, angry over the legislature taxing their pensions and Perpich unplugging their coffeepots, are also believed to have voted Republican in much greater numbers than was typical.

"You had the Bob Short and Don Fraser fight [and] you had the primary battles. Wendy was in trouble on the BWCA," remembered state senator Roger Moe. "I just think it was a combination of our own arrogance, double-digit inflation, 20 percent interest rates, midterm on the national election—all negatives, and they were all in our columns."[58]

Lola and the Perpich family believed that abortion had been the key factor in her husband's defeat and that the leaflets distributed by Quie's campaign staff were "an emotional smear sheet." Two weeks after the election, Lola uncharacteristically let her emotions show in a personal letter written to the *Minneapolis Star* in which she blasted Quie for carrying a "Bible in one hand and a bucket of mud in the other," and for implying that he "is a Christian and that Rudy is not."[59]

"Many people have asked my feelings about the Nov. 7 election," Lola began her letter. "What concerns me the most about that election, as it should concern all Minnesotans, is that Mr. Quie interjected religious judgments into a political campaign for his own personal gain.

"Rudy has been an active Christian since childhood. He doesn't believe in using religion as a political ploy. The standard Webster definition of a Christian is having loving qualities demonstrated and taught by Jesus Christ as love, kindness, humility—a decent, respectable person."

The one-page letter on white stationary was written under the Minnesota first lady's unaided initiative and concluded with a simple question: "Who then is the true Christian?"[60]

Gretchen Quie, signing a private handwritten letter on behalf of herself and her husband dated December 10, 1978, addressed to Governor and Mrs. Perpich, acknowledged that "over-zealous supporters" had used religion as a political advantage during the campaign.

"We regret the last-minute tactics by the groups you mention," the letter conceded.[61]

None of it would heal the wound created between these two men, and none of it could invalidate Quie's victory. Rudy Perpich had lost.

CHAPTER 9

Rudy Returns and Minnesota Pivots

"You wake up one day in November, and in sixty days, you're
no longer going to be holding elective office. So, what is it
that you're going to do with your life?"

—*Lynn Anderson, assistant to Governor Perpich*

The Minnesota Massacre set off fractious recriminations within Minnesota's
DFL. Some, like Perpich, used the defeat as a time to step away from politics.
Days after the 1978 election, Perpich visited the executives of Minnesota-based
Control Data, a mainframe and supercomputer firm in Bloomington, with his
hat in hand. "I will be governor for another month, and then I will be out of
work. . . . I need to work," he said.[1]

The loss devastated Perpich. He was not angry with the voters and was not
bitter, but he was shattered that his life's political goal was gone. Perpich would
move his family across an ocean because he refused to look back and always
propelled himself forward. He believed that if he remained in Minnesota, he
would be seen as a political "has-been." Perpich understood that no governor
in Minnesota history had ever lost the office and returned to serve another
term. Conditions would have to be perfect for him to have a second chance
at the job he had worked so long to achieve, and even if they were, there were
no guarantees that the DFL would support him again. In politics, four years is
a lifetime, and in November 1978, Rudy Perpich realized that his political life
might have ended. It was time to start anew.[2]

Those closest to Perpich had witnessed time and again the zeal with which
he embraced a challenge. The chapter in his life that followed the 1978 defeat
was no exception. During a cross-country skiing excursion that winter on Lake
Esquagama, close friends were not surprised when he and Lola told the group
that had advised them since the days of their first school board campaign that
the Perpich family was going to Vienna.

"We kidded Lola that maybe the sewing club would be in Vienna next year,"
remembered Norma McKanna years later.[3]

Rudy Abroad

Perpich called Control Data founder and CEO Bill Norris shortly after the '78 election. During his first term as governor, Perpich occasionally met with Norris and Norbert Berg, deputy chairman of Control Data's board of directors. He was comfortable with the company's leaders. He had remarked to another business leader that the pair from Control Data were the only two business leaders in the state he trusted or believed.[4]

Norris, a progressive visionary who grew up on a farm in Nebraska, was introduced to computers while serving as a code breaker in the US Navy. He founded Control Data in Minneapolis in 1957 and by 1978 had established the company as one of the world's most respected and innovative computer firms. At first, Norris found the call from Perpich curious, but the lame-duck governor wasted no time getting to his point. He wanted to represent Control Data in Eastern Europe. Perpich told Norris he had family ties to the region and spoke the language.

After Perpich called, Norris walked into Berg's office and told him the governor wanted to meet with them.

"He said he spoke Croatian and was a citizen over there because his dad was. He was the highest-ranking Yugoslavian (I think he said Yugoslavian and not Croatian) in the United States, and the people over there know that," Berg remembered of the first meeting with Perpich.[5]

"The first day I was over there, I would be dancing with the people in the streets. I have a lot of capability you can use," Perpich told the pair.[6]

"Then he said, 'So, what do you think?' Just like that. 'What do you think?'"[7]

Norris and Berg were impressed and intrigued by the idea and arranged a meeting between Perpich and the marketing staff that oversaw the company's European sales division. The team was equally impressed. The two executives quickly agreed that Perpich's proposal would be a good fit for the company's fledgling operations in the region. They offered Perpich $50,000 plus housing and travel expenses. It was less than the $58,000 he had earned as governor, but Perpich was eager for the opportunity and embraced the challenge.

"That's good, that sounds fine. And maybe if I do a good job, I will get some more," Berg remembered Perpich's response to their offer. "I said, 'You understand this capitalism thing, don't you?' He liked that."

When asked by the media how his new salary compared to what he earned as governor, Perpich replied: "I am not telling you what I am going to get paid, but I can tell you this: My dad thinks it is more than I deserve and Lola thinks it's less than I deserve, so it is probably just about right."[8]

Rudy moved with Lola and the kids to New York for six months while undertaking a short course on world trade before the family relocated to Europe. Perpich spent the next three years based in Vienna, Austria, as a Control Data trade envoy in Eastern Europe. He traveled throughout Hungary, Czechoslovakia, and Poland, making sales and establishing connections with government agencies in the region.

The former governor worked within a division of Control Data called WORLDTECH, where he was involved with scouting technologies that could be utilized in different industries and regions of the world. Additionally, he helped introduce technologies from around the globe to Eastern European companies. He also participated in a system of countertrade that allowed companies burdened by a shortage of hard currency in the struggling Eastern European economy to purchase Control Data technology and services through an arrangement where they would infuse cash into the company by purchasing products as varied as greeting cards, sporting goods, precious stones, or cement.[9]

Many close to the former governor referred to the experience as Control Data University, which exposed Perpich to global business and cutting-edge internal trade technologies. It wasn't just others who noticed the experience's impact on the former governor. Berg remembered the change Perpich recognized in himself.

"Berg, you have got to understand. You are talking to a kid who used to throw rocks at the shack where the mine superintendent was. They were the enemy," Berg remembered Perpich telling him. "It was Governor Perpich's first real insight into how business operates and who the people are in business. He was much less suspicious of businesspeople. He was more trusting. By his own admission, he had a different feel for business after this.

"He understood a lot more about job creation and where jobs came from and what things would make [Minnesota] prosperous and keep the people employed. Control Data University took a real active, fertile mind and bombarded it with all these experiences."[10]

Rudy was also profoundly influenced by the social welfare structure he witnessed in his travels. The lack of homeless and hungry people on the streets of Vienna gave Perpich inspiration that the public programs and goals he championed were achievable. His belief that government could improve people's lives was reinforced. He saw what was possible when people were fed and clothed and had a safety net—a society where people had jobs, and the elderly were cared for. He saw beautiful cities with public spaces and low crime rates. He witnessed government-created social structures and public programs that took care of people. But he also saw the downside of government being overly involved in business, the high taxes required to support Europe's robust public programs, and the corresponding strain they put on their economies. The educational systems in Scandinavia enthralled Perpich, but the government's control over industry turned him off. He wondered whether Minnesota could prove that a society could have one without the other.[11]

Exposure to so many different systems and structures of public and private enterprise in such a short time was invaluable—particularly for someone who kept alive the idea of returning to the Minnesota Governor's Residence if the stars aligned. Perpich firmly believed that his loss in '78 was a fluke and that he had been caught in the cross fire of voter anger that hadn't been intended for him. He recognized that the more the Minnesota economy struggled, the more those same voters would realize their error and long for the economic stability of 1977–78. He was constantly in contact with friends and political allies back home, and there was heavy pressure from the Iron Range for him to return. The longer he was away, the stronger his belief in the direction he could take the state if given a second chance in the governor's office grew.

"The travel alone, the exposure to different educational systems, different transportation systems, different health delivery systems, socialized government versus [capitalism]. It was an incredible knowledge base for him to bring back in '82," recalled Lynn Anderson, one of several members of his first administration with whom Perpich kept close contact while in Europe.[12]

"Some of the conversation was political, that he really wanted to come back. Some of it was personal-political; 'don't make any commitments, don't rule me out,'" Anderson remembered of the long-distance conversations. "He talked a lot about what he saw in education and the cultural environment he [was] exposed to. Minnesota had a very good cultural core here, but he [saw] how much more we could do and how we could tie that more to education. You could see, early on, that a lot of [a future] agenda was being formed. The one thing, very firmly, he could see is how Minnesota could have a place internationally, and he could see how to take the state in that direction."[13]

The time abroad introduced the former governor to global business, trade, and government, and exposure to the arts, culture, and history of Europe transformed the entire Perpich family. Rudy and Lola could enjoy each other's company in a way they couldn't as Minnesota's governor and first lady. The couple explored their adopted home of Vienna and spent long weekends traveling across Europe. They took in the architecture and art galleries of Europe's finest cities, frequented theaters and operas, and soaked in the culture and food of their ancestors. It was a time that could only have seemed more than a world away from the stresses of St. Paul and the limits of the Iron Range.[14]

"I had dinner with them there one night, and they were like a couple of kids on their honeymoon," remembered Norbert Berg. "We went for a leisurely walk after dinner. They were at peace, and they were almost at home. They were relaxed. They were happy. It was a wonderful experience for them, but it was also, obviously, a broadening experience for them."[15]

"I remember being in Vienna and taking a course in opera and falling in love with it. Every night that we could, we'd go to the opera," remembered Mary Sue Perpich, who, along with her brother, spent time studying and visiting the sites of Europe with her parents. "I think a lot of the appreciation [for the arts] came when we were living in Vienna. My mom and dad realized they couldn't live without the stimulation of the opera and concerts. When they came home, they knew they had to have the [arts] school."[16]

But there were mounting pressures from back home. The people of the Iron Range desperately waited for their hero to return. Ron Gornick traveled to Dubrovnik, Croatia, to visit Perpich in early 1982. With their feet dangling in the Adriatic Sea, the two talked politics and contemplated Rudy's return. Perpich said that he had had his chance, that his new life was rewarding, and that his wife, Lola, especially enjoyed Vienna. But Gornick detected that Rudy wasn't at peace with his decision. A few days later, Perpich told Gornick he wanted to be Minnesota's governor again.

Gornick had one requirement: "If you want to be governor, you have got to promise me that you will be a candidate if the people want you."

"Go find out, Gornick," was Rudy's reply. It was all Gornick needed to hear. He returned to the Iron Range with the news everyone had been waiting for.[17]

Perpich's time in Europe expanded his horizons and developed his world-view. He was exposed to international culture, history, and industry and returned to Minnesota with a vision of the state as a global leader in the arts, education, tourism, and trade. And as the political stars began lining up, Perpich was ready to ask the voters of Minnesota for a second chance to make his vision a reality.

Rudy Returns

In the spring of 1982, Minnesota was at a crossroads. The national economy had endured a prolonged period of double-digit inflation; the state's economy had hit its lowest point since the Great Depression. Minnesota's state government budget crisis began in the fall of 1980. Recurring deficits required the legislature to add six special sessions to reach a remedy. Republican governor Al Quie had entered office in 1979 with a $250 million surplus, allowing him to enact campaign promises of tax cuts and reduced expenditures. Ultimately, those tax cuts, plus a series of inaccurate budget forecasts, sent the state's government into a fiscal tailspin.

Minnesota enjoyed national renown as a state where government worked.

A strong agricultural economy had helped shield it from previous recessions. But when the downturn of the early 1980s simultaneously hit three leading industries—farming, manufacturing, and mining—the entire state was in peril. Quie announced his decision not to seek reelection in January 1982, after realizing the state's fiscal calamity would require him to break his campaign pledge not to raise taxes.

After Quie's exit, Attorney General Warren Spannaus was the DFL heir apparent and, given the Democratic Party's rebound in state and national polls, the presumed next governor. He was a popular figure within his party, though some felt his liberal policies—particularly on gun control—would make it difficult for him to connect with voters outside the Twin Cities metro area. Any challenger to Spannaus would need a statewide platform to succeed.

That political reality was not lost on a core group of Perpich supporters, many of whom had known Rudy since childhood. They refused to believe that Perpich's political career had ended with his 1978 defeat. While Rudy was in Vienna, they met in Chisholm, Minnesota, in a room above the Deep Rock gas station, owned by Gornick. It was hot and uninsulated, but it was secluded from the press. The group consisted of friends like Gornick and Frank Ongaro; family, including three different George Perpiches—his state-senator brother, his hockey-coach cousin, and his cousin's son; Iron Range politicians, including legislators Doug Johnson and Joe Begich; and union leaders like Baldy Cortish and Joe Samargia. They came to be known as the Monday Night Gang. To keep interest alive, they put signs in storefronts across Minnesota's Iron Range asking, "Where is Rudy?" In the summer of 1981, they mailed flyers across the state, hoping to generate buzz for a Rudy return.[18]

When Gornick returned from visiting Perpich in Vienna with a mandate from the former governor to "go find out" his chances at making a comeback, that was all the Monday Night group needed to hear.

Rudy would stay in Europe as long as possible while his friends sowed intrigue back home. Word of the clandestine gas station meetings leaked to the press. When local and state news outlets began contacting members of the group, Gornick was outraged. But then it became clear that the leak was an opportunity. The nascent Perpich campaign had stumbled into a wealth of free advertising. Newspapers across the state picked up the story. CNN reported that a "renegade ex-governor" would return home to take on the machine.[19]

In April 1982, the *Minneapolis Tribune* and the *Minneapolis Daily Star* merged, becoming the *Minneapolis Star and Tribune*. The editors wanted a splashy front-page story to launch the combined paper and preview the coming political season. So, for the Easter Sunday edition, young journalist Lori Sturdevant was assigned to cover the return of Rudy and Lola Perpich stateside.

Members of the Monday Night Gang. Mark Phillips (with glasses) is seated at center, and "Big" George Perpich is at the head of the table. Continuing clockwise: Joe Drazenovich, Gary Lamppa, Frank Ongaro, Bob Scott, Joe Moren, George Perpich Jr., Dana Miller, John Ongaro, DeLyle Pankratz, [unidentified], Ron Gornick, Phil Landborg, and Jeff Petrack. Sawmill Saloon owner Andy Shuster is seated to the right, and standing behind him is noted accordionist Oskar Frykman. *Courtesy Minnesota Discovery Center*

Perpich had left Minnesota's political scene in January 1979 with graying hair and a feeling that his opportunity to shape Minnesota had been lost. He had worked his entire political career to become governor, only to lose the office two years after attaining it. Still, his exile proved transformative. Living and working in Europe broadened his horizons and opened his mind to the potential of Minnesota as an international player. But none of this—save for a change in the color of the former governor's hair—was immediately apparent when Sturdevant sat down with Rudy and Lola at the Russian Tea Room in New York City for their interview.

As he answered question after question, the change in Perpich began to emerge—and it was more than his hair, which was now dyed jet black. Sturdevant remembered him as an Iron Range folk hero during his first term—colorful, unique, and always good for a quote, though sometimes tongue-tied and unfocused. Now he was a polished international businessman, presenting ideas not being talked about by other state political leaders. He argued that state government could propel Minnesota forward via international trade, better use of natural resources, and technology-driven economic diversification.

In response to Sturdevant's questions about the state's chronic budget deficits, Perpich said the first thing was to "realize that the real villain is energy." The state needed to lean into alternative energy ideas, Perpich said. He talked about timber, peat briquettes, pig farms, and opening Minnesota's agricultural markets to the world.[20]

On tax relief, which both political parties were proposing to aid the struggling economy, Perpich was dismissive. "I don't think that works. Spannaus is talking about a 75 percent tax cut the first year for a new business. A new business doesn't make any money the first year to tax!" Instead, Perpich would take a page out of the playbook of Control Data, a company that had started with eleven employees and had grown to 60,000 in forty-seven countries. "Why?" Perpich asked. "Because [they're] marketing worldwide, and that's what we have to help other Minnesota industries do."[21]

If the solutions were so simple, Sturdevant asked, why hadn't they been tried already? Why was no one else talking about this? Perpich said that political leaders "take too narrow a view of the world." He added, "I used to be like that, too."

Jobs, Jobs, Jobs

It became apparent that, while overseas, Perpich had never closed the door to a political comeback. Through weekly calls to his close friends and political allies, he kept apprised of the political and economic situation in Minnesota. He knew that some Minnesotans felt their Republican governor had led the state into financial ruin. This feeling was especially strong on Minnesota's Iron Range, where job losses were staggering.

Perpich saw economic distress as his political opening and an opportunity to unite the state. DFL front-runner Spannaus's message was murky at best and held little prescription for the state's economic pain. Perpich's message would be simple: Jobs, Jobs, Jobs.

In 1982, Minnesotans' hearts and minds were with the Iron Range. The mining industry was in shambles, with some economists forecasting that the jobs were gone for good. Families were devastated and communities were decimated. Statewide, unemployment rose to nearly 10 percent; but some Iron Range communities saw unemployment rates as high as 50 and 60 percent. Churches all over the state were sending food and were worried about finding jobs for unemployed Rangers. Against this backdrop, Minnesotans were ready to listen when Perpich talked about an economic development strategy for the whole state, with a particular understanding of what the Range needed.[22]

Perpich formally announced his candidacy for a second term as governor during a press conference at the Minnesota Press Club in Minneapolis on April 22, 1982. "I want to be Minnesota's number one salesman, number one fan, and number one promoter," Perpich said. His campaign message would incorporate natural resources, education, high tech, medicine, alternative energy, and tourism—but it all came back to one thing: providing jobs for Minnesotans. He wanted to reach the dairy farmer in southern Minnesota as much as the miners of the Iron Range. He needed the union leaders of Minneapolis and leaders of business across the state. The state must leverage what it had to avoid spirals of increasing taxes and reducing services, he argued.[23]

Employment was important to Perpich, going back to his childhood at Carson Lake. As a kid, seeing his father's lunch pail on the counter meant his dad was out of work. It meant his family wouldn't have money to provide the necessities for Rudy and his three brothers. But the Rudy of 1982 was a far cry from the kid who threw rocks at the mine supervisor's front door when his father was out of work. His Vienna experience had taught him to engage with the business community, while still relying on support from labor. "This campaign is about jobs," he said. "We have got record unemployment. . . . What I'm going to do is bring Minnesota back to the position it was in when I was governor. . . . If I take care of that, many of the other issues will take care of themselves."

Business leaders noticed Perpich was acting like a governor, a leader. He was involved. He was talking trade initiatives. Perpich introduced executives from St. Jude Medical, TELEX, and other Minnesota corporations to trading companies from the former Yugoslavia. One executive from St. Jude said afterward that his company had been trying to get into Yugoslavia for years without any success. Now Perpich was bringing them to the front door.[24]

Across the state that spring, Perpich fan clubs began popping up, each with their own initiatives and reasons for supporting Rudy. Somebody in Rochester loved him because he was committed to keeping the state hospital open. Somebody in Worthington because he understood the impact that neighboring states and businesses have on local economies. Farmers in western Minnesota, miners on the Range—all had their issues, and he spoke to them all. Rudy and his message of "Jobs, Jobs, Jobs" began appearing on buttons across Minnesota.

Single-Issue Politics

Like today, the political parties of Minnesota and the nation in 1982 were divided on gun control and abortion. Lola believed that abortion had been the key factor in her husband's loss in the 1978 election, when anti-abortion groups distributed leaflets in church parking lots on the Sunday before the election. The Perpich family believed the leaflet mischaracterized Rudy's position.

Perpich said that while he was personally pro-life, he would not be defined by a single issue.[25]

Gun control was equally divisive, and it was a topic Perpich wasn't afraid to use against Spannaus. Gun control had played a central role in Spannaus's twelve years as attorney general. In 1975, he had backed a major gun law requiring waiting periods and background checks for firearms purchasers. The legislation made him a target for gun-control opponents. Perpich argued that Spannaus had divided the rural and urban areas of the state, which Perpich saw as a trap. He believed that arguments about guns and abortion wouldn't make a better Minnesota. "This campaign is about jobs. We have got record unemployment," Perpich said to deflect controversial topics. "Our single issue is jobs, jobs, jobs."[26]

Perpich had no illusions where his positions left him with the DFL Party. Ever since he began considering a return to politics, he understood that single issues, along with the DFL's support for Spannaus, would require him to avoid the party's endorsement process and take his campaign straight to the people. His renegade approach wasn't without cost. The party shunned him at its state convention in Duluth. On Saturday, June 5, party activists removed Perpich signs and did anything else they could to discourage delegates from noticing Perpich's candidacy. Later that day, Spannaus was endorsed, winning 81 percent of the delegate votes. Even former governor Wendell Anderson, under whom Perpich had served as lieutenant governor, gave a speech that chastised Rudy for running against the party's endorsed candidate.[27]

Convention organizers finally agreed to allow Perpich to address the delegates on the last morning of the convention, when attendance would likely be sparse. Rudy Jr., who along with his sister accompanied their mother and father onstage, watched in surprise as Spannaus supporters jumped up from the audience, shouting so Rudy could not be heard. The Perpiches were appalled by such rudeness, later recalling, "He got about halfway through and turned and walked off. And we followed him. That was the end of it."[28]

Perpich left the convention abruptly and spent the rest of the day at his home near Hibbing. Ultimately, all the drama proved little more than theater for political junkies. The average Minnesotan held little regard for political conventions, something Perpich understood perhaps better than those who held leadership posts in the DFL Party. His focus was on the September 14 primary election.

RVs and Renegade Rangers

The fledgling Perpich campaign avoided the DFL Party machine, with its county and district chairs and perennial operatives. "We . . . didn't pay attention to them because they weren't with us anyway, and they could only hurt us—we didn't trust them," said campaign chair Eldon Brustuen. "We just simply ignored them and went to the people."

Brustuen saw the campaign as seven separate organizations: Minneapolis, the Iron Range, St. Paul, the unions, the anti-abortion Minnesota Citizens Concerned for Life, southeastern Minnesota, and the Seventh District. He noted, "Anytime we would bring the leadership of them all into one room, it was a disaster. It was chaotic. It just absolutely wouldn't work."[29]

Perpich saw a simpler campaign. He saw his path to a 1982 primary victory starting in the Eighth Congressional District, which included Duluth and the Iron Range, and then flowing to the rest of the state. His core supporters on the Range were already organizing the Eighth District, allowing Rudy and Lola to focus on the remainder of Minnesota.

Every weekend, members of the Monday Night Gang joined the Perpiches to canvass the state. Traveling in a handful of RVs plastered with signs and pictures of Rudy, they shouted, "Get out and vote! Get out and vote!" They went to county fairs, church suppers, picnics, and coffee parties—in the suburbs, in the inner city, throughout the countryside. Like a campaign for local office on steroids, "The campaign was very naive, innocent, and filled with down-home, folksy people," Brustuen recalled.[30]

Part of the campaign's advertising and endorsements came from small daily newspapers, such as the *Swift County Monitor* and the *Faribault Daily News*. In Sleepy Eye, one of Rudy's vehicles appeared unannounced at the radio station and went live on the air within five minutes. In a front-page article titled "Perpich Campaign Comes to Our Town," the next day's newspaper reported that this was the first time a governor's campaign had visited Sleepy Eye.[31]

Perhaps the biggest benefit of the RV campaign was the perception that Rudy and Lola were everywhere. Lola was critical to the campaign. "During that '82 election, if Lola was there, we knew we were going to get attention. . . . People liked Lola," remembered Ongaro. When Connie Perpich, wife of Rudy's brother George, waved out their RV window, the crowds mistook her for Lola. Joe Begich, who shared Rudy's same curly black hair, said, "I think I could pass for Rudy." When either of them was behind the wheel with the sun visor down, most spectators couldn't tell the difference. According to radio reports, Rudy and Lola were in Austin, Roseau, and Moorhead all on the same day.[32]

Once at a campaign stop in southwestern Minnesota, Perpich spoke to a group of forty to fifty people. After the speech, he saw an advertisement for a polka, which turned out to be a political event. Of course Rudy wanted to go. "It was incredible," Bob Scott, one of the original members of the Monday Night Gang, said. "People were packed in there, and of course every woman wanted to dance with him. . . . The entire campaign was magic," he recalled. Not brilliant, but magic. "Everything that campaign touched turned to magic, except not a lot of money came in."[33]

Creating Opportunities

The Perpich campaign was grounded in creating opportunities, and opportunities began with education. This principle was ingrained in Rudy by his parents—particularly his mother, Mary, who had been forced to quit school and give up her dream of becoming a teacher after her marriage at age sixteen. Her children became the focus of her own unrealized educational aspirations. Mary Perpich told Rudy and his brothers, "It would be better to be dead than not to be educated." Rudy wanted to ensure the next generation wouldn't need to make the sacrifices his mother had.[34]

Perpich saw Minnesota as the brainpower state and proposed the Minnesota Job Skills Partnership—a collaboration between the private sector and higher education—to beef up the training and retraining of the state's existing workforce. He wanted Minnesota to be world class, and he shared that vision with everyone he met: teachers' unions, farm interest and commodity groups, Main Street shop owners, and everyday people at the local cafés—Perpich wanted everyone involved.

Perpich's closest political confidant, Lola, believed defeating Spannaus would require a platform that included greater opportunity for women. They committed to choosing a woman as his running mate, which, if successful, would mean the first female lieutenant governor in the state's history.

Perpich's first choice for a running mate was Minnesota's second female secretary of state, Joan Growe. His campaign manager remembered the day Growe approached Perpich and, with typical Joan Growe class, said, "I need to be able to say that I wasn't asked, so before you ask me, Rudy, you need to know that if you did ask me, I would have to turn you down. . . . I have a political future in front of me, and I cannot run on an unendorsed ticket." Perpich also asked Lori Sturdevant about her interest as a possible running mate (she demurred), and he considered Emily Anne Staples, a former Republican elected in 1976 as the first female DFLer in the Minnesota Senate.[35]

On Wednesday, May 26, 1982, the *Minneapolis Star and Tribune*'s front-page headline read, "Spannaus Chooses Rep. Carl Johnson; Feminists Unhappy." Spannaus tapped Johnson, a farmer and long-serving legislator from St. Peter, as his running mate to add "geographic and occupational balance," the newspaper reported—much to the disappointment of not only feminists but also Growe admirers across the state who believed she would be selected.

Spannaus's press conference was interrupted by Minnesota Women's Political Caucus members, who told him they were "very, very disappointed that [he] did not choose a woman."[36]

Spannaus's choice for running mate provided an opportunity for Perpich. He blasted Spannaus, saying the attorney general had committed a political blunder. He called Growe "the most popular woman in state politics." On June 8, Sturdevant wrote a story recapping the convention and reporting Perpich's commitment to selecting a female running mate.[37]

Madame Lieutenant Governor

Businessowner Marlene Johnson, a founder of the bipartisan Minnesota Women's Political Caucus, sat in her office at the Minnesota Building on Fourth Street in St. Paul considering the news of Perpich's campaign promise. The move had her full support. Later that night, she wrote in her journal, "If he really wants to win, he will call me."[38]

The next day, Perpich called Johnson. On June 9, the two met at the Brother's Delicatessen in Southdale shopping mall. Rudy ate cake piled high with ice cream and whipped cream, telling Johnson about his vision for governing and how he had always wanted to be governor. He told her he had run for lieutenant governor in 1970 knowing there was no way a "hunkie from the Range was going to be elected governor of Minnesota." The lieutenant governorship had opened the door to his governorship, and he felt the same could happen for women.[39]

"As liberal a state as Minnesota was, there was a conservative bent here that was going to make it next to impossible for a woman to be elected governor for the first time," Johnson later recalled. "It meant a lot to him that he opened the door for women in the courts, and he wanted to do that for the governor's chair."[40]

Johnson had not held elected office, had no baggage, was active in the business community, and had many political friends. She was savvy and had a good reputation. Perpich also felt that she was closer to the party than he was. Spannaus may have had the DFL endorsement and the traditional party machine, but the party included many younger female voters who were increasingly active and were turned off by the status quo.[41]

Perpich believed Johnson could help him carry St. Paul. Minneapolis primary voters would stick with Spannaus, but it was possible for a Perpich-Johnson ticket to carry both St. Paul and the Eighth Congressional District—and that could win him the primary. When Perpich offered her a spot on the ticket, Johnson said she needed a week to decide. He said she could have a day. The next day, Sturdevant got the leak that Marlene Johnson was Perpich's choice for lieutenant governor.

Perpich's choice of a capable and accomplished woman may have been critical to his success. Some political observers believed that had Spannaus chosen a woman as his running mate, he would have won the primary and been elected governor. Marlene Johnson provided Perpich with political balance, gender balance, and geographic balance. She was strong on issues like pay equity and women's rights, appealing to female voters across the state. Carl Johnson, on the other hand, could provide Spannaus only with votes from St. Peter.

A Patchwork Quilt

Perpich had lived the immigrant experience. His father had emigrated from Croatia and his mother was the child of Croatian immigrants. Following passage of the US Refugee Act of 1980, many Hmong immigrants sought a home in the Minnesota metro area. During his 1982 campaign, Perpich wrote that Minnesota "will welcome any and all." He knew Minnesota could not reach its economic potential without embracing diversity. He also understood that this integration required overcoming cultural barriers, language barriers, and challenges to educational delivery. Perpich's future chief of staff, Lynn Anderson, later recalled, "I think he saw Minnesota, coming from the Iron Range, not so much as a melting pot, but as a patchwork quilt."[42]

Perpich's deeply held belief in the responsibility of community was driven by his experience and those of other immigrants and their strong ties to family. Education had been his "passport out of poverty" and fueled his core conviction that no child should suffer from their parents' unemployment. Public initiatives had allowed Perpich and his brothers to advance beyond the simple life of a mining location upbringing, and he wanted to ensure that all Minnesotans had that same opportunity, regardless of their birthplace. Years later, Minnesota US senator Paul Wellstone would say of Perpich that "everything had to do with education and opportunity. That was the core value. He never forgot his own immigrant experience."[43]

Primary Night

The Monday Night Gang's final meeting before the primary election was nerve-racking. Rudy's brother George warned that the northwestern section of the state was critical to victory. They needed one final push of advertising to secure a strong turnout. With no time to lose, $12,000 was needed for the media campaign. Those who could wrote checks for $1,000. Those who could not were as loyal as ever, some offering their hunting rifles and shotguns as collateral for quick loans.[44]

The night of the primary election was unseasonably hot and muggy across Minnesota. Perpich's campaign gathered in Eveleth at the Rustic Rock restaurant, which was jammed full of supporters. Polka music blared from the speakers, and TVs played in every corner. Doug Johnson, Gary Lamppa, and Tom Rukavina took turns working a single phone set at a center table—with a cord going straight through the ceiling. When a member of the press asked Lamppa where the line went, he told them, "Right to heaven. Right to heaven."[45]

But as the early Twin Cities returns came in, it looked bleak for Perpich. Pessimism snowballed, and even diehard supporters thought the campaign was lost. They could not make up 100,000 votes! Casual supporters thinned out as the night wore on, and only the most ardent remained. George and Connie Perpich were sitting at the bar crying. Ron Gornick joined them.[46]

Rudy had left the party early for the quiet company of Lola at their cabin on Esquagama Lake. But things started to change. Sometime after midnight, returns came in from Rochester, where Perpich did extremely well, thanks in part to the support of former Rochester state senator and lieutenant governor Sandy Keith. Then came returns from St. Cloud and other outstate areas, where Perpich picked up ground. The Iron Range results roared in around two or three in the morning.

Even with its limited number of votes, the Iron Range carried a disproportionate influence, particularly in primary elections. The Range was known for some of the best voter turnout in the nation for primary elections—sometimes 80 percent compared to the rest of the state's 20 percent. But this election was special.[47]

The 1982 Minnesota primary voter turnout was the highest it had been since 1970, at 31.1 percent, which has not been matched to this day. In the Eighth Congressional District, registered voter turnout was more than 49 percent. In St. Louis County, which includes Duluth and the bulk of the Iron Range, more than 87 percent of primary voters cast their lots for the DFL, with Perpich picking up more than 82 percent of those votes. The Eighth District put Perpich over the top in the 1982 primary election—exactly as he had predicted at the beginning of the campaign.[48]

Loyalists at the victory party tried to call Rudy, but he had taken his phone off the hook. His brother George rushed to the cabin but got no answer at the front door. He pounded on the window, saying, "Rudy! You won! You won!" In a short time, an overwhelmed Rudy was back at the Rustic Rock with his friends. Perpich had beaten Spannaus by more than 28,000 votes, 275,920 to 248,218.[49]

The General Election

The morning after the primary, the general election race for governor took shape as Rudy Perpich vs. Republican Wheelock Whitney, a wealthy retired investment banker. "It was hard to imagine two more opposite people," remembered Tom Triplett, who would become Perpich's revenue commissioner and, later, executive director of the Minnesota Business Partnership. "George Perpich would say, 'Rude, just keep reminding folks that Wheelock plays polo on weekends. Use that. Polo. Polo. Folks out there aren't going to like someone that plays polo on weekends.'"[50]

After his primary victory, Perpich turned his focus to reuniting the DFL Party. He wanted to avoid the kind of division that had contributed to the Republicans' Minnesota Massacre victories in 1978. He met with Mark Dayton, the DFL's candidate for US Senate and a future Minnesota governor. Dayton showed up for a simple meeting over coffee to find Perpich with *Minneapolis Star Tribune* reporter Jim Klobuchar and a newspaper photographer. Their meeting, with a smiling photo, made the front page, and the next Saturday, at a DFL Central Committee meeting in St. Cloud, Dayton gave an impassioned speech in support of Perpich and the unification of the DFL. Perpich was endorsed by 80 percent of the delegates.[51]

Perpich with future senator and governor Mark Dayton (center), September 1982. *Photo by Stormi Greener, Minneapolis and St. Paul Newspaper Negatives Collection, MNHS*

It soon became obvious to the state's veteran political observers that the general election contest for governor would not be close. Perpich knew it too. He began to use campaign stops to recruit key personnel from across the state for his upcoming administration. Unlike his first term as governor, when critics accused his administration of favoring close friends and allies, now Perpich sought a diverse range of viewpoints from both business and labor. In so doing, he not only revealed a much more confident Rudy than the man who had been defeated in 1978 but also signaled that his administration would be engaged with constituency groups from all regions of Minnesota.

Perpich and Johnson went on to beat Whitney and his running mate, Lauris Krenik, by 1,049,104 votes to 711,796—a margin of nearly 20 points. At a critical moment in state history, Perpich returned home with a vision for Minnesota as a world-class economic actor, renowned for its well-educated and productive workforce. The campaign would foreshadow the work of his second administration and change the trajectory of Minnesota.[52]

Rudy Perpich Jr. later remembered the 1982 campaign as the culmination of his parents' work over the previous thirty years. "My father had a very simple message," he noted. "It was 'jobs, jobs, jobs.' People knew him, they loved him, and that was what took him to victory."[53]

Lola, Rudy, Mary Sue, and Rudy Jr. celebrate with supporters at the Sawmill Saloon in Virginia, Minnesota, on November 2, 1982. *Courtesy Minnesota Discovery Center*

– CHAPTER 10 –

The Education Governor

> "Last time, I knew where I was from, but that was about it.
> Now, I know where I'm at. That's a mighty big difference."
> —*Rudy Perpich, January 1983*

If Rudy Perpich's first inaugural address was an homage to his hometown delivered at the seat of Minnesota political power, his second inaugural, delivered in his hometown, was an indication of what he planned to do with that power. His three-minute inaugural in December 1976 portended a burst of energy but lacked focus and confidence—at times feeling parochial. His second inaugural established a clear vision for the entire state, foreshadowing what would be among the most impactful four years of any governor in Minnesota history.

On Monday, January 3, 1983, Minnesota's 34th governor became Minnesota's 36th governor in the ornate auditorium of Hibbing High School. Perpich defended the unusual location by emphasizing the school's history of academic excellence and long list of successful alumni, to include all four Perpich brothers, who were in attendance. The brothers' parents, Mary and Anton, watched the ceremony on television at home a short distance away.

The location of "his oath of office was unprecedented historically," remembered longtime top aide Lynn Anderson. "The swearing-in had always been at the state capitol. He was sworn in on the stage of Hibbing High School because, to him, that represented how he got to the governor's office."[1]

Justice Rosalie Wahl administered the oath, while Rudy placed his hand on the white family Bible that Lola held—with Rudy Jr. and Mary Sue looking on from beside their parents. Former Hibbing superintendent Jim Michie, wearing a Perpich campaign button, watched with a smile as the student to whom he delivered a diploma on the same stage thirty-seven years earlier now delivered the inaugural address as governor of Minnesota.

Considering the setting, the speech predictably focused on the new governor's lifelong commitment to education and his campaign pledge of creating and defending jobs. "I want to call a halt to the wholesale cutting of classroom

Perpich taking the oath of office for his second gubernatorial term, January 1983. *Photo by Darlene Pfister, Minneapolis and St. Paul Newspaper Negatives Collection, MNHS*

teachers whenever school budgets get tight," he told the audience of primarily local students and teachers.[2]

Perpich sounded familiar themes such as the environment but also championed technology and international trade as critical to his second term. He proposed that school district state aid be contingent on the adoption of energy conservation actions, including converting to nonfossil heating fuels by 1985. He urged schools to invest in computers and science, strengthen their foreign language programs, and commit to producing students better prepared for a global job market.[3]

More than two dozen former teachers of Rudy or Lola were in attendance, invited so that he could publicly thank them for "making an extra effort for a bunch of kids from a ghetto."

"He said the only thing he kept in his desk drawer was a list of all the teachers he ever had," recalled Perpich's education commissioner, Ruth Randall. "He said he would never have been governor of the state had it not been for his teachers."[4]

Afterward, the Hibbing High School Band and a mixed chorus performed patriotic songs, the "Yugoslav Polka," and Aaron Copland's "Fanfare for the Common Man," before the event concluded with a lunch of chicken soup and peaches in the school cafeteria.[5]

New Plans, Familiar Surroundings

At the capitol two days later, Perpich's newfound self-assurance was unmistakable during his State of the State address before a joint session of the legislature. He laid out a vision of Minnesota in ten years becoming a national center of high tech, a global magnet for medical care, an agricultural processing hub, and a tourist destination drawing crowds from Asia, Europe, and the surrounding region.[6]

Perpich pledged closer relationships between the state and local governments; simultaneously, he warned that reductions in local aid would have to continue if state revenues kept falling below projections. He warned against raising state income taxes more than they had already been raised in 1982 and reducing assistance to industry. Both, he said, would be critical to Minnesota's rebound from the nasty recession of 1981–82.

"The best thing we can do with our taxes is stay someplace in the ballpark of other states," Perpich said. "We've got to keep watching our income taxes."[7]

He called for a closer relationship between business and the state's higher education institutions and the need for training and retraining programs to meet the demands of a rapidly changing global economy.

"Our schools need to be flexible enough that with thirty days' notice, they can bring in workers and retrain them to fit a specific job."[8]

But Perpich's trademark spectacles were not rose-colored. He assessed the state of the state as "not good" and planned partnerships among the private sector, labor, and "all levels of government" to fix the ills. He also called on all levels of government to join with churches and nonprofits to establish "the greatest self-help operation this state has ever seen" to address the combined crises of homelessness and hunger facing Minnesota.[9]

Perpich promised he would be willing to make the tough political decisions necessary to make his vision a reality—such as requesting the legislature to voluntarily reduce its size—even if it meant that his second term as governor would be his last.[10]

There was plenty in Perpich's speech for Democrats to approve. Senate majority leader Roger Moe said it "set the tone for the session in just the right way," while house speaker Harry Sieben said he had heard "more new ideas in the thirty minutes Perpich spoke than in the last six years."[11]

There was even more for Independent Republicans to like, including Perpich's plan for reducing government bureaucracy, lowering employers' workers' compensation rates, and government support for job creation. One Republican house member went so far as to depict Perpich's State of the State address as a "good Republican speech by a governor who I think is looking for help from the private sector."[12]

While politicians and the press were trying to figure out how to label the returned Rudy, Perpich's 1983–85 budget proposal was as much a reflection of his values as it was a fiscal document. Perpich pledged to "make Minnesota work again" through a $75 million jobs program in place of welfare, property tax relief for small businesses, and a return to the "real DFL" ideals of government helping those most in need through tax refunds and increased financial aid for lower- to middle-class families and students.[13]

One thing was apparent to all about the second Perpich administration: the new governor had a clear vision of where he intended to take the state and a willingness to work with anyone, of any party, to reach his aims. He also had a renewed confidence that impressed even those who knew him best—especially those who had worked with him in the first administration and members of the press.

"The first term, everybody thought he was just a 'bohunk' from the Range, and he was fighting that. After he came back [from Austria], he was a different person," said Ray Bohn, who served in the governor's office during that first term. His "infectious" confidence changed the administration and its reception, Bohn said, inspiring belief in Perpich's vision and ability to get things done.[14]

"He gained enormous breadth and stature during his four years away," recalled Mark Dayton. "In retrospect, it was the best thing that could have happened to him. He was a very different man when he returned from Europe. Lola was a very different woman. They came back with a worldview. They came back with a real idea of where he wanted the state to go."[15]

This new dimension in leadership enhanced the ingrained populism that had brought Perpich close to the voting public and launched him improbably back into the governor's office. Perpich was overflowing with enthusiasm and eager to get to work for the people of Minnesota when he left the house chamber three days into his second term as governor.

"He was hugging everybody he could grab," remembered journalist Lori Sturdevant. "He was so excited about his own performance and so up about the whole thing. He even grabbed me and gave me a hug and said, 'Now tomorrow. Six-thirty. We are in the air. We are going to take this message' around the state."[16]

Perpich indeed took his message straight to the people, beginning a flurry of campaign-like stops in Worthington, Austin, Rochester, and Winona before heading north to Alexandria and St. Cloud. He canceled a ten-day trade mission to Asia in March "so I can get in my car and hit the coffee shops for a few weeks." He likened the task of getting his ambitious agenda passed in the face of ongoing economic uncertainty and legislative resistance to his incredible comeback campaign the year before.[17]

Perpich and his wife, Lola, share a kiss at the inauguration ceremony, January 1983. *Photo by Darlene Pfister, Minneapolis and St. Paul Newspaper Negatives Collection, MNHS*

"I was further behind last April, on that campaign, than I am on getting this budget passed," Perpich said in February 1983. "I'm very optimistic—I think I'm going to come very close to getting the whole thing."[18]

Yet Perpich was also realistic, recognizing his greatest challenge would be convincing skeptical legislators to invest scarce public dollars in his vision of jobs, education, and international trade. To do so, the new Perpich accepted that convincing the public in gymnasiums and coffee shops across the state would not be enough and that a close courtship of the legislature—something he had failed to understand in his first term—would be critical for success in his second term.

It wasn't easy.

"This time, Perpich rode close herd on lawmakers," a *Star Tribune* headline read days after the session concluded, noting the difference between the Perpich of 1978, when he had gone home to Hibbing in the waning days of the legislative session. The 1983 Perpich was everywhere but his hometown—facilitating conversations between key legislators and interest groups on bonding projects, education, tourism, jobs, and international trade in his office at the capitol, dropping in unannounced at house and senate offices, and "jawboning conferees" in the middle-of-the-night hours before the constitutionally

mandated end to the session in mid-May. When that end came, Perpich succeeded with 55 of the 63 initiatives he recommended to lawmakers.[19]

The success was acknowledged uniformly by all sectors of political insiders
in St. Paul. Perpich's command of the office was "vastly improved" compared
to five years earlier, noted the president of the Minnesota Association of Commerce and Industry. The president of the Minnesota AFL-CIO agreed, saying
Minnesota's first second-time-around governor was "much more aggressive"
than in his first term. Even Republican lawmakers admitted Perpich's performance was "well above average."[20]

Perpich's steady hand led to sweeping victories in areas as wide ranging as
total spending, taxation, worker's compensation, and school funding.

"The minor stuff, what the heck, it's a give-and-take business. You let that
go," Perpich remarked. "But there are certain things that, if you stick to them,
the rest of it kind of falls into place. You decide ahead of time what that's going
to be." For Perpich, those "certain things" included a budget of no more than
$9.9 billion, no change in federal income tax deductibility, and a workers' com-
pensation bill.[21]

House speaker Harry Sieben credited the successful session to the way
Perpich interacted with the DFL majorities in both chambers. "He didn't try to
dictate to us much, but he made a point of being there when we needed him."
Chief of staff Terry Montgomery agreed, appraising the interactions between
Perpich and his DFL colleagues in the legislature as "comfortable, professional
relationships."

"It was a fantastic session," Perpich enthused while sharing credit with the
legislature. "Take just about any area—energy, education, international marketing, taxes. The legislature has given us the tools necessary to get out and sell
Minnesota."[22]

Building the Brainpower State

Over the next seven and a half years, Perpich would use these tools to mold Minnesota to realize his vision where students prepared for jobs at "world-class" universities and institutions, the state's businesses participated on the global stage,
and the educational opportunities he had been given as a child were available to
all. Collectively, the pieces of his vision would come together to make Minnesota
into what Perpich referred to as the "brainpower state." This clarion call was first
introduced by Perpich in September 1984 during a speech to educators in St. Paul
and would be the all-encompassing catchphrase for Perpich's far-reaching educational proposals for the remainder of his time as governor.[23]

Perpich realized that the team around him, which he had begun assembling

during the last days of the '82 campaign, would be critical in the battles ahead
to achieve his goals.

"As soon as we won the election, he began to put together his cabinet," recalled Lynn Anderson, who helped lead the transition. "It was the first time
that he could really put his own team together. He had to be very thoughtful
and selective. He knew he had an awful lot he wanted to accomplish and he was
going to be dependent on his commissioners to do that for him."[24]

Most staff and cabinet members he hired in 1983 would stay through the
entire second and—later—third term, although not all would stay in the positions to which they were initially appointed. Perpich freely moved staff and
cabinet officers around to where he felt they were most effective at the time.
His independent streak was evident in the fact that he named few political
patronage appointees to top-level posts.[25]

"He wanted as many women and minorities as was possible. But, beyond
that, there was little in the way of political screenings," recounted Tom Triplett,
who coordinated the hiring of key policy staff and commissioners in addition to working on the budget for the new administration before serving as
commissioner of the Department of Finance. "I think that's in large part his
ambivalence towards the party and party politics. He felt he won the primary
by opposing the party. So, he didn't feel he owed the party anything."[26]

And once in place, Perpich gave his commissioners the responsibility and
authority to do their jobs without interference.[27]

Ray Bohn, who served in the governor's office during both the first and
second terms and later as commissioner of two departments under Perpich,
described it this way: "I'll tell you what he told me—the only thing he told me.
[My] job was regulating utilities, a five- or six-billion-dollar-a-year business—
big business. He would look at me and look at my shoes. He said, 'The only
thing I'm going to tell you, I don't want you coming back in my office wearing
$200 shoes.' It was his way of saying, 'I don't want you to go down there and
get bought off.'"[28]

As Bohn recalled it, Perpich expected his commissioners to run a tight
ship—and to let him know first if there was a controversy headed for the press.
Of course, sometimes it was Perpich's decisions that invited controversy, like
his appointment of Roman Catholic sister Mary Madonna Ashton as the commissioner of the Department of Health.

"For obvious reasons—her background and her beliefs—people were very,
very concerned about what direction that would take the Department of
Health," Lynn Anderson remembered of the appointment of the anti-abortion
Catholic nun. "What were the governor's motives? Everything came into question. But the bottom line was that the governor believed that he was absolutely

appointing the most appropriate, the finest person, to that role." From experience, Perpich was certain that with time, the public and media would see the prudence of his appointments—after the sensation settled down.

"The fact that she was a Catholic nun was not how she would be defined," Anderson said, noting that Ashton would go on to serve the department for a full eight years. "He really gave Sister Mary Madonna Ashton, as well as a lot of other people, opportunities to show that they shouldn't be judged by what they did for a living. What their beliefs were. Where they came from. He asked people to put all of that aside. That genuine faith in people and their ability to rise above politics set the tone for the administration."[29]

Minnesota's commissioner of education was one of the positions critical to fulfilling Perpich's vision. That appointment, however, was made by the Minnesota Board of Education and confirmed by the senate, in accordance with state law. In January 1983, when the governor heard Rosemount–Apple Valley–Eagan School District superintendent Ruth Randall give a speech to the legislature, he set out to rewrite the law.

One of only five female superintendents in Minnesota's 434 school districts, Randall spoke about the obstacles facing education in the 1980s and Rosemount's innovative solutions. She talked about her district's efforts to empower parents and teachers to be part of budget, staff, and curriculum decisions usually reserved for administrators. She discussed collaborations between schools and the business community, including a partnership with Control Data to develop educational courses. Her district was recognized as a technology leader within the state's schools, and she promoted foreign languages being taught in kindergarten.[30]

In short, she was exactly what Perpich was seeking. He understood that it would be easier to achieve his education goals by working with his education commissioner directly—especially if that commissioner could be someone with whom he agreed so fundamentally, as he did with Randall—rather than working through a state board.

Perpich got his wish after an uphill battle, winning the right to appoint his own education commissioner as the 1983 legislative session came to a close. "I was told that the legislature held that hostage until they could get some things they wanted from him because it was so important to him," Randall remembered. Following the appointment, she became the first woman in the state's history to hold the position.[31]

"Excellence in education is a keystone of my program, and Dr. Ruth Randall is the perfect choice. In only two years, she earned a reputation for drawing students, teachers, and parents into a drive for innovation and excellence," Perpich told reporters on May 17 as he introduced his new education commissioner moments after signing the law that allowed him to do so. "Her assignment is to spread that gospel throughout the state, by giving direction where needed but also by encouraging schools, teachers, and administrators to branch out into innovative programs of their own."[32]

Randall had worked in rural, suburban, and urban school districts with children of all socioeconomic and racial backgrounds. She would become one of Perpich's most trusted and influential advisers amid a group of commissioners known for loyalty to a boss who showed them "110 percent support."[33]

"She is extraordinary. She came up with some excellent ideas," Rudy Perpich Jr. recalled of Randall. "[My father] had a commissioner of education who understood what he wanted and who was able to get it done."[34]

Access to Excellence

For Minnesota to find its place as a technological center and "the brainpower state of the nation," Perpich insisted that the government would need to do more than maintain the status quo. "We must lead the way in instructional technology, not just in new things to be taught but in new ways to teach," he told a crowd of public and private postsecondary representatives on September 5, 1984, in what his office called "the largest gathering of higher education officials ever convened by a governor." Perpich set the expectation for postsecondary schools to attract more students and improve their educational offerings.

"I will not hesitate for one second to recommend the closing of one institution or ask more to be closed. Our resources are limited, and we have competition," he warned.[35]

During the first years of his second term as governor, Perpich shepherded bills through the legislature that invested in technology for K–12 classrooms, increased general education funding that allowed teachers' salaries to as much as double in some districts, developed international curricula in math, science, and social studies, and supported professional development programs for teachers.[36]

But Rudy Perpich's lasting impact on education would be educational choice for students, and one of the pivotal moments of his time as governor came in January 1985 when he released what would come to be known as the "Access to Excellence" program for school reform. In it, he laid out many of the components that would define his legacy as an education governor. Perpich promoted his proposal on "the single theme of accountability." According to Perpich, the state would be accountable for providing funding, school districts would be accountable for the quality of educational opportunities they provided, and parents would be accountable for the education of their children.[37]

The proposal would increase the state's portion of total school costs from 63 percent to more than 80 percent in exchange for cities and counties picking up the homestead and agricultural credit property tax relief programs. A "learner outcomes" system to measure student achievement would be established and required to be published for all schools. Perpich proposed eliminating all other state mandates, including curriculum requirements.

"I personally will propose only one mandate: statewide evaluation using state-designed tests," Perpich said, adding that "local districts must have the flexibility to determine their own curriculum."[38]

The impetus for Perpich's program was personal. During a speech to the influential Citizens League, the governor strayed from his prepared remarks to describe his public education as a "passport out of poverty" and how he and Lola had chosen a school district for their children first and a house second when they moved to the Twin Cities during his time as a state senator in the 1960s.

"The reason we got to choice in education was because of the experiences that he had had with his own children when he was in the senate and the lieutenant governor's office," remembered Anderson. "He had enrolled them in one school district and found out that they just were not being challenged. It was not a bad district. It was just that coming out of the Hibbing school system, which was very progressive and very strong, the kids were not being challenged. So, he wanted them to have the ability to go to another school district, whether it was to take additional language classes or more extensive math or sciences or whatever, and that ability wasn't there—that mobility between districts."[39]

"I want all Minnesotans to have that kind of choice," Perpich told his audience. "Research shows that when families are permitted to select the public school of their choice, parents become more satisfied with the educational system, student attitudes improve, teacher morale goes up, and community support for schools increases."[40]

Choice would be the defining element of Perpich's education legacy. The "Access to Excellence" he described in January 1985 would take the rest of his time as governor to fulfill, but its impact has been felt ever since in school districts throughout Minnesota and across the nation. Under his plan, K–12 students would be able to attend the public school of their choice, with state aid following them. Juniors and seniors would be allowed to enroll in public postsecondary courses for college credit. And model schools would be developed, including district-operated "magnet" schools for math and science and a state-run school for the arts.

"Choice was absolutely our battle cry on all of this," said Barbara Rohde, who headed up the governor's Washington, DC, office during the second and third terms. "Choice. Magnet schools. But choice more than anything, because he was such a believer in the marketplace for education. That was our main issue."[41]

"The sky was the limit. He didn't want to be challenged by barriers—traditional educational barriers. What he wanted was for everyone to think about the children and to give parents an opportunity to make a decision in their child's education," Anderson elaborated.[42]

The *Star Tribune* editorial board cautioned that "critical appraisal" was needed and that there were definite "drawbacks" to Perpich's proposal, but they also praised the plan's audacity and the governor's boldness. Perpich's dream of Minnesota as the brainpower state would fundamentally alter the definitions of public education responsibility, the board argued. The choice offered to students and their parents by the governor's plan would incentivize school boards, superintendents, principals, and teachers to ensure their schools were in line with student expectations and provide motivation for each district to excel. The plan was a powerful agent for "grassroots educational change" and an antidote for ever-increasing money and mandates as the answer to better outcomes.[43]

Perpich's plan for what became known as "open enrollment" was met with resistance from many educators and school administrators—particularly those from smaller districts, who feared that the proposal was a consolidation bill in sheep's clothing and that the loss of even relatively few students and accompanying state aid to open enrollment would make their districts unviable.

Members of the Minnesota School Boards Association, meeting in Minneapolis less than two weeks after Perpich unveiled his "Access to Excellence" plan, gave Ruth Randall an icy reception as she addressed the group to explain the plan and calm the fears.

"It could be disastrous for us," one member of the Buffalo Lake School Board told Randall.

"It could be instant disaster for rural areas," the Moose Lake superintendent remarked during the two-hour session.[44]

In February, Perpich appointed a panel to recommend how the plan might be implemented. Instead, the panel offered an alternative plan of their own, proposing that students be allowed to change schools only for classes or programs not offered in their home district. Perpich's "School-Choice" and "Access to Education" bills, which included the open-enrollment and postsecondary issues, passed a key committee in the DFL-controlled senate in late March, but Perpich knew the road in the Independent-Republican-controlled house would be more difficult.[45]

It was the unlikely team of Perpich and Independent-Republican majority leader Connie Levi, of Dellwood, the first female majority leader in Minnesota history, who steered the open-enrollment bill through the house's Education Aids Subdivision, which many believed to be its toughest hurdle. In her fourth term, Levi was well liked and respected by members of both parties, noted for both her effectiveness as a spokesperson and her subtle ability to twist arms. In the male-dominated Minnesota House of the mid-1980s, Speaker Dave Jennings gave her high marks, saying his deputy "had to be better than her male counterparts to succeed—and she's done it."

But climbing Minnesota's political ladder did not appeal to Levi, who was being increasingly mentioned as a possible candidate for statewide office. "More pay and more power doesn't interest me. Public service does," she said during the 1985 legislative session.[46]

In order to get the proposal through the subcommittee, Perpich and Levi agreed to eliminate any references to students other than juniors and seniors and also to provide additional funding to small districts that might be disproportionately affected by losing students and the accompanying state aid. Levi credited the Minnesota Business Partnership, whose proposal to restructure junior and senior high schools to provide students in grades seven through ten a foundation of core classes first before allowing juniors and seniors to specialize by attending the school of their choice had been the basis for Perpich's "Access to Excellence" proposal, with swaying the votes in the house subcommittee.

Many school officials, educational lobbyists, and the teachers' union came out strongly against the changes, while groups such as the Citizens League and the Minnesota Business Partnership, which had funded a study of the state's public education that recommended similar opportunities for choice and mobility of students, hailed the governor's proposal as "historic."[47]

Perpich, Levi, and the partnership were taking on much of the education establishment. The Minnesota School Board Association and the Minnesota Association of School Administrators all opposed the plan and argued it would lead to chaos and confusion rather than educational excellence. The issue was "close to the boiling point," Superintendent Harold Larson of Glyndon-Felton Schools said the same week it passed the subcommittee, warning that the proposal would be the "greatest tragedy for rural education that our state has ever seen."

"By and large, the educators were not for all the aspects in his speech except for the secondary school principals. They were somewhat supportive. But the rest of the educational leadership were not supportive of choice," remembered Randall. "The policy entrepreneurs, the Citizens' League, the Business Partnership, and other groups like that were very supportive and had had a strong hand in helping design the 'Access to Excellence' speech. It had a difficult time in the legislature. That was when we did a lot of traveling around Minnesota."[48]

"It was terrible in '85. The teachers' unions made awful threats to the governor. And, of course, you couldn't threaten him. They went out and publicly said they would no longer support the governor in his programs because they didn't believe in this. They really, in my opinion, pulled out all the stops," Randall said. "But, I still knew he would come through on it."

Resistance from the unions tugged at Rudy, who remembered what union membership had meant to his father and the value it had provided for miners and their families on the Iron Range. The union pushback caused considerable controversy, forcing Perpich to repeatedly rethink his approach in hopes of finding a solution.[49]

Perpich countered the resistance by doing what he did best—taking his message directly to the people and selling his vision in personal terms. He made stops across the state, telling students, teachers, and administrators about his struggle to find the best education for his children when his family moved to the Twin Cities and about his belief that rural districts would not be decimated because of the excellent educational opportunities offered in rural districts such as the one he himself attended.[50]

Lewis Lehr, chairman of 3M, who said in 1983 that the company would "find it difficult to justify any further investment in Minnesota" after his public feud with Perpich over the governor's signing of the hazardous waste "Superfund"

Governor Perpich visits a classroom during his second term. *Courtesy Minnesota Discovery Center*

law, joined forces with Perpich in April to support the school choice proposal
in Minnesota's major media markets of the Twin Cities, Rochester, Duluth,
and Fargo-Moorhead. Past disputes over taxes and environmental laws were
off-limits at the press conferences, with Perpich rebutting critics' assertions
that the new law would be detrimental to small school districts and open the
door to private school vouchers.

"Once you give people an option, they'll come back to the public school
system," Perpich said, referencing studies showing magnet schools in St. Paul
drawing students from private schools.[51]

By the end of April, much of Perpich's school choice proposal was all but
dead, as the senate Finance Committee stripped the provision allowing juniors
and seniors to attend the public school of their choice from their omnibus
education bill. Perpich had fixed his hopes on the DFL-controlled senate after
the Republicans removed the proposal from the house omnibus education bill
earlier in the month. The proposal failed after coming under attack from nearly
every corner of the education establishment.[52]

Only a couple of elements in Perpich's plan remained—creation of a high
school for the arts and a toehold on school choice known as the "postsecondary option."

A School for the Arts

By pushing his proposal so forcefully in the face of fire from typically friendly
forces, Perpich demonstrated his genuine commitment to education reform,
along with his independence from education "special interests." He also displayed his capacity to work with business interests and to cross party lines for
reforms that he believed in. Following the proposal's defeat, Perpich reiterated
his conviction for putting principles before politics.

"I just believe in it," Perpich said. "Who knows about the political side? A
full generation has gone through the schools since I've been [in state govern-
ment], and the problems are still the same. We've got to break into this system
and make some changes.

"This is like a prairie fire that's roaring across Minnesota," and its opponents
would soon feel the heat, Perpich said.[53]

Senate Democrats, as if to ease the blow to the governor, included the plan
for a state arts high school in their proposal, which First Lady Lola Perpich had
championed and which was seen as a pet project of the governor's.[54]

According to Anderson, the Perpiches had seen the success of a similar
school in New York and had witnessed the impact of targeted educational opportunities, nationally and culturally, throughout their travels. Both Rudy and

Lola felt such a school could work well in Minnesota, but what they had to begin with was an early concept that needed work.[55]

Perpich had first proposed the idea for a state arts high school as part of his 1984 education budget, where he included $148,000 in planning money for the idea. It was met with opposition from both sides, with the DFL chair of the house Education Committee admitting there was "not much love" for the proposal among committee members. His counterpart in the senate, also controlled by DFLers, agreed. Nonetheless, Perpich remained "absolutely committed" to the idea, according to his top policy adviser, Tom Triplett. Perpich touted the arts high school as a lure for businesses to locate in Minnesota.[56]

"The school for the arts had been his love, but it had also been Lola Perpich's love," remembered Randall. "Lola came to the legislature and lobbied. Her lobbying, oftentimes, consisted of sitting in the front row of the hearings. . . . Her personality and her character and all—people liked her a lot. . . . Sometimes at legislative hearings, you can have some rancorous and caustic things said. . . . When she was there, I don't believe they became quite so mean-spirited. . . . And, of course, the governor lobbied ceaselessly for the school for the arts."[57]

Anderson, meanwhile, recalled that the push by Perpich came at a time when arts and music programs were often being cut out of district budgets. Perpich hoped his school for the arts might ensure the students seeking those programs weren't deprived of an opportunity to explore their passions.[58]

"What Rudy used to say is, 'I know what it is like in those small towns. You get someone who is a really gifted artist or something, they sometimes don't fit in. And they don't get what they need,'" remembered Ray Bohn.[59]

In the face of stiff opposition to the open enrollment provision of his school-choice legislation, the arts school remained a top priority for Perpich throughout the 1985 session. So did his proposal to allow juniors and seniors to enroll in public college or university courses while still in high school. Perpich's postsecondary enrollment options proposal would use state aid currently going to high schools to pay the cost of students' college tuition, textbooks, and transportation. This drew criticism from school officials who argued that funding for secondary education should not be diverted to pay for college tuition. But Perpich did not back down, reasoning that granting high school students more access to university courses was part of the larger goal of providing greater access to educational opportunities at all levels.[60]

"Everyone trained their guns on open enrollment, and the postsecondary options program somehow slipped through," Perpich later recalled.[61]

The arts high school became the key bargaining chip in the final negotiations of a $2.5 billion education bill as the legislature neared the end of its 1985 term. During a special session, Perpich said he had "released" the proposal to break a deadlock over the bill. In the end, the DFL senate and IR house agreed to a bill that included Perpich's proposal for postsecondary options for high school juniors and seniors along with $2.7 million for the development of a state arts high school and an associated resource center.[62]

"I think it was going out to the public to talk about it," remembered Randall.

Not just to talk about choice. Talk about all the components of the "Access to Excellence" speech. My recollection is that we went to fourteen different areas of the state . . . we went to a number of places around the state and talked about all the components of "Access to Excellence." Rep Connie Levi, who was a Republican, took the leadership in the house. And Senator Tom Nelson, who was a Democrat, took leadership in the senate. And those two people worked very, very closely with Governor Perpich, and they deserve the credit for actually getting the postsecondary-options portion through the legislature.

Representative Levi and Senator Nelson were of different parties but of a common mind on what needed to happen.[63]

While the pared-down legislation was a far cry from the sweeping vision laid out in his "Access to Excellence" speech six months earlier, it laid a founda-

Governor Perpich with the Lake Harriet Suzuki Strings. *MNHS collections*

tion for something more. At the signing ceremony that followed, Perpich said the legislation would "put Minnesota in the forefront of educational policy." Perpich predicted the new postsecondary options would "ease the transition between high school and higher education" while reducing the costs of college for families and keeping more Minnesota students in state schools.[64]

Legislators from both parties shared the stage with Perpich as he signed the bill. During the ceremony, the governor made it clear that he was far from done fighting for education reform. In addition to continuing the push for open enrollment, Perpich said that all-day kindergarten and schools for four-year-olds would be part of his upcoming agenda, with a further hope for increased early foreign language education. He also planned to increase high school students' overseas opportunities and develop "satellite facilities in other parts of the world" for Minnesota's colleges and universities.[65]

"International education was a very big desire of his, languages being paramount," remembered Randall. "He had great foresight in seeing how much we were coming into an international economy and a global world, how technology and rapid communication was bringing us together."[66]

Alternative Learning

Another educational program that Perpich supported but that failed to pass the legislature in 1985 was a "second chance" bill, which would have allowed troubled students to take courses in a school district deemed most appropriate by a neutral committee, with state aid following the student. In November, Perpich visited the Area Learning Center in St. Cloud, which had become a model for teaching students who had failed in traditional educational settings. But resistance from regional school boards, afraid of losing coveted state per-pupil funding, limited the number of students who were able to take advantage of alternative learning.

"We're going to work on that," Perpich told school officials as he toured the St. Cloud school and mingled with students. He praised two teenagers making plans for careers in law enforcement and signed an excuse slip so that a student attending courses could return to the Stearns County Jail after class.[67]

"Governor Perpich was strongly behind the idea that any young person who had not earned a high school diploma should be able to come back and do so on state aid," remembered Randall. "They should be able to do that in high school if they choose to do that. Or, if not, they could go to one of these alternative learning centers."[68]

"He looked at at-risk students and looked for ways to make sure that we could protect and capture them and keep them," Anderson recalled. "He didn't want to lose students in the process. If they were having trouble learning, if they weren't being challenged, if they were preoccupied, if they had financial obligations that they felt that they had to meet to their family—or whatever. What could be done to make sure that we could offer them alternative education?"[69]

In August 1985, just months after the legislature had approved Perpich's postsecondary options program, more than 1,200 students across the state were taking college courses funded through state school aid. Perpich continued promoting his school choice agenda by sending a letter to 170 school districts ahead of the 1985–86 school year, asking them to voluntarily implement open enrollment for high school juniors and seniors to "make it easier for the legislature to make the best decision." However, only ten school districts had implemented his suggestion by February of the following year.[70]

While not openly opposed to the voluntary adoption by those districts with educational effectiveness programs or state-designated technology demonstration sites, the Minnesota School Board Association and Minnesota Education Association remained steadfastly against a mandatory system.[71]

Early revenue projections signaling a shortfall of as much as $915 million for the upcoming biennium led Perpich to call for possible spending cuts, including to educational programs, in the '86 session to help offset a budget deficit. These potential reductions, coupled with a reelection campaign, eliminated Perpich's signature school choice proposal from consideration during the 1986 session. In May, despite his statements during the previous legislative session that he did not want the endorsement of the teachers' union for his reelection bid because of their staunch opposition to the proposal, Perpich stunned many when he announced he would not push mandatory open enrollment in 1987 if reelected. Critics contended that he was making a plea for the teachers' union endorsement amid his DFL primary challenge, from St. Paul mayor George Latimer.[72]

"As you know, I have supported that program and worked hard to secure its passage," Perpich told representatives of six educational organizations conducting interviews with potential DFL and Independent-Republican candidates. "I also recognize the opposition to it. . . . I believe that whenever you force something, you have problems. So the [open-enrollment proposal] I believe, should be on a voluntary basis. But let me add this: I believe if we had [open enrollment], you'd see a return to the public schools like never before in the history of the state."[73]

In August, the Minnesota Education Association (MEA) and the Minnesota Federation of Teachers (MFT) endorsed Perpich's reelection. The MEA had endorsed Perpich in 1978 and again in 1982 after his primary victory over Spannaus, but the support of both influential organizations had been considered unlikely because of the tussle over enrollment and Perpich's openness to consider cuts to school aid to help offset the budget deficit. (Elementary and secondary public schools were ultimately spared from the cuts, but post-secondary colleges and universities were not.)

"Although, like anyone else, you don't agree with someone on every issue, overall his record has helped the children of Minnesota to continue to receive a very, very excellent educational program," said MFT president Dick Mans.[74]

The endorsements were important to Perpich not only for his reelection campaign but also for the legacy he saw for himself as Minnesota's chief executive.

"I want to be known as the education governor from the brainpower state," Perpich declared.

Lasting Legacy

More than three years after his "Access to Excellence" speech, Minnesota became the only state in the country to allow parents broad discretion to send their children to the school of their choice when Perpich signed his signature educational proposal into law at a ceremony in Hibbing on Friday, May 6, 1988. The bill would also allow those over the age of twenty-one who had not graduated to return to high school to earn a diploma at state expense, another provision that was a first in the nation.[75]

"He announced choice and then he had to build on it," remembered Rudy Perpich Jr. "It took three years or more for all of his choice programs to be instituted. He did it step-by-step. He always said, 'start small and just get them a little bit excited.'"[76]

Perpich had worked hard to put together committees, task forces, and "blue ribbon" commissions with people representing every possible education interest group. Anybody who cared about education was allowed a seat at the table—teachers, parents, business interests, and education reformers. The groups labored to hammer out details on different proposals, but direction came from the governor. Perpich established criteria that required stepping away from the status quo and toward access. It was all part of the governor's plan to bring people, however incrementally, to see his vision for what choice would mean for Minnesota's educational system.[77]

"He was always taking baby steps, taking little pieces and then allowing them to grow and snowball—to prove themselves so people would have confidence so that the next thing offered up wouldn't be so daunting," Anderson recalled of Perpich's approach. "If you could get your hands around open enrollment, could you then get your hands around postsecondary options? And

The Perpich brothers at Hibbing High School, January 1983. *Photo by Darlene Pfister, Minneapolis and St. Paul Newspaper Negatives Collection, MNHS*

then, could you begin to see where alternative learning centers were valuable? Or could you understand how you could have a school for the arts and not have that liberal arts education abandoned?"[78]

"Let's see if we can't serve students better," Perpich would suggest. "See if we can't make sure that we don't have so many sixteen-year-olds dropping out— that they feel like, if they can't make it, they have some choice."[79]

Perpich returned to the school where he had received his diploma forty-two years earlier to sign the open enrollment bill into law. He explained to the audience of nine hundred students how his parents had instilled in him the value of education, while Anton, who was eighty-nine years old, and Mary, seventy-five, sat quietly beside him.[80]

CHAPTER 11

Labor, Latimer, and Supersalesman Rudy Perpich

"Wendy Anderson told me once, the greatest governor would be one who lost and then came back. I think he was right. I know now it's not the end of the world when you lose—in fact, the world gets better in some ways."

—*Rudy Perpich, 1983*

The economic downturn of 1981–82 was the worst recession in the United States since the Great Depression. National unemployment rates reached nearly 11 percent, the highest since World War II. Among those hardest hit were blue-collar workers in manufacturing and construction.[1]

The hardship was felt acutely in Minnesota and led to a state budget crisis—something new to Minnesota in the early '80s. A robust income tax had historically grown apace with the economy—an economy predominantly consisting of mining, agriculture, and manufacturing, buttressed by a sales tax in 1967—and had kept state coffers full for decades. Even in previous recessions, such as the mild one in 1974–75, Minnesota's agricultural sector held up, leading people to believe the state was immune to deep downturns.

Governor Al Quie repeated a general consensus among lawmakers and the public that the trouble they were witnessing was not possible in Minnesota. People thought: "It can't be anything wrong with our economy. It must be some incompetence or something." When Quie's finance commissioner, Wayne Burggraaff, testified before legislative committees about falling revenue forecasts, members laughed and teased that there was no way Minnesota could experience revenue shortfalls.[2]

The 1981 recession was a different animal. Experts attribute the crisis to reduced state revenues, caused by the indexing of personal income taxes in 1979; excessive spending commitments as the result of a compromise Quie made with Democrats for property tax relief to get his indexing proposal through the legislature; and a faltering national economy that would cost Minnesota an estimated $800 million in lost taxes.

It all added up to $2.2 billion, a massive downturn in a state whose 1980–81 general fund budget was only $7.2 billion.[3]

The pain was especially acute on Perpich's Iron Range. Minnesota's north-eastern seven counties had an unemployment rate of 18.5 percent, more than double that of the state as a whole. The region also saw shutdowns at seven of the eight major mining facilities, and, by mid-1982, 12,000 of the area's 14,000 mining workers had been laid off.[4]

Perpich then, in his 1982 campaign, ran on a platform of "jobs, jobs, jobs." But he wasn't the first. In September 1981, President Ronald Reagan said that "jobs, jobs, jobs, and more jobs" would be the goal of his economic agenda. Four months later, Governor Al Quie sounded a similar appeal but in a much less confident tone during his 1982 State of the State address, saying that "jobs, jobs, jobs" were necessary "or else everything falls apart." Even the president of the once-socialist Sri Lanka, Junius Richard Jayewardene, described the top three priorities of his newly elected administration as "jobs, jobs, and jobs."[5]

It seemed the same thing was on everyone's mind.

Perpich campaigned on jobs as a way to restart the economy but was also quick to highlight Minnesota's fiscal health when he exited office in 1979, leaving Quie with a $250 million budget surplus.

"Take a look at state government now, and then tell me who's flaky," Perpich said to reporters, still chafing over Quie's use of the term to describe him in 1978. "You never get ahead by trying to get even," Perpich liked to say, but certainly winning the 1982 contest would prove a little bit of payback. "If the economy in this state was doing well, I wouldn't be running," Perpich quipped. "Al Quie is leaving—God bless."

When asked by a reporter if that was "God bless Al Quie" or "God bless the fact Al Quie is leaving," Perpich paused before responding, "Both."[6]

To Perpich, finding a solution to the unemployment crisis was more than a slogan or even a platform; it was personal. As a child, he had witnessed the pain in his parents' eyes when Anton was sent home from the mine without work, and he had felt the hunger in his own stomach.

"He cared viscerally about jobs and peoples' opportunities to have jobs. He talked all the time about his own experience growing up," remembered Mark Dayton, who would join the Perpich team as commissioner of a newly imag-ined economic development department shortly into the second term. "What a difference it made for his family and for him if his father's lunch pail was on the kitchen counter. That meant he was working and those were good times. If the lunch bucket was on the shelf, that meant his father wasn't working.

[Rudy's childhood experience] meant there was nothing he wouldn't do, no-where he wouldn't go, in order to bring jobs to Minnesota."[7]

In December of 1982, the governor-elect visited with out-of-work miners at a hockey arena in Eveleth but was so moved by their desperate stories that he "couldn't carry on without crying" and had to leave. His administration's number one priority would be bringing hope and help to those miners and the unemployed across the state.[8]

"There were not two faces to Rudy Perpich. When he cried about his fellow men being out of work up on the Range, those weren't crocodile tears," remembered Joseph Alexander, who served as commissioner of the Department of Natural Resources in all three of Perpich's terms. "It wasn't a front. When people were in tough shape, tears would come."[9]

Perpich put jobs at the top of his list and said he'd do the hard work himself by representing Minnesota to the world. "I want to be the No. 1 salesman, the No. 1 fan, the No. 1 promoter," Perpich said early in his comeback campaign. "The governor can't sit in that office and hope that something falls down from heaven. The governor has to get out and promote the state."[10]

In the first State of the State address of his second term, Perpich proposed a state loan fund for new alternative energy businesses and a quadrupling of the state's tourism spending—including a focus on overseas tourists. He under-scored the elevated priority his administration would give state tourism pro-motion by assigning Lieutentant Governor Marlene Johnson to spearhead the effort. He also proposed a major increase in the promotion of Minnesota prod-ucts to foreign markets, assigning himself as the state's "supersalesman" while detailing four "selling" trips scheduled for the coming year.

"What he did was very smart because he used the jobs umbrella and eco-nomic development to set the agenda," remembered Lynn Anderson. "Every-thing grew out of that."[11]

"It was so constant, he was upbeat [and] would talk about what was right and what was good about the state," explained senate majority leader Roger Moe. Perpich would say, "We can be better. Here's what we have to do. We have to understand the world is changing. We have to focus on bigger markets. We have to understand that we are becoming more diverse."[12]

Perpich detailed a task force led by Mark Dayton and charged with growing Minnesota's medical technology industry and promoting the state's health facil-ities worldwide. "I'm going to work hard on that," he said. "One thing I learned while I was in Europe—whether you're communist, fascist, or whatever—you're interested in living longer."[13]

He created similar commissions to study wood products, high technol-ogy, film and graphic arts, and agricultural processing, predicting that by 1993 high-tech, health care, and wood products industries would play a much larger role in the state's economy. Perpich envisioned that tourism and the arts would continue to grow while mining and manufacturing would decline. Agriculture, however, he believed might be saved by agri-processing and overseas marketing, to remain a mainstay of the Minnesota economy.

Perpich recruited Minnesota's top CEOs and business leaders to serve on these "blue-ribbon" economic development commissions. The panels of industry experts would develop reports and make recommendations on specific issues they were charged to study. Some of the groups generated ideas that led to policies and projects; others were simply a means of engaging leaders of important industries. The commissions succeeded in building nonpartisan relationships with key stakeholders who helped to bring about consensus across the state and promote Perpich's idea that all things were possible for Minnesota.[14]

Brighter Skies Ahead

Minnesota's economic outlook remained shaky as Perpich began his second term. The forecast released by the Minnesota Department of Finance the previous November predicted unemployment in the state would rise beyond the record numbers set in 1982. While the nation's economy as a whole began to rebound in 1983, Minnesota remained stuck in the doldrums it had been mired in since 1979, further debunking the myth that Minnesota was recession-proof.[15]

Compounding the problem was that many of Perpich's job proposals, such as loan funds, lower interest rates, and expansion of vocational training and small business centers, would require large amounts of state funding—which was in short supply in January 1983. Democrats in the legislature, who just a few years earlier proudly boasted about the government programs their party championed in the 1970s, now openly endorsed a "conservative approach" on all state spending.

The 1983–85 state budget was forecast to produce a $750 million to $1 billion shortfall under the current levels of revenues and expenditures. Closing that gap would be essential to Perpich's jobs agenda. All options were on the table, including increases to income and sales taxes, lower local government aid, reduced spending on social programs, and possible closures of state hospitals and college campuses.[16]

Despite continued bad news on the state economic front, Perpich was confident that the relationships his administration was building between the legislature and the public and private sectors would pay dividends to lift Minnesota out of the economic slump it had been mired in for much of the previous two years. By the end of the first legislative session of his second term, that plan paid off, setting the stage for a rebound of Minnesota's economy.

On May 23, 1983, the legislature approved a bill establishing the new Minnesota Energy and Economic Development Department. The department would be charged with providing loans, loan guarantees, grants, planning, and technical assistance to the private and public sectors to carry out the Perpich jobs agenda. The legislation also aimed to expand markets for state trades by providing funding to establish a Minnesota office in Washington, DC, and creating a commission to study the building of a world trade center in Minnesota and a council to develop Minnesota's film and television industries.[17]

"He wanted people back to work, and he wanted to do a full-court press on the business leadership in Minnesota," Mark Dayton, commissioner of the new department, later explained. "If he saw or heard of an opportunity to get a Louisiana-Pacific wood-processing plant or he heard that there was a possibility of one of the taconite operations on the Range being shut down, he was on a plane instantly."[18]

The self-appointed state supersalesman was determined to attract business, educational, and even scientific opportunities to the state. The results were mixed. For example, in November 1983, he wrote a letter to the US Department of Energy asking that it locate a $2 billion proton accelerator supercollider in rural Minnesota.

"The population of Minnesota is well-educated and is oriented to technological innovation," Perpich wrote in an attempt to persuade Energy Department officials. "We have willing workers who are skilled in heavy industrial construction. Minnesota has ample supplies of water for cooling, a climate without excessive heat, good transportation, and a moderate cost; ample electrical supply with limited summer peaking." Despite Perpich's efforts, the project was eventually sited in Texas.[19]

He was similarly outgunned when, during the 1985 legislation session, he pushed a bill that would provide $1.2 billion in incentives to attract a $3.7 billion state-of-the-art General Motors Saturn plant. After seven months of intense competition involving three dozen states and hundreds of proposed sites, Spring Hill, Tennessee, was ultimately selected as the site for the plant that opened in 1990 and employed more than 3,900 workers.[20]

But Perpich scored a major victory that summer. He promoted another state-of-the-art idea: a $1.35 billion "megamall" with retail shops, a convention center, and an indoor amusement park on the site of the old Metropolitan stadium in Bloomington.[21]

While Perpich's efforts to land an atom smasher or lure an auto plant were unsuccessful, his programs were putting Minnesotans back to work. In January

1985, he noted that 170,000 more Minnesotans were working than when he delivered the first address of his term two years earlier.

Yet Perpich worried that rural portions of the state were being left behind. Two years into his second term, in his 1985 State of the State address, Perpich described the state's economic condition as "greatly improved," but he also warned that Minnesota was "becoming a two-economy state, with prosperity in the metropolitan area and depression in many parts of rural Minnesota."

The first signs of a rebound began in mid-1984 when state revenue collections were more than $128 million higher than forecast. This, combined with the reserve fund that Perpich had raised to $375 million, would put the state $500 million in the black by the end of Perpich's first biennium budget.

"There's no doubt the economy is still burning rubber," state finance commissioner Gus Donhowe said, but warned that two-thirds of the jobs created by the recovery were in the Twin Cities metro area.[22]

"Although there are now 57,800 more Minnesotans working than ever before in our state's history, that is no consolation to the steelworkers on the Iron Range, to the woodworkers in International Falls, to the implement dealers in Dawson, or the farmers in Fairmont," Perpich said in his annual message to legislators. The problems the state's rural economies faced "will require a massive bipartisan effort that includes a major commitment from Washington. . . . I will not rest in my effort until all Minnesotans share in our improving economy."[23]

Internationally Minded

Perpich maintained his commitment to selling Minnesota to international markets through his second term. He had brought a firm conviction in the promise of international trade back with him from Europe and saw investment from foreign business as a source of job creation at home and an expansion of markets to Minnesota businesses abroad. He purchased season tickets to the Minnesota Orchestra to win over international trade envoys and asked the legislature for funding to upgrade the governor's residence budget for china and silverware as part of an effort to entertain foreign delegates with polish. (Perpich withdrew his request for the enhanced dinnerware under heavy IR criticism.) He also asked the legislature for an increase in the budget of the state's international trade office to $3.5 million for the '83–'85 biennium, up from $130,000 spent from '81 to '83.

"International trade is like a romance," the governor justified in his request. "If you don't make the phone calls and don't send the flowers, they're not going to be at the church."[24]

Following an eighteen-day trade mission to China early in his first term, Perpich was confident that his administration's commitment to international trade put the state on the right path. "Our strategy in Minnesota is correct," he said. "We have to concentrate on high technology and agriculture." The governor announced his intention to open a trade office in Hong Kong similar to the one the state had recently opened in Sweden.

"I don't know who will be governor by 1995, but he'll have a nice job because of the work we're doing," Perpich predicted.

When the legislature approved Perpich's request for additional funding, the governor recruited former Pillsbury executive William Dietrich, who had extensive experience in foreign trade, to head the expanded international marketing office, and convinced Honeywell to loan Perpich's 1982 campaign manager, Eldon Brustuen, who was now an executive at the Minneapolis multinational conglomerate, back to the governor's office.[25]

"We were fiftieth out of fifty states in export promotion when he became governor," Brustuen said. "We were the bottom of the line; I mean, Tennessee and Mississippi were spending more money than we were. Rudy came in with a vision.

"His idea was to get small and medium-sized companies exporting, and the other idea was to get the big companies to big brother the little companies. And these companies bought in. . . . It seemed like everywhere he would go, it would be like a tidal wave that would go out from this guy. That energy, and that character, and that charisma would flow," Brustuen recalled.[26]

After trade trips to ten foreign countries during the first year of his second term, and with criticism growing from opponents and the general public who failed to appreciate his vision for Minnesota's expanded presence in an increasingly global marketplace, Perpich testily announced that all out-of-state travel would be paid for with campaign funds and vowed his foreign travel "won't cost taxpayers a cent."[27]

"He built a group of about a dozen businessmen, top-level people, and he built an economic development support committee," Anderson explained. "The commitment was that those individuals would raise money to fund his travel. He had Mike Wright from SuperValu. Curt Carlson chaired it, from Carlson Companies. He had Harvey Mackay. He had key businesspeople from all industries on this committee."

The group raised significant funds and also provided in-kind contributions such as corporate jets—all of which saved taxpayers a significant amount of money. The arrangement provided the flexibility Perpich needed to execute his out-of-state marketing and recruiting agenda, but Anderson said that it also "was a signal to the business community that he really was there to work with them."[28]

Two years of increased spending under Perpich put Minnesota near the top of the list of state foreign trade promotion (nearly $3 million annually). The boost in financial resources, along with increased staffing from eight employees in the Quie administration to thirty-four under Perpich, helped Minnesota's trade office produce results. The state was the first to guarantee working capital loans for exporters and reported increased agricultural exports to Asian markets. Perpich boasted that during the first two years in office, the increased spending allowed the office to confirm Norwegian investment in southern Minnesota's Hutchinson Manufacturing Company and Swedish investment in the development of the peat industry in the northern region of the state. The sprawling Japanese conglomerate Mitsubishi had opened an office in Bloomington, and the low-cost People Express Airlines would serve the Twin Cities.

However, not all of Perpich's attempts to market Minnesota were successful, such as his championing of a chopstick factory on the Iron Range, which garnered intense criticism from political opponents and the press. Condemnation over the failed plant—opinions he felt were ill founded and out of proportion—would sting Perpich deeply and sow the seeds of resentment between Perpich and the press.[29]

"One of the things that I always resented was the label that he got on the chopstick factory," protested DNR commissioner Joseph Alexander. "That was not a Rudy Perpich, one-person-type thing. That was a cooperative effort by a bipartisan group that had all the potential of doing pretty well. In the meantime, we had five or six paper plants, fiberboard plants, strand board, chipboard, and various other plants that came into the state—increased the wood production and put people to work. But we didn't hear much about that; we heard about the chopstick factory that didn't go."[30]

In many ways, at least with regard to international relations, Perpich was years ahead of his fellow governors.

"He was ahead of the curve in terms of the global expansion and development that was coming and was determined to position Minnesota to take advantage of the opportunities in the international marketplace," remembered chief of staff Terry Montgomery. "He had that exposure. He also had a great self-confidence which goes with having operated in that arena."[31]

"At the time he started, probably one or two other governors were starting to come up with the idea of doing what, in their mind, were maybe junkets, but it was practically unheard of," Brustuen remembered. "To the point where within one year of [Perpich] being governor, the governor of New Jersey brought approximately forty business leaders from New Jersey into Minnesota for a two-day symposium of what today we call benchmarking."[32]

All of Perpich's work with business and international trade affected his public perception, with some claiming the business community had bought out Rudy. But to Perpich, business meant jobs, taxes, and growth. He believed the state needed a business climate that attracted foreign investment to realize his vision of Minnesota, and with the correct policies, everything could fall into place. The investment and talent of his "brainpower" state could complete the loop by creating further investments.

"He came a long, long way from his knee-jerk, antiestablishment upbringing," recalled Control Data chairman Norbert Berg. "The business community had a begrudging respect for him, which became less and less begrudged. He came in as a Democrat. Then he was a Democrat with some funny ideas. Then, he was their governor. He earned the respect of the business community, and he had to come a long way to do that."[33]

Still, Perpich hoped to win reelection in 1986, meaning he would need the support of labor as well. His battle with the teachers' union over open enrollment was not the only confrontation with labor that threatened his reelection.

The Hormel Strike

In August 1985, at the Hormel Foods Corporation's company headquarters in Austin, Minnesota, nearly 1,500 members of Local P-9 of the United Food and Commercial Workers (UFCW) union walked off the job—many of them never to return. The strike would become one of the longest and most contentious in state history, lasting thirteen months and roiling the rural community of 22,000, eventually gaining national attention.[34]

It began in the late 1970s when Hormel announced it would build a new plant but threatened to move its meatpacking operations out of Austin. To keep the plant in Austin and the 1,500 union jobs, Local P-9 approved a contract with concessions to management, including a wage and benefit freeze, giving up incentive earnings, and agreeing not to strike until at least three years after the plant was opened. The $20 million in concessions helped finance the new $100 million facility.[35]

The new plant opened in 1982, and soon afterward, Hormel announced plans to cut wages by 23 percent. Workers were outraged but bound by their 1978 agreement not to strike. The wage cut, from $10.69 to $8.25, went into effect in October 1984. Workers, along with their families and supportive members of the community, formed Austin's United Support Group to raise funds and public support for the workers' cause.[36]

It was a difficult time for the meatpacking business. The national economy had increased competition in the industry, with many smaller companies going under and others cutting and freezing wages and benefits. Tensions between labor and management continued to escalate over safety and working concerns in an industry notorious for dangerous and unsanitary conditions. One source sympathetic to the plight of the workers cited a 120 percent increase in worker injuries at the new factory.[37]

Perpich traveled to Austin in February 1985 to meet with union and company officials in hopes of staving off an escalation of the worsening situation. He appointed a task force led by the director of state mediation services to meet with both sides to find a resolution to the dispute.[38]

"The seriousness of the situation in Austin must not be underestimated," Perpich told reporters. "I have a great concern about the potential loss of jobs in the community. Austin has only one real large employer and that's Hormel. If a sizable number of jobs are lost here, we have the makings of an economic disaster in Austin."

Perpich tried to put his best face on a situation he knew was quickly deteriorating. "The fact that both sides are opening this up to us is a very positive step," he said, adding that he had achieved his goals for the trip. But those closest to the governor knew he realized tensions were intensifying.[39]

"First, we went down and met with the union [and] the company—before they went on strike," recalled Joe Samargia, who directed the Jobs and Training Commission in the Perpich administration and was present on the trip to Austin. "Everybody knew this thing was just going to be a mess. I remember we left Austin knowing that . . . neither side was listening to us. We were just wasting our breath."[40]

In August, union members, citing cuts to benefits and concessions on seniority, rejected a contract offer by a vote of 1,261 to 96. With the "no-strike" clause of their 1978 agreement expired, P-9 president Jim Guyette told his members to prepare for the picket lines. At 12:01 A.M. on Saturday, August 17, Local P-9 United Food and Commercial Workers went on strike.

Hormel management, meanwhile, had anticipated the walkout by moving production of one of their most popular new products, "Frank 'N Stuff" chili-infused hot dogs, to Houston, Texas. They also purchased $80,000 worth of barbed wire and entered into an agreement with a packing plant in Dubuque, Iowa, in the event the Austin plant was forced to shutter operations.[41]

"The result is not surprising in view of the attitude of the union over the last few months," said Hormel vice president Charles Nyberg, acknowledging that the Austin plant would be shut down in the short term but that the company was committed to having the facility operating in the near future.[42]

Tensions continued to escalate over the next several months as picketers blocked the entrance to the plant and union members voted down a mediator's proposal to end the strike. That November, despite the closure of the plant, Hormel announced record earnings for the year and the quarter ending October 26.

Hormel reopened the plant on January 13, 1986, with five hundred P-9 union members returning to work, causing tremendous division across Aus-

Striking P-9 members barricade the entrance of the Hormel packinghouse in Austin, Minnesota, January 1986. *Photo by Marlin Levison, Minneapolis and St. Paul Newspaper Negatives Collection, MNHS*

tin. Five hundred forty nonunion employees, mostly Mexican migrants, were also hired to bring the plant to full capacity. A week later, Mower County sheriff Wayne Goodnature described the deteriorating situation as "mob rule" outside the factory as protesters used a blockade of several hundred cars to shut down the plant again.[43]

Austin mayor Tom Kough, a striking P-9 member, along with the sheriff and chief of police, asked Perpich to intervene on January 20.

"At the request of Austin Mayor Tom Kough and Chief of Police Donald Hoffman and Sheriff Wayne Goodnature, I have authorized the Minnesota National Guard to provide assistance to local authorities in Mower County to maintain the peace," Perpich said in a statement. "At about 3:15 P.M. today, we were informed that the situation in Austin had exceeded the capabilities of local officials. As governor, I have a constitutional responsibility to protect the lives and safety of Minnesota citizens, and this action is taken to fulfill that responsibility."[44]

By ten o'clock that night, the first of four Minnesota Army and Air National Guard units arrived in Austin.[45]

Perpich had been prepared for weeks to use the guard to keep the peace, and he did so within seconds of receiving the request from local authorities. He had kept an opinion from a chief deputy attorney general on his desk for ten days detailing exactly what he could and couldn't do if a request came in. He was advised that he could deploy the National Guard for peacekeeping purposes only at local law enforcement's request and not by request from Hormel or union officials.

Perpich's deployment of troops to Austin was the first time a Minnesota governor used the National Guard in a labor disagreement since Governor Orville Freeman called out the guard during a December 1959 strike at the Wilson meatpacking plant in Albert Lea.[46]

Perpich was aware that Governor Freeman had lost to Elmer Andersen in 1960 at least in part due to his actions in response to the strike in Albert Lea. The guard acted as an ally of the striking union to close the plant, and twelve days after Freeman declared martial law, his action was overturned by the courts as executive overreach. Perpich was careful to avoid a replay of that situation.

"My only concern is for the safety of those people," Perpich said.[47]

Perpich was swift and certain in his action, but the decision carried weight for the son of an iron miner and lifelong friend of labor. His face was tense at a hastily called press conference. When reporters asked if the circumstances alarmed or disturbed him, Perpich tersely answered, "Yes," before referring other questions to his public safety commissioner, Paul Tschida.

"It was very difficult," Perpich admitted later that evening. "But when you get the call from the chief of police, the sheriff, and the mayor, constitutionally, you do what has to be done."[48]

Perpich took some heart knowing that Austin's Mayor Kough, one of the three making the request, was a member of Local P-9.

"When even he said they needed the help, then . . . it had to be done," Perpich rationalized.

Incidentally, Hormel chairman Richard Knowlton had requested that the state patrol be sent to Austin earlier that morning. The governor refused the company's urging, but there was no equivocating once local law enforcement made the same call for aid.

"We handled it in a very straightforward way," said chief of staff Terry Montgomery. "We've operated from one basic premise: to do what's necessary to preserve the lives and property of the people of Austin."[49]

A Terrible, Emotional Period

On January 28, acting on a letter from the mayor of Austin, Perpich ordered three hundred guard members to return home and deployed the remaining five hundred troops away from the Hormel plant to the Austin Armory.[50]

On February 18, just under a month after Perpich ordered the National Guard to Austin, he began phasing out their operations. "We have come through this extremely tense situation with no serious injuries, and that was the sole purpose of our response," Perpich said. "I want to underline once more that our concern was for the safety of all citizens."[51]

With the guard removed, Perpich was more upbeat than he had been in weeks. The decision to send the National Guard to Austin had taken a toll on the governor—who had long considered organized labor an ally.

"If you're hurting about something, you wake up in the morning knowing something's bothering you," Perpich said at the end of February 1986. "There it was, every morning. First thing, call and see what's happening in Austin. I couldn't be happy. That went on for a good three weeks."[52]

"He struggled with Hormel. He'd be in tears about it," remembered longtime ally and state representative Tom Anzelc, who served as an assistant commissioner in the Perpich administration. "He'd tell us about Floyd B. Olson, who was one of his heroes, and how Olson didn't call out the guard during the [1933 Austin Hormel] strike. It was a terrible, emotional period in his life."[53]

After the National Guard had been sent home, violent encounters occurred between protestors and local law enforcement. On April 10, police used tear gas on strikers, and nine police officers were injured during a riot outside the plant. The violence in Austin and a widely publicized boycott of Hormel products across the country garnered national attention. Two days after the riot, the Reverend Jesse Jackson arrived to mediate between Hormel and the P-9 union. He delivered an extemporaneous sermon when strikers met him at the airport to welcome the civil rights icon and Baptist minister to Minnesota. Five thousand people descended on Austin in the week following the riots in support of P-9 strikers.[54]

Unfortunately for the strikers, the UFCW parent union sided with Hormel management throughout the conflict. UFCW national leaders had initially ordered P-9 officials to end the strike in March, but the local leaders refused. In May, a judge denied a P-9 restraining order, giving the UFCW control of the local union. Striking P-9ers were evicted from the Austin Labor Center on July 3, leaving them without economic or organizational assistance. The strike was all but over.

On September 13, 1986, P-9 workers voted 1,060 to 440 to accept a contract agreement with Hormel, but many were left on callback lists, with only 20 percent of the striking employees getting their jobs back.[55]

The strike had lasting impacts, changing the culture of an Austin icon and the region's largest employer and helping transform the racial composition of the southern Minnesota community. Old-timers remembered a small-town, protective company that took pride in the home of its corporate headquarters and took care of its employees. Younger workers had seen a Hormel job as the best job in Austin. Some of those perceptions changed during the strike when Hormel hired replacement workers, many of whom were immigrants, at lower wages. Today, more than 25 percent of the city's residents are minorities.[56]

The decision was "extremely difficult for any governor to make," remarked former representative Tom Berg, "and very difficult for this one who had close ties to labor." But, Berg said, Perpich had a constitutional responsibility to the people of the state that demanded his action.[57]

Personal Connections over Political Solutions

If Perpich was worried about the political fallout with the unions after his decision to call out the guard in Austin, he didn't show it. Three weeks later he endorsed an unemployment compensation bill that organized labor vigorously opposed. Perpich was convinced that his longtime friends in labor would see that with the jobless bill, as with the strike in Austin, he was simply making the best he could of a bad situation. Throughout his time as governor, Perpich would show the strength of his convictions to do what he believed was right, even in the face of opposition from political allies. A $181 million shortfall in the state's unemployment insurance fund had led to a standoff between labor, which opposed any benefit reductions to unemployed workers, and business interests, which were against any increase in taxes to pay for the deficit.

Perpich's bill would cut benefits by $110 million over five years, significantly less than Republicans were proposing in several bills making their way through the legislature, but momentum was on the side of the businesses. Republicans had taken control of the Minnesota House in the 1984 election.[58]

"At the time, the number one issue in the business community was unemployment insurance. It was out of hand, too expensive," remembered Joe Samargia, a close confidant of the governor who had also served as president of the largest local union on the Iron Range and whose father had worked in Milwaukee's packinghouses. "The commissioner that was there for economic security at the time, Barbara Beerhalter (Chapman), tried to get a deal cut with the employers and the unions. Nothing could be done. They just used it as a political battering ram."[59]

The legislature passed a bill that cut benefits an estimated $361 million over five years and cut taxes on employers by $14 million over the same period. It was a bridge too far for Perpich, particularly the provisions that harmed seasonal agriculture, forestry, mining, and construction workers. He vetoed the bill.[60]

"If you were laid off for a part of a year, the next year when you calculated your unemployment, you calculated based on a formula," remembered Samargia. "What would happen is that a construction worker or a steelworker on the Iron Range who was working seasonally would end up getting just a terrible whack on the number of benefits that they would get. So, he vetoed it. He was really worried about what the political fallout was going to be. And there wasn't any."[61]

"It is a political solution rather than a responsible solution. It does not meet the test of what is fair and what is right," Perpich said at a press conference announcing his veto. He believed the bill would "impose hardships on those Minnesotans who can least afford it."[62]

When reporters asked whether the veto was an attempt to court labor after his decision to use the National Guard during the Hormel strike, Perpich defended his decision on more personal terms, evoking an emotional connection to the "movement of his iron-miner father and laundry-worker mother."[63]

"I benefitted by unemployment insurance," Perpich said. "My parents went through that. It's not something that's abstract that we're talking about. It's something that we literally experienced, and I tell you, it kept us out of the welfare lines."[64]

The Latimer Challenge

Regardless of Perpich's sentimentality, he was still a practical politician running for reelection in the spring of 1986. He had watched with the rest of Minnesota during the televised inauguration of the 100th anniversary of the St. Paul Winter Carnival when the union tradesmen who built the carnival's ice palace enthusiastically cheered Perpich's unofficial DFL primary challenger, St. Paul mayor George Latimer.[65]

The affable Latimer grew up in Schenectady, New York, before moving to St. Paul in 1962 to work as a law clerk. He and his wife fell in love with the history and neighborhoods of Minnesota's capital city, where they returned after he graduated from law school. Latimer ran for mayor of St. Paul in 1976, vowing to bridge the differences between the city's corporate leaders and the heavily entrenched DFL establishment at city hall.[66]

In the early days of 1986, Latimer kept everyone guessing on his future political ambitions, playing coy about plans to run for an unprecedented sixth term as mayor of St. Paul or to challenge Perpich for the job many saw as his ultimate goal. Three days after Perpich's State of the State address, Latimer gave no signs that he would challenge the governor, instead offering his praise.

"I think the major themes of his administration have been excellent," Latimer said, commending Perpich for restoring fiscal responsibility to the state, his push for tax reductions, and his drive to expand the exporting of Minnesota products. "If you look at the two or three major thrusts of the governor's career, they've been right on, just what was needed for the state."[67]

"George Latimer doesn't do things without a real good reason, and there's not a real good reason [to run for governor]," said Latimer ally and former chief of staff Dick Broeker. "He's satisfied with Perpich."[68]

At an earlier press conference, Latimer ruled out seeking the DFL endorsement, refused to discuss divisive issues such as gun control or abortion, and hinted at a third-party run as an Independent.

Then, on March 12, Latimer declared that he would not challenge Perpich as an Independent. But he added to the intrigue by noting that he had not ruled out the DFL primary.[69]

Political insiders observed how Perpich had begun incorporating a standard line into almost all his public appearances, noting the 180,000 jobs that had been created during his administration compared to the 3,000 jobs that had been lost in St. Paul, along with the capital city having the highest property taxes in the metro under Latimer's leadership.

"[Latimer and St. Paul] have been financing these developers, and the taxpayers in St. Paul have been paying for it," Perpich said in March. "I think part of his effort to be governor is to get the treasury to bail some of that out."[70]

Perpich acknowledged a Latimer primary bid would be his biggest challenge in 1986, dismissing Independent Republicans' chances against him in the general election. Latimer was both better known and better liked than the three Independent Republicans who were running to unseat Perpich, according to a December 1985 Minnesota poll.[71]

Despite a mounting farm crisis, a state revenue shortfall, and stubbornly high unemployment in rural parts of the state, Perpich remained optimistic. "I feel very confident, I really do," he told reporters. "We are still gaining jobs almost every month."[72]

The threat of a Latimer challenge gave the governor a new focus. Those close to Perpich initially weren't convinced that he was committed to running for a third term, but now they saw a renewed commitment to keeping his job and building closer ties to the DFL Party than he had enjoyed in nearly a decade.

"I suppose [Latimer and his supporters] are half convinced that I'm 50–50 on the race and that if they make life miserable for me, I'll drop out," Perpich said at the end of 1985. "But, I'll tell you, it's just happening the other way. Just the opposite. It's solidified my family even."[73]

"Nothing inspires the Perpiches like a challenge," remarked one Perpich aide.[74]

In December, Perpich said he wanted a "united DFL front" in his reelection campaign, signaling that he would seek the party endorsement and crediting newly elected DFL chair Ruth Esala as a "rallying point" uniting disparate voices within the party.

"She gives everyone an opportunity to come home—including me," Perpich laughed.[75]

Latimer was using Perpich's 1982 campaign against Spannaus as a model for his own bid to unseat Perpich, touting himself as an outsider with fresh ideas challenging the status quo and party establishment.

Latimer was one of multiple Democrats who had put their gubernatorial ambitions on hold in 1982 to clear the path for Warren Spannaus, the presumed DFL standard-bearer, only to watch Perpich mount a successful primary attack. By 1985, Perpich, an incumbent governor who had repaired his relationship with the DFL and particularly with legislators, found himself as the establishment candidate against Latimer. This would have been hard to imagine for those who remembered Perpich as the candidate who inaugurated his career with a long-shot bid against a twenty-two-year incumbent DFL state senator and then spent a career causing headaches for party leaders before defeating the DFL machine in 1982.[76]

In early 1986, with one eye toward reelection, Perpich called for a $604 million cut to state personal income taxes and a greatly simplified tax filing form in his State of the State address to the legislature.

"Our first priority, our first action, must be a major reduction in personal income taxes," Perpich said, touting the proposal as the largest tax cut in state history. "Minnesotans want, need, and deserve tax reduction and simplification."[77]

Perpich said the state had made "great strides" in creating jobs and turning the economy around, but a major reduction in personal income tax would ensure a strong economy. "We have proven that that government can be lean without being mean," he said. "Minnesota will do well because knowledge will be the steel of this post-industrial economy. Minnesota has the potential to become the number one brainpower state in the nation."[78]

Those closest to Perpich were bullish on his odds at reelection.

"By the time he was running in '86, look at all that had changed—both for Minnesota and nationally," Lynn Anderson remembered. "The economy was strong again. Business was good. Everything was turning around, and you declare victory, you seize the moment."

"He would drive around and count the number of construction cranes, and that, to him, was the best indicator," remembered State Planning Agency director Tom Triplett.[79]

Perpich continued his calls within the DFL for a broad-based coalition. "I want people to get out to their caucuses, so we have their input. The more input, the better," Perpich said as his party prepared for their precinct gettogethers. "Then you won't get the single-issue stuff that divides us. Then we'll have the DFL Party we want, a party of jobs and education and taking care of the less fortunate."[80]

Finally, on the last day of March, after four months of teasing a gubernatorial run, Latimer formally announced his plans to challenge Perpich in the DFL primary.[81]

The governor brushed off the news. "I look forward to an interesting summer and fall," he said with a knowing grin.[82]

The Campaign Trail

Perpich confronted Latimer's challenge with typical zeal. One weekend in April, the governor went on offense on Latimer's home turf, leading reporters on a tour of projects in the capital city which Perpich said benefited from the work of his administration. The bus tour included the future site of the World Trade Center, the World Theater, Como Park, and the St. Paul campus of the University of Minnesota.

"I'm the best governor St. Paul's ever had," he told reporters. "Instead of a thank you, I got a kick in the shins."[83]

Perpich spent the rest of the weekend attending party conventions in Proctor, Duluth, Nashwauk, Hoyt Lakes, and Virginia and at the Fond du Lac Reservation.

"Our focus has to be on jobs and economic development," Perpich said. "This isn't going to be a party of one issue, but it's going to be a unified party working for job creation."[84]

The following week, Perpich positioned himself squarely between his DFL and GOP opponents, characterizing both Latimer and house speaker and potential general election challenger David Jennings as too extreme for Minnesota voters.

"The people of Minnesota are not going to either a candidate like George Latimer, whose economic development policies depend on high taxes and large government subsidies, or David Jennings, whose irrational opposition to state programs will destroy the public–private partnership that all of us worked so hard to forge, and which have made us one of the most successful states in the nation," said Perpich, who touted his centrist credentials and thought he would be reelected because "I believe government must be both efficient and compassionate, lean but not mean, and because I'm neither to the left nor the right, but forward."[85]

Perpich won a notable but not overwhelming endorsement on June 13 at the DFL state convention in Duluth, with 72 percent of delegate votes. The first-ballot tally was comfortably more than the 60 percent required but far short of the 81 percent backing they had given the last endorsed candidate for governor in 1982, Warren Spannaus.[86]

Nevertheless, a successful vote signaled, for the time being, an end to the schism between Perpich and the party, providing his campaign with a "shot in the arm."

"We're going to win big," Perpich told the delegates during his acceptance speech, which was interrupted by applause twenty-five times and followed by cheering and parading for more than five minutes when he finished.

US senator and potential 1988 presidential candidate Joe Biden of Delaware gave the convention's keynote address, praising Perpich as ahead of the national party and condemning the Republican message as encouraging Americans to "look to themselves first and their nation last. . . . That's a mean-spirited view of the American character."[87]

Perpich crowed to the convention that his administration had balanced the state budget while reducing personal income taxes, restored the state's credit rating, and held state spending growth to the lowest levels in twenty years. He also touted the fact that 100,000 more Minnesotans were currently employed than at any previous time in state history, along with his increases in education funding and his push for pay equity for women.

He left the convention wondering what could be left for the Latimer campaign. "The only thing left for him to do is damage me going into the general [election]. My advice to him would be to continue as mayor of St. Paul."[88]

In July, Latimer and the leading GOP primary candidates criticized Perpich for his economic development policies and the five hundred Iron Range workers recently unemployed as a result of Reserve Mining's closure of facilities in Babbitt and Silver Bay.[89]

A Star Tribune poll showed Latimer closing in on Perpich, but, despite a worried meeting of Perpich's team to discuss the numbers, Latimer's gains wouldn't be enough.

On Tuesday, September 9, 1986, Perpich soundly defeated Latimer in the DFL primary, 293,426 votes to 207,198. On the Independent-Republican side, endorsed candidate and former legislator Cal Ludeman defeated Bloomington mayor James Lindau. The endorsed candidates, both former legislators from rural parts of the state (Ludeman was a farmer from Tracy), bested their more liberal big-city mayor rivals.[90]

Exit polls on election night gave Perpich a 3–1 advantage outstate, but he was especially proud of the support he enjoyed in the Iron Range town of Babbitt, where he received nearly 95 percent of the vote. "I have tried very, very hard" to save their jobs, Perpich said on election night. "It's approval of the effort I have made."

Ludeman

The ultraconservative Ludeman, who was referred to as "Mr. No-Man" because of his voting record in the legislature, called Perpich an "old and tired politician who has made our state vulnerable." The thirty-five-year-old had surprised many by outmaneuvering the more experienced House Speaker Jennings and former state senator Mike Menning for the IR endorsement before defeating in the primary James Lindau, who had bypassed the IR endorsing process due to his belief that a moderate candidate could not win endorsement from a party becoming increasingly dominated by hardline conservatives and the religious right.[91]

"The race against Ludeman was quite interesting because he had such a conservative record. I was very pleased when they chose him," remembered Tom Berg, who served as chair of Perpich's 1986 campaign. "Ludeman was a nice man. Honest man. Nice family. And totally out of touch with Minnesota. And we just hammered that home."[92]

The young archconservative IR candidate faced the same challenge that vexed the liberal Latimer: articulating a persuasive argument as to why voters should dump Perpich. Minnesota voters were notorious for giving incumbents the benefit of the doubt unless there was a compelling reason not to. Many voters felt a personal connection to Perpich and, as a result, were more willing to judge him apart from policies they didn't agree with—a relationship much like national polls indicated President Ronald Reagan enjoyed.[93]

"I think people will say, 'I don't agree with everything he does,'" Perpich said during the campaign. "'But he works hard, he's fair, and he loves Minnesota.'"[94]

Perpich exited the primary and entered the general election race in a stronger position with voters than he had had in nearly a year. Polls throughout the fall continued to show the governor with a commanding lead. Ludeman struggled to break through, remaining a little-known entity, as voters' confidence in the direction of the state grew. Less than half the state saw Ludeman as qualified to be governor, as compassionate about the less fortunate, or as in harmony with the electorate on issues. Polls showed Perpich ahead of Ludeman among several constituencies not typically part of a DFL governor's base, including voters whose number one concern was the level of state taxes, which favored Perpich by 29 points. He also led by nearly 10 points among "born-again Christians" and 13 points among supporters of Republican US senator Dave Durenberger.[95]

The week before election day, confident of his own reelection, Perpich sought to lend some of his political capital to his party's legislative candidates, who were trying to recapture control of the Minnesota House and free the logjam that had been blocking some of his signature proposals. "Don't tie one hand behind my back by not giving me a legislative majority," he told a Worth-ington rally in a string of stops that included Mankato, Marshall, Fairmont, Winona, and Willmar. Perpich hoped for the DFL Party to retake the Minne-sota House, which then had a 65–69 minority.[96]

"Jobs, jobs, jobs" was a recurring theme in his campaign against Ludeman. When the IR candidate questioned the incumbent governor's assertion that the state had gained 205,000 jobs since his administration took over in January 1983, Perpich sent the Ludeman campaign a list of more than three hundred companies his administration had assisted directly. The support from the state development programs created by Perpich accounted for the creation or reten-tion of more than 29,000 jobs, and Perpich himself worked with sixty-four of the companies, the letter stated.[97]

While campaigning, the governor pledged to remove Minnesota from the top ten list of states in income and commercial industrial property taxes and to forge public-private partnerships focused on rural economic development through the creation of a "Greater Minnesota Corporation." Perpich in-voked the importance of election day to his immigrant parents to encourage voters to the polls. "I would see my mother and father in work clothes all the time, and then they would be dressed up in their best on Tuesday when they went to vote because it was a very, very special day," he told the crowds.[98]

Perpich's campaign in 1986 was a sophisticated and effective political ma-chine that used his incumbency as an advantage. He generated favorable news through visits to farmers, seniors, teachers, and labor groups while releasing a steady stream of positive statistics and honors the administration had earned.

Ludeman and the Republicans had counted on a divided DFL Party after the primary against Latimer and an unfocused Perpich susceptible to sticking his foot in his mouth. Neither materialized. In fact, Perpich stayed on task and used the primary to paint himself as the moderate—first against the more lib-eral Latimer, and then against the ultraconservative Ludeman.[99]

Despite record low turnout, on Tuesday, November 4, Perpich easily won reelection—56 percent to Ludeman's 43 percent. After a bomb threat canceled a planned appearance at the DFL election headquarters at the Radisson Hotel in downtown Minneapolis, Perpich headed for the Iron Range to take in the returns at an election party in Eveleth.[100]

He watched as DFL legislators rode his coattails to a landslide victory, re-capturing control of the house by picking up 18 seats and an 83–51 majority and padding their cushion in the senate with a 4-seat pickup and a 47–20 margin.[101]

Arne Carlson, the lone Independent-Republican bright spot in 1986, won election to his third term as state auditor, claiming 55 percent of the vote. "The party has to improve its mechanics," Carlson said following his victory. "We have to be more of a centrist party, more of a people party."[102]

Perpich enjoys the Mesaba Button Box Club on election night in Eveleth, November 1986. *Photo by Tom Sweeney, Minneapolis and St. Paul Newspaper Negatives Collection, MNHS*

Minnesota attorney general Skip Humphrey, who also won reelection, credited Perpich with bringing the DFL closer to the political mainstream. "Exactly where we need to be," he added.

Some DFLers at the election night celebrations wore buttons reading "Rudy Perpich on to Iowa," referring to the host state for the precinct caucuses that traditionally open the major-party presidential nominating process. When asked about his presidential ambitions, Perpich replied simply and straightforwardly: "I want to be governor, and that's it for me."[103]

Those closest to Perpich felt that the idea of him running for president was often fueled by speculation that he would attempt to move up following the completion of his second full term as governor. Few successful two-term governors were not at least mentioned as potential White House candidates. But in late 1986, Perpich felt the idea was too far in front of him and realized his growing animosity with the press would be problematic to a presidential run. While Perpich often employed a "stop it some more" approach and continued to flirt with the idea, it was never formalized into an official operation.[104]

Perpich delivered a speech the day after the election in Hibbing in which he laid out the priorities for his upcoming term with a legislative mandate. These included completing his unfinished education agenda, tax reductions, and investments in programs to move people off the unemployment rolls and into productive employment. All the governor's proposals sounded a familiar chorus of economic development and job creation. He wanted to leave office with "everybody working" and wanted Minnesota known throughout the country as "the brainpower state."[105]

Prior to Rudy Perpich, no governor in Minnesota history had served longer than six years. As Perpich looked forward to his historic third term, he could look back on one of the most successful four-year gubernatorial administrations in Minnesota history.

On taking office in January 1983, facing the biggest economic downturn since the Great Depression and unprecedented state budget deficits, Perpich turned those shortfalls into surpluses and created a $450 million reserve fund by 1985, while providing the largest personal income tax cut in state history that same year. The 10 percent income tax surcharge levied in 1982 could be repealed, and nearly 100,000 more Minnesotans were employed than at any time in state history. The relationship between the business community and state government was demonstrably improved.[106]

"We don't have that antibusiness stigma any longer," Perpich exulted. "We are competitive now."[107]

He limited state spending growth to its lowest level in twenty years, all while increasing spending on K–12 education by 23 percent and postsecondary schools by 10 percent. He was instrumental in establishing engineering schools at St. Cloud State University, Mankato State University, and the University of Minnesota Duluth. He championed state bonding to build laboratories across the state college and junior college system and pushed for an electrical engineering and computer science building at the University of Minnesota.[108]

Perpich significantly increased the state's attention to tourism, resulting in a doubling of inquiries from out-of-state visitors. His centrist brand of DFL populism would also leave an indelible mark on the state's court system, with Perpich appointing more than one-third of the state's 240 judges, including all of those newly appointed to the state court of appeals.[109]

Even Perpich's foes had to appreciate what the Iron Ranger had achieved during his second chance. "He responds to people, he's available, and he has a vision of the problems of the common man," former IR senate leader Robert Ashbach appraised his one-time adversary.[110]

For Perpich, the achievements of his second term were a source of pride and would provide a foundation to build upon in a third term.

CHAPTER 12

Hits and Misses

"Minnesota is a remarkable state. Minnesotans are
exceptional people. And I am deeply grateful and honored
for the opportunity to serve longer than any other governor
in the history of this state."

—*Rudy Perpich, 1987 State of the State address*

"The governorship is important, but my family is more
important."

—*Rudy Perpich*

Rudy Perpich began his seventh year as Minnesota's governor in high spirits
and approaching the peak of his political power. Like the state he had led for
the previous four years, Perpich's political fortunes had weathered the economic crisis of the early 1980s, and the governor and his team were optimistic
about an unprecedented third term in the governor's office. Perpich's 1987 State
of the State address stood in marked contrast to the address he had delivered
four years earlier.

"I can report tonight that the state of our state is sound," Perpich told the
joint legislative assembly on January 7. "We have overcome major adversities,
we are meeting remaining problems boldly, and we are placing Minnesota
squarely on course for a stable and prosperous future."[1]

From the challenging economic times of the early '80s through the remainder of the decade—including the good times of 1987—the fundamental goals
of Perpich's administration remained the same: job creation and increased opportunities for all Minnesotans to succeed. He believed that growing the economy and expanding the tax base was the surest path to providing government
services and delivering on DFL priorities.

The 1987 address focused primarily on tax reform. Minnesota had established the income tax while Floyd B. Olson was governor in 1933. Since then,
the tax had increased considerably as a source of revenue for the state. By

Perpich's second term, Minnesota's income tax raised 41 percent of the state's tax receipts. As the income tax assumed greater progressivity, Minnesota moved up the national ranking of highest-taxed states. By 1984, Minnesota ranked second in income taxes per capita and led the nation in income tax per $1,000 of individual income.[2]

Rudy had a more extensive view than simply following DFL dogma of taxing wealthy individuals and corporations to maximize revenues to provide services. He saw a bigger picture of how, through more business-friendly policies, Minnesota could be attractive to national and worldwide capital that would drive revenues and investments in his vision of a "brainpower" state.

Perpich was now ready to spend whatever political capital was necessary to ensure that "no longer will Minnesota tax rates be in the top ten in any major tax categories." He appreciated Minnesota's reputation as a state where government worked. However, he recognized that Minnesota was developing a reputation around the country and the world as a state that taxed its corporations and individuals at an unreasonable level to pay for that functional government. Rudy's time in Vienna only strengthened his belief that Minnesota's tax policy put the state at a competitive disadvantage.[3]

In January 1985, Perpich had quickly seized on the opportunity presented by the Republican gains in the legislature to enact tax reforms that would align Minnesota's tax system with his idea of a more business-friendly environment. He proposed a $604 million income tax cut and simplification of the state's tax system. Members of his own party immediately opposed the plan. When the dust settled on the 1985 legislative season after a June special session, Perpich signed an $866 million tax cut that he boasted was a boon for business.[4]

But now it was 1987 and the actions of his second term were insufficient to bring about the full scope of the changes he envisioned. He promised the state would "harness the momentum of federal tax reform to initiate a major overhaul of our entire tax system." Perpich proposed to return to Minnesota taxpayers the estimated $719 million in state tax revenues that would result if the state fully conformed its policies with the Tax Reform Act of 1986 signed into law by President Reagan the previous year.[5]

Perpich sought agreement wherever he could. Those who agreed with him on little else continued to embrace his tax ideology. "The atmosphere that Minnesota is not going to be a high-tax area . . . do I love that? I'm with the governor all the way," said businessman and Mankato IR state senator Glen Taylor in response to Perpich's State of the State address.[6]

To many, Perpich's call to "get to work" sounded strange coming from the leader of Minnesota's DFL party and seemed more in line with the traditional Republican mantra. The governor's budget proposal contained the lowest state spending increase in over two decades. His speechwriter emphasized four sentences in the speaker's copy of his address:

WE ARE PROPOSING TAX REFORM THAT REWARDS WORK
WELFARE REFORM THAT ENCOURAGES WORK
RESEARCH THAT CREATES WORK
AND EDUCATION REFORM THAT PREPARES FOR WORK

Perpich proclaimed these stances to his joint-legislative audience at the capitol while simultaneously signaling to business leaders across the state that he would continue to push for reforms to Minnesota's tax system, including reducing the top corporate tax rates from 12 percent to 9 percent.

At the same time, Perpich reinforced his independence. He differentiated himself from many Republicans who supported his tax proposals by calling for increased environmental regulations, improved childcare assistance for low-income families, and a robust public works spending package. He also reiterated his core belief that a strong state government and public education system are critical to a vibrant state economy.[7]

Perpich called for the creation of a "Greater Minnesota Corporation" to fund research and product development at state and private colleges, as well as grants and venture capital for startups as a result of that research. The speech was part of inaugural week activities the Perpich team was calling the "Best of Minnesota."[8]

"We must have a tax system that is competitive, honest, simple and fair, an education system that is committed to excellence, and a climate of research that will yield the products, ideas, and jobs of tomorrow," Perpich said with an air of contagious optimism while highlighting his love for all things Minnesotan.[9]

Perpich would praise the work of the 1987 legislature as "one of the greatest sessions in our history." The session produced the largest budget for education in state history, including increases to elementary, secondary, and post-secondary public education. The tax bill raised taxes by $690.5 million over the upcoming biennium, but cut income taxes for two-thirds of Minnesotans and simplified Minnesota's tax-filing system through conformity with federal tax law, returning the resulting $660 million to Minnesota taxpayers. The bill, which Perpich ally and senate Tax Committee chairman Doug Johnson called "the most significant reform in the history of the state, and probably the most significant reform any state has enacted," reduced Minnesota's top corporate tax rate from 12 percent to 9.5 percent and the top personal income tax rate from 14 percent to 8 percent and provided $25.5 million in property tax relief for small businesses.[10]

"We are fast becoming the best state in the nation," Perpich, flanked by

Lieutenant Governor Marlene Johnson and commissioners Tom Triplett and Ruth Randall, told reporters at the capitol.[11]

"We had a very, very good legislative session in '87," remembered Lynn Anderson. "And then towards the end of '87 and the beginning of '88, the dynamics all began to change."[12]

Few observers would have guessed that Perpich was reaching the height of his political power and that troubling times lay ahead.

Family Matters

Among the changing dynamics was the increasing role that Rudy's family played in his administration. Family was at the core of who Rudy Perpich was, and his children, Rudy Jr. and Mary Sue, had regularly accompanied their parents across Minnesota since the state senate days of the early 1960s. Both were veterans of countless county fairs and DFL bean feeds, often wearing sandwich boards and passing out campaign literature.

As Perpich had climbed the ranks from state senator to lieutenant governor to governor, Rudy Jr. and Mary Sue changed schools more than a dozen times, switching back and forth between Hibbing and various schools in the Twin

Mary Sue, Rudy Jr., Lola, and Rudy Perpich take a break from the 1982 campaign.
Courtesy Minnesota Discovery Center

Cities. This itinerant lifestyle and the demands of political campaigning knitted them together more closely than most families. After the 1978 defeat, their ties grew tighter when the children switched colleges three times to be with their parents first in New York, then in Austria, and finally back in Minnesota.[13]

Shortly after the 1986 election, a front-page *Star Tribune* headline read: "The Perpiches: The Governor and a Family of Advisers." Independent Republicans levied charges of nepotism against the governor, criticizing him for including Lola on international trips, accusing him of a "breach of trust" for hiring Rudy Jr. as a campaign adviser, and condemning his appointment of Mary Sue to a committee charged with bringing an Olympic training center to Minnesota.[14]

Rudy Jr. defended his role in the campaign, saying he had been providing political advice to his father for years. Perpich's son had returned to Minnesota after graduating from law school at Stanford University midway through his father's second term and held a bachelor's degree in political science in addition to his law degree. Shortly after his return, however, he was stricken by a mysterious viral infection. Diagnosis proved elusive, and he remained weak and bedridden for months at a time.[15]

"These were parents, Rudy and Lola, who would do anything for those kids. They were so tightly knit," remembered Lori Sturdevant. "[Rudy] felt he had to do anything he could to help Rudy Jr. have a full and normal life, and that would include giving him the sense that he was his close and trusted adviser. Well, then he became, in all reality, a close and trusted adviser."[16]

Rudy was proud of his children's contributions to his administration, and he resented the scrutiny and accusations that followed as an attack on him and his family.

"He was a great father and husband. He and Lola, I think, every day they were more in love," remembered senate majority leader Roger Moe. "They were just a wonderful couple. They had such high regard for one another and complemented one another.

"But I think he was overly protective of his children. Then his son had health problems, and I think that wore on him. The press would try to get in there—stick their nose in and find out what was going on. Rudy would try to get his son more involved, and then the press would pick on [Rudy Jr.]. Rudy would say his family was off-limits. The press would say, 'Well, you got him involved. You are bringing him into the limelight.' "[17]

"He seemed to lose focus," observed Sturdevant, "and I think the single biggest contributor to that was his concern about his son's health."[18]

"Is Perpich Losing His Political Touch?" a headline in the *Star Tribune* asked in September 1987. Less than a year removed from the '86 election, it appeared to friends and foes alike that the "master has lost his touch." The story demonstrated the growing discord between the governor and the press. The piece described Perpich as "more isolated, more unpredictable, and more prone to political misjudgment than at any previous point in his seven years as Minnesota governor."[19]

Perpich was criticized for his judicial appointments, a scrum with Minnesota's DFL-led congressional delegation over federal contracts, resuming his international travel, and skipping the Great Minnesota Get-Together (the Minnesota State Fair). But more than any of these self-inflicted missteps, the press criticized Perpich for removing the experience and know-how of the advisers who made up his successful second term's inner circle. The mounting criticism was more about personality than it was about policy.

"That inner circle has been shrinking and appears to be dominated by members of the Perpich family, particularly his son, Rudy Perpich Jr.," wrote *Star Tribune* reporter Betty Wilson.[20]

Yet the younger Perpich had the complete confidence of his governor father, who considered his son a "brilliant strategist and writer" and credited Rudy Jr. as "the brains" of the widely acclaimed 1986 reelection campaign, including its "Making Minnesota Work" theme.[21]

Rudy Jr.'s increasing role, which began in late 1985 when the governor had reached career-low poll numbers following a poorly received trip to Austria, had come as Rudy's senior aides were being reassigned to responsibilities farther and farther from the governor's office. The press and fellow DFLers alike worried aloud that the administration was adrift and would flounder without the stabilizing presence of more senior officials.[22]

"A governor must be an administrator and executive [and] must have the follow-through as well. When Rudy had the best of his administration around him, the follow-through was there in the persons of those strong commissioners and that strong gubernatorial staff. Part of what happened to him in that third term is that those people went away, and he was unwilling or unable to replace them with people of similar caliber," Sturdevant remembered of the changes to Perpich's inner circle.[23]

Most concerning was the distance developing between Perpich and his core supporters. There were moans among DFL legislators that the governor was losing the backing of rural Minnesota over a lack of highway funding and rumblings on the Range that their favorite son had forgotten where he came from.[24]

"His third term as governor is when he almost disappeared," remembered *Hibbing Tribune* editor Al Zdon. "I would guess you could go a year between when I saw him at those times. You would see him at a function in the Twin Cities or something, but his trips to the Range became fairly infrequent."[25]

The increasing strain that Rudy Jr's illness was placing on the governor was evident in nearly every facet of the administration.

"He wasn't making decisions from his own instincts. He wasn't following his own advice. One of his great strengths had always been that he did follow his own drummer," remembered his lieutenant governor Marlene Johnson. "He lost the joy of it in the last couple of years. Everything revolved around whether he could fit it in between going off to meet researchers or people who were interested in the issue or the health of his son. And no one wanted to begrudge him the concern for his family. On the other hand, everybody really wanted to keep governing in a positive way, and it became very difficult to do that because he was not consistent."[26]

Healing for the Harmed

Perpich may have come under fire for the role of his children and family in his administration, but there were successes as well. When Rudy Perpich Jr. approached his father with the idea to build a center for victims of torture, political consultants advised against the project because it lacked a natural constituency. "My father said, 'Yes, there is no constituency, and, yes, I am going to get hurt [politically], but there are people out there who need [help],'" recalled Rudy Jr.[27]

"[My father] saw government as almost adding yeast to society—fermentation, experimentation," the younger Perpich explained years later. "Government could do things that the private sector couldn't. A lot of times people say that the private sector can try things that government can't. It is true in many areas. But we came at it from the opposite tack, that the government has the ability to try things that the private sector can't."

In early 1985, Perpich appointed a task force to study the feasibility of building a center for victims of torture in Minnesota. When the committee released its recommendation in May of that year that a center be built because "there is no such center in the United States nor is there likely to be one in the near future," Perpich pledged to personally lead the fundraising effort.[28]

"The Center for Victims of Torture was Rudy Jr.'s idea, but it resonated with his father's basic sense of compassion and justice," remembered chief of staff Terry Montgomery. "It was hard to describe to the public and, therefore, controversial, but both father and son were right."[29]

"He was so proud of the fact that his son was a policy adviser and he believed that he really was very good and very bright. The victims of torture center is one of those [ideas]," Anderson remembered. "But, at the time, if you said that you were going to establish a center for torture victims, what a wonderful cartoon opportunity for the media. It was so visionary, people couldn't fathom what did that have to do with Minnesota? Who were these people? And how would we serve them?"[30]

Perpich believed Minnesota's rich and complex cultural history, innovative

Perpich speaking at the opening of the Center for Victims of Torture, with Buddhist monks in the background, May 1987. *Photo by Regene Radniecki, Minneapolis and St. Paul Newspaper Negatives Collection, MNHS*

industry leaders and entrepreneurs, and empathetic tendencies as demonstrated by other successful social programs would make the state an ideal location to provide physical, psychological, and rehabilitative support.

"It's highly appropriate for Minnesota to join in the struggle [for human rights]," Perpich told reporters the day the task force report was released.[31]

The center opened with one counselor in May 1987 in a house on the edge of the University of Minnesota campus. As cars and buses rolled past, Perpich spoke to a small gathering on the front lawn of an unremarkable house on Southeast Fulton Street.

"The work of the center can convey to the world Minnesota's spirit of compassion," Perpich said. "We envision a place where people from around the world will be trained in order to return to their communities to treat victims there in the most supportive environment."[32]

Since that time, the center has helped foster and champion the international torture rehabilitation movement and provided care and healing to tens of thousands of survivors of torture. With a budget today of more than $28 million, the center provides care and support for more than 5,000 survivors and 20,000 family members annually and employs more than 300 staff around the world.[33]

"He was one of the strongest supporters of human rights I've ever seen," remembered Tom Triplett. "The Center for Victims of Torture is the crowning piece of all that."[34]

Super Bowl

Rudy Perpich thought big—"in global terms [and] in grandiose ways," recalled Montgomery. "He was one of those people who always felt 'nothing ventured, nothing gained' and was willing to take a chance. He was also willing to risk the embarrassment of something not working out. Many politicians won't do that. Sometimes he was irritated by the criticism he [received], but he was still willing to do it."[35]

Often, he took those risks to bring people to Minnesota. Perpich saw sporting events as a piece of that puzzle, though he never ran up and down the aisle waving the flag for sports in the way he would for education, children, or the marginalized. Still, he had long recognized the potential of large sporting events to gain attention for the state and to provide a significant stimulus to the state's economy through tourism, hospitality services, and other business.[36]

During his first term as governor, Perpich named Minneapolis businessman and former Chamber of Commerce president Harvey Mackay to chair a task force charged with studying a domed stadium. A brouhaha over the stadium was just heating up when Perpich entered the governor's office in 1976, but he realized the long-term impact the issue represented for the state. Minnesota's professional baseball and football teams had come to the state on "fifteen-year or twenty-year leases," Mackay remembered. "So, in the late '70s, they had the right to leave our community. There were cities beckoning; it was a very, very serious challenge."[37]

In a speech to the Minneapolis Chamber of Commerce, Mackay warned that "if the Minnesota Twins and Minnesota Vikings are to leave our community, we are on our way to becoming a cold Omaha."[38]

Mackay delivered hundreds of similar speeches across the state on the importance of a domed stadium to ensure professional sports endured in Minnesota. One person understood that concept better than anyone—Rudy Perpich.

Perpich traveled to New York with Mackay to secure a commitment from the NFL that Minnesota would get a Super Bowl if they built a domed stadium. The NFL was noncommittal, but the seeds had been sown. Perpich similarly urged Mackay to write a letter to NFL commissioner Pete Rozelle requesting the NFL guarantee Minnesota the Super Bowl if the state built a domed stadium, which resulted in a reply from Rozelle indicating, according to Mackay, an "extraordinarily high" probability the NFL would come through. Mackay circulated the letter to hundreds of people and used the correspondence with Rozelle in his attempt to sway legislators to support a year-round facility in the Twin Cities.[39]

The Hubert H. Humphrey Metrodome opened while Rudy was making his comeback in 1982. By the time he resumed his duties in the governor's office, he was ready to make a Super Bowl in Minnesota a reality. When Perpich went public, the press was predictably pessimistic.

"They all said, 'Man bites dog. No way. Impossible,'" Mackay recalled.[40]

In the fall of 1982, governor-elect Perpich asked the energetic, charismatic, and indefatigable Marilyn Carlson Nelson to chair the effort. Nelson was the daughter of Minneapolis businessman Curt Carlson, founder of the Radisson Hotel Group and Carlson Companies.

"Extraordinarily bright. Very creative," remembered Mackay. "She was the catalyst that made it happen with the vision coming from Rudy Perpich."[41]

Nelson was considered a Republican, but Rudy believed she knew how to get things done and was the right person for the post. "There was no political affiliation," Perpich friend, Democrat, and Metropolitan Sports Facilities Commission chair Ron Gornick remembered. "She may have been a Republican, but Rudy [could not have] cared less. It was who was going to get the job done."[42]

Nelson was the chair of Scandinavia Today—a National Endowment for the Arts and Humanities project commemorating the contributions of Scandinavian artists, athletes, architects, and academics. The opening event of the nationwide celebration was the first non–sporting event to be held at the recently opened Hubert H. Humphrey Metrodome. The event was an enormous success, and featured a world record 10,000 voices from Minnesota school, church, and community choirs singing Aaron Copland's "The Promise of Living" as part of the world's largest choir.

Basking in the success of that event, Nelson received a call from the governor.

"Marilyn. It's Rudy. I've got an idea. I think you should chair a task force to bring the Super Bowl to Minnesota," she recalled the conversation. When she told him he must be kidding, Perpich replied, "What do you mean kidding?" Nelson suggested that January wouldn't be the best time for Minnesota to host the world, to which the governor quite simply replied, "Why not?"

"And that is when I learned about Rudy Perpich, [that] he always asked 'why not?' He really never asked 'why?'"[43]

Nelson was won over and formed her committee, and the governor provided the support they needed. When the group traveled to make their first presentation to the NFL in 1983, Rudy Perpich was in the room—the only governor to personally support their state's bid.

"When the governor of Minnesota walked in there, you could have heard a pin drop," Ron Gornick recalled. "They were absolutely beside themselves—surprised and elated. The first time a governor ever came to talk to them about a Super Bowl."[44]

Nelson remembered being seated between Pasadena and Miami during their first bid. As the NFL owners rifled through questions about types of lighting and number of seats, the questions shifted to climate. Pasadena and Miami both expected January temperatures in the 70–75 degree range.

When asked, "Mrs. Nelson, mean January temperature in Minnesota?" Nelson, nervous and uncertain how to respond, instead made a clever play on words. "Mean January temperature?" she had been asked. "Yes!" she exclaimed, laughing. "Rudy laughed. Everyone in attendance laughed. And that triggered the beginning of what was the Minnesota campaign for the Super Bowl," Nelson recalled years later.[45]

The press wondered aloud, "What if the world comes to Minnesota, and there is a storm, and it is a disaster?" But Perpich thought about the taxicab drivers, the bus drivers, and the bellmen. He thought about the opportunity to invite 70,000 people from around the world to spend money and visit the state's museums, theaters, and restaurants; to cross-country ski, ice skate, and fish on frozen lakes—most importantly, to experience the people of Minnesota.

It would take six years and six ballots, but ultimately, Minnesota would win the prize. At a 1989 owners' meeting in New Orleans, the NFL announced that Minnesota would host the 1992 Super Bowl. Just as in 1983, Perpich was there with his wife and team. When the results came back after six rounds of voting, "Nelson clapped and shrieked for joy, [and] Perpich punched Lola on the shoulder. Football's jewel event was headed for Minnesota in the dead of winter."

Economists estimated the event would generate $120 million in direct economic activity for the state. An estimated $260 million in new convention business came in subsequent years as a direct result of the 1992 Super Bowl.[46]

"I guess that is another characteristic of Rudy Perpich," Nelson remarked. "He never, ever gave up. It really started with Rudy's trust. Rudy never doubted that, if we were successful, the people of Minnesota would win the hearts of the NFL."[47]

Nelson related that sentiment through the story of a "slick, seen-it-all-sophisticate NFL executive" who arrived at the MSP airport a few days before the big game, cynical about the Super Bowl being played in the Twin Cities. "How could it be fun? How could it be successful? How could it possibly enhance the NFL's image?" Catching a taxi to his hotel, he asked the cabbie, "So, what's the big deal about Minnesota?"

The cab driver turned to say, "Are you kidding? Would you like to see Minnesota? Would you like to know why it is going to be a success here?" When the executive said he would, the cabbie turned off the meter. "The NFL executive thought he was being kidnapped," not imagining "anybody caring so much about their community that they would turn off the meter. Instead, [the cabbie] turns around and introduces himself, and offers to show the executive his town."

"That is Minnesota. That is what Rudy Perpich knew in his heart. That is what he believed in, and that is why, ultimately, we were successful," Nelson recalled.[48]

It wasn't just America's largest sporting event that Perpich and his team sought to land. They went to Colorado Springs in an effort to secure an Olympic Training Center on the Iron Range. They went after lacrosse and swimming events. There was an Olympic oval and bandy rink in Roseville that came out of Perpich's dream of hosting the Winter Games, as well as the National Sports Center in Blaine.[49]

Perpich traveled with Gary Lamppa and other Iron Range delegates to the cross-country skiing world championships in Seefeld, Austria, in January 1985 to personally lobby the Nordic skiing world governing body for an event in Minnesota. The effort was successful, and Giant's Ridge in Biwabik hosted a World Cup race in December 1985.[50]

Perpich traveled with University of Minnesota president Ken Keller and Ron Gornick in 1986 to Monterey, California, to pitch the NCAA on the Metrodome hosting college basketball's showcase event.[51]

"They were absolutely blown out of their shoes when Governor Rudy Perpich came there to make a presentation for the Final Four," remembered Gornick. "These guys went bananas—'we have never, ever, ever had a governor of any state come here looking for the Final Four.' The Final Four got to Minnesota because of Rudy Perpich. There are no two ways about it."[52]

Nelson's father, hospitality industry entrepreneur Curt Carlson, had chaired a commission on tourism and economic vitality that recommended Minnesota invite large, national events to the state that would build economic vitality.

"It was really out of that, I think, that Rudy not only issued the invitation to the Super Bowl, but to the Special Olympics, the Summer Olympics, the Final Four," Nelson remembered. "Who would have ever guessed that we would have been successful in so many ways? The Super Bowl was not an end in itself. It was a means to an end, just as the Special Olympics were. They were the means to an end. The end, of course, was the economic vitality of the state."[53]

Castles in the Sky

Tangible antagonism between Perpich and the press began in 1985 over two separate international trips: one to search for a castle and one to lure a megamall to
Minnesota. Both combined elements of Perpich's unique blend of futuristic
thinking, folksy and sometimes clumsy delivery, and tendency toward frus-
tration when the press failed to recognize his brilliance. Perpich was roundly
criticized for both projects in 1985, but history would vindicate his vision.

In late October 1985, Perpich made a sudden and unannounced trip to
Austria to meet with industry leaders and investors in hopes of persuading
them to bring their businesses to Minnesota. He also met with education leaders about the development of a Minnesota education center that would be
sponsored by the University of Minnesota along with private colleges. Lola accompanied him on the trip, their third to Austria that year and the governor's
tenth overseas excursion since taking office in 1983.[54]

On the trip, Perpich visited an eleventh-century castle in Petronell that was
being offered by the Austrian government for free. The governor saw it as
a possible site for an education center. Perpich met with Austrian president
Rudolf Kirschläger in hopes of negotiating Austrian investment in the idea.

"I think it would be a real advantage to them if we could get our professors
from Minnesota teaching here," Perpich said while in Austria.[55]

Republican criticism was to be expected, as when Cal Ludeman, jockeying
for position with the crowd of IR hopefuls lining up to challenge Perpich the
following year, lashed out at the governor. "Is he over there looking for a retirement home? Just exactly what is he there for?" asked Ludeman. "If he's going to
look for a castle, for goodness sakes, he should know the serfs are a little restless
back home. I think it's embarrassing that the governor acts this way."[56]

But when DFL allies such as senate majority leader Roger Moe questioned
the motives of Perpich's trip, the governor became increasingly defensive. Moe
wondered if the trip wasn't "more R & R [rest and relaxation] than it is real
substantive business."[57]

Many in the press agreed. "That was probably as much personal vacation to
satisfy Lola as it was anything else, but he was too proud to admit it," remembered Sturdevant. "He said he never took vacations, but he should have. He
needed to take more vacations. He needed to step back more often than he did.
So, he went off and did this sort of fanciful thing—looked at this castle, [and]
probably had a few nice days in Vienna."[58]

Perpich would pay a political price for the trip. The excursion reminded
people of the unpleasant memories of his actions during his first administration, unpredictably appearing in unanticipated and odd places. The Austria
trip brought people back to a time and behaviors they thought Perpich had

matured beyond. Some close to Perpich point to this time when the governor and his brother, George, who had been one of his closest political advisers, had a falling out that took years to repair. It was not that people close to the governor did not see the value in the Minnesota education center or even a castle in a foreign country for the university. Still, the way he was going about it reminded them of how Perpich could, at times, be his own worst enemy.[59]

"Rudy was kind of stumbling a little bit in the fall of '85," remembered Sturdevant. "The castle thing was a big part of that. His reaction of pique to the way that that got played. Saying that he was going to pull back on some of his travel when, in fact, what he should have done at that point was say, 'Listen. What I am doing is good for Minnesota. And it's the way governors ought to behave.' Instead, he got mad and was huffing and puffing."[60]

Perpich was ultimately vindicated when his administration used the same concept to establish Minnesota State University's Akita, Japan, campus. The Akita program grew out of the 1985 Vienna concept, as well as trade summit meetings in Japan the following year. The campus opened as a partnership between Akita Prefecture and the State of Minnesota in 1990 and operated as a model of cross-cultural exchange between Japanese and American students to foster global-minded future leaders who would study English as a second language, along with general college courses. Unfortunately budget pressures within the Minnesota State Colleges and Universities system forced its closure in 2002.[61]

"The Akita campus in Japan really grew out of the castle in Vienna controversy," remembered Lynn Anderson. "It was one of those things that we appeared publicly to back away from but very quietly set in motion, doing ultimately what he wanted to do."[62]

Perpich was promoting Minnesota's role in a global economy and using international studies and the state's university system as a venue for international education. But he often had trouble communicating those ideas to average Minnesotans, and the press regularly amplified his critics, increasingly frustrating Perpich.

"That castle was every bit as viable as the Akita University," remembered Eldon Brustuen. "The press often was better informed than they pretended to be. They would play to the guy sitting in Monticello, Minnesota, at the barbershop who is reading it and saying, 'What is this guy doing?' By the same token, sometimes Rudy could be his own worst enemy on these things."[63]

Mall of America

Perpich showed the same combination of visionary leadership with a tendency to shoot himself in the foot in his attempt to land America's largest mall in

Minnesota. As usual, the public, the press, and his political adversaries failed to see his vision and were late to the party.

It began in the summer of 1982, when a series of gubernatorial forums were held featuring candidates from both parties. One of those seeking the IR endorsement was former governor Harold Stassen. During the debates, Stassen talked of his friendship with Walt Disney, who had been dead for more than sixteen years by then, and of Stassen's own idea of building a "Disney World of the Winter Kingdom" in Minnesota. The audience, press, and fellow candidates rolled their eyes and chuckled aloud—all but one, that is. Stassen was competition and likewise a past governor trying to reclaim the office, but Rudy Perpich listened with rapt attention.[64]

A Republican, Harold Stassen was elected governor of Minnesota in 1938 at the age of thirty-one. One of the youngest governors ever elected in the United States, the "Boy Wonder" moderated but did not abandon the progressive policies of the Farmer-Laborites that preceded him and that Floyd B. Olson had cemented as the bedrock of Minnesota politics. Stassen modernized how state government delivered services, initiated civil protections for state workers, and pushed employment laws that lessened acrimony between business and labor and reduced the number and frequency of strikes in the state. He was elected to a third term in 1942, even after declaring his intention to resign in 1943 to join the navy during World War II. In 1945, President Franklin D. Roosevelt recruited him to help draft the United Nations charter.[65]

Stassen was a serious candidate for the Republican nomination for president in 1948 and 1952, although his eventual nine bids in six different decades ultimately left him a tragic and comic side note in American political history. Stassen ran for high office, again and again, to draw attention to his ideas, including national health care for children, full employment through public works jobs, low-interest federal support of family farms, a national childcare initiative, and increased US participation in the United Nations.[66]

Perpich admired and, arguably, identified with Stassen's creative approach to public problem-solving, even if he recognized that the former governor was often years or decades ahead of his time. In 1983, Perpich tapped Stassen to head a task force to study the feasibility of a graduate-level school of international business in Minnesota.

"Harold Stassen is the most brilliant governor we've ever had," Perpich said in July 1983. "He's very creative, very honest. He's ahead of his time. We haven't recognized that man's talents the way we should."

Stassen employed what he called his "creative center approach" to public life, "working with both sides, never going to one extreme or the other." The moderate Republican, who had been willing to work with Democrats throughout his long career, returned Rudy's compliment.[67]

"I worked a lot with President [Franklin] Roosevelt, but I kept my independence," Stassen said. "Roosevelt respected that. Governor Perpich does, too."[68]
If Stassen's "Disney World of the North" was a bit ahead of its time, Perpich appreciated the creative genius of the concept. By the summer of 1985, Perpich would have his opportunity to put his own mark on the idea.

Perpich kept the concept in the back of his head "until the Ghermezians came along in '85," Sturdevant remembered. "They were going to be building 'Harold's Disneyland.' I remember that is one of the things Perpich said to me. 'Only it is not going to say Disney. It is going to say Ghermezian.'"

"It was like the economy was finally good, and the state was going well. We needed a diversion, and along came the Ghermezians," Sturdevant laughed. "We needed a break from reality, and here came these people talking about building Disneyland in our midst. And Rudy thought that was the greatest thing."[69]

"I'm so excited I can't sleep," Perpich said in July 1985 after returning from a trip to Canada to meet with the Ghermezian brothers and tour a similar, enormous mall they had developed in Edmonton. By the time he returned to Minnesota, Perpich had already directed state officials to expedite the permitting process required for the project. It would be located on the site of the old Metropolitan Stadium in Bloomington, which had become obsolete when the Twins and Vikings had moved into the new Hubert H. Humphrey Metrodome in downtown Minneapolis in 1982. The Old Met was demolished in January 1985.[70]

When enthusiastic about something, Perpich often didn't think clearly, or necessarily care, about what was feasible. He would promise the moon and then figure out some way to deliver it later. But the press and even Perpich supporters and fellow DFLers were not nearly as energized by what they saw as the governor's latest harebrained idea. To them, the $1.5 billion megamall was a boondoggle.

"It was an avalanche of criticism. In fact, it almost became a political liability of major proportions near the end," remembered Montgomery. "Once the Ghermezians hit town, because they were so personally controversial, it became a political nightmare. It just kept getting worse. And we were going right into that critical election. I remember [Minnesota Twins owner and financier] Carl Pohlad calling. Carl Pohlad was one of Perpich's business supporters. Pohlad was kind of apolitical, but he liked Perpich and he supported him. I remember Carl calling, just tremendously distressed, saying, 'You have got to get him off this megamall. This megamall is killing us. You have got to tell him to quit talking about the megamall.'"[71]

"My gut feeling is I wish he wasn't out there," Second District DFL chair Harold Windingstad said, evoking memories of the 1978 Minnesota Massacre.

He and others saw the issue as a potential Achilles' heel for Democrats in the 1986 election.[72]

"In rural Minnesota, we are facing the worst family farm crisis we have ever had, and small businesses are having some real economic hardship," DFL state senator Joe Bertram of Paynesville pleaded. "People would say, 'You mean that megamall is more important than our farms and businesses?' "[73]

The governor was also plagued by scorching statewide editorial criticism that he had reverted to his "shoot-from-the-hip" style which had contributed to an overwhelming Republican victory in 1978.[74]

A strongly worded report commissioned by the Met Council in October 1985 downplayed the potential impact of the proposed project, arguing that retail and amusement would simply capture already projected growth and that tourism would be limited to the first year or two, when "public curiosity was at a peak."[75]

Perpich stuck to his guns.

"When that [megamall] was proposed, what I saw was 9,000 or 10,000 construction jobs—1,100 of them up North, by the way—that's the equivalent of two taconite plants," Perpich defended the project in January 1986. "I also saw a lot of people working there, tourists coming in—a real plus to the [state] economy."[76]

When Arthur Naftalin, a university public affairs professor and interviewer for public television's *Minnesota Issues*, questioned the project's economic benefit and attempted to debate Perpich on the finer points of fiscal disparities tax-sharing, the governor was fed up with what he saw as an esoteric exercise in intellectualism.

"The difference is you're getting a check every two weeks. Well, 110,000 people in Minnesota are out of work," Perpich rebuked Naftalin. "It's easy to be theorizing when you're getting paid. But you talk to my people up north, and they are losing everything. You talk to the people in western Minnesota who are losing everything, and then they're going to say [something] about this theory of fiscal disparities. I'm offended by that."[77]

Today, the Mall of America is host to more than four hundred events each year, including everything from concerts, live television, and touring circus troupes to superstar appearances and fashion shows. More than forty million people from across the globe visit the mall each year, producing $2 billion in annual economic impact for Minnesota.[78]

Pursuing a Vision Others Could Not Yet See

International trade was central to Perpich's vision. Consequently, departments within his administration jockeyed to position foreign trade under their jurisdiction. The international trade office started under the Department of Commerce, then moved to the Department of Agriculture, and finally landed in Commissioner Mark Dayton's Department of Employment, Trade, and Economic Development.[79]

Perpich recognized Minnesota's diverse economy of agriculture, high tech, health care, and manufacturing as crucial to the economic well-being of the state and saw the potential for the expansion into global markets as critical to Minnesota's future. A World Trade Center that could promote the state government's trade and export programs organized under one roof with the private sector could position Minnesota as a national leader in global trade—a one-stop shop where businesses could coordinate international finance, translation, export management, and potential clients.

Early in his second term, Perpich established an advisory committee on the creation of a World Trade Center Minnesota and traveled to Melbourne, Australia, to secure approval from the World Trade Center Association for a Minnesota franchise. Representative Jim Rice served on the governor's World Trade Commission and accompanied Perpich on the trip to Australia. The Minneapolis DFLer served as chair of the house Appropriations Committee and would be critical to the fulfillment of the governor's vision.[80]

Of course, not everyone agreed. "We had this real prairie skepticism," recalled Brustuen, who was working in the governor's trade office. "A World Trade Center in Minnesota? Come on!"[81]

But Brustuen and others continued to push forward the governor's idea. DFLers Glen Anderson, who served as chair of the Local and Urban Affairs Committee in the house, and Mike Freeman, who served on the senate Local and Urban Government Committee, carried the legislation. When their bill was about to be defeated in Representative Phyllis Kahn's committee, Brustuen grabbed Jim Rice, who wrote a note to Kahn on the back of an envelope that Brustuen hand-delivered to the chair:

"Phyllis, I want the World Trade Center to pass. This one has to pass. If you can't do it, see me. —Jim."

"We were seconds away—seconds away—from that one dying. They were pulling the sheet over the World Trade Center for that session," snorted Brustuen years later.[82]

The legislation passed, and competition for the center was fierce. Duluth, Rochester, Bloomington, and Minneapolis all vied to be the epicenter of global trade in Minnesota before Mayor Latimer and the City of St. Paul won the coveted prize. The thirty-seven-story, $130 million World Trade Center, built of Finnish granite, opened ahead of schedule and under budget in September 1987.[83]

The World Trade Center was a major victory for Perpich. The Minnesota Trade Office, located within the center, provided export training, education on product packaging and licensing, and assistance in promoting products inter-nationally and networking with foreign governments and housed the Minne-sota Export Finance Authority along with an international trade library. The Minnesota World Trade Conference Center sponsored more than two hun-dred international businesses and 10,000 businesspeople in its first year of operations.[84]

But there was also controversy. "I was out there touting the thing, and I would pound on the soapbox that this World Trade Center is not going to take *one* nickel of state funds. This is going to be self-supporting; it won't take *one* nickel."

"I didn't know how right I was going to be—it took *millions* of nickels," Brustuen recollected with a laugh.[85]

There was also political controversy when the first president of the World Trade Center, Dick Broeker, who was responsible for shepherding the orga-nizational formation and physical construction of the center, left the post to run Latimer's '86 campaign against Perpich. When Perpich supported Eldon Brustuen, who worked in the governor's trade office and had chaired his '82 campaign, to succeed Broeker, the press had a field day criticizing Perpich.

But ultimately, it was the press's criticism of the governor's international travel that irritated Perpich enough to skip the grand opening of one of his sig-nature accomplishments. He returned to Minnesota the week of the scheduled ceremonial opening of the center with Lola from an international conference on technological innovation and entrepreneurship in England. The press met him at the Minneapolis–St. Paul International Airport, where he told them he would skip the opening due to their negative coverage of the project and fre-quent criticism of his foreign travel to promote international trade.

"It was like guerrilla warfare. The papers were constantly attacking, attack-ing, attacking," Perpich told reporters.[86]

Perpich believed that distancing himself from the opening ceremonies and his growing animosity with the media would benefit the new venture. In his absence, he asked former vice president Walter Mondale to welcome the more than forty ambassadors and trade dignitaries to Minnesota.

Yet some saw it as the most public example of the growing disarray within Perpich's administration—and a harbinger of the personal turbulence that would plague the governor's third term.

Richard Nolan, who had succeeded Broeker as president of the World Trade Center, tried to make the best of the situation. "Everybody's writing, this is the most important thing since statehood, and the governor should be there," he said. "Prior to this, most media coverage was either critical or questioning."

The week before the scheduled opening, a *St. Paul Pioneer Press Dispatch* editorial called the governor's actions "petty and juvenile," referring to Perpich's "childlike attitude" that would "embarrass the state if he is absent." The *Star Tribune* editorial board agreed, writing that Perpich "has no good excuse for missing the opening."[87]

"It was nice that Mondale was there, and it was nice that I was there," Lieutenant Governor Johnson recalled. "But neither of us were the governor. He just lost his way and was making choices that were not the choices of a leader who was following his own vision."[88]

A Vision Shatters

Perpich's vision for Minnesota was all encompassing. It was a statewide approach to positioning the state as a national leader in an increasingly global economy. This included the arts and humanities, sports and tourism, and business and geopolitics. But it never stopped including jobs.

Perpich made developing a Greater Minnesota Corporation (GMC) the centerpiece of his revamped economic development initiative for his third term. Created during the 1987 legislative session, the GMC was established as a "quasi-public corporation," intentionally free of the regulations governing most state agencies but still relying on state dollars. The new venture would

Governor Rudy Perpich (standing) with former governors, left to right, Al Quie, Harold Stassen, Harold LeVander, C. Elmer Anderson, and Wendell Anderson. *Courtesy Minnesota Discovery Center*

begin with guaranteed funding of $12.5 million from the legislature and up to $120 million of any undesignated state surplus. It would have a statewide aim, but, as the name clearly indicated, it would have a specific focus on communities beyond the state's metropolitan core.

Building upon partnerships between the private sector, public universities, and laboratories, Perpich believed the GMC could revitalize rural areas of the state while strengthening Minnesota's position to compete nationally and internationally, nurturing burgeoning industries, expanding rural markets, and growing jobs.[89]

"So much emphasis had always been placed on what was happening in the metropolitan area or major corporations," remembered Lynn Anderson. "And yet, the strength of the state has always been, in many ways, what Greater Minnesota had to offer. That was the focus.

"The resources in Greater Minnesota were changing. The mining industry was changing. The forestry industry was changing. Agriculture was changing. What were we going to do to make sure [Greater Minnesota] stayed vital? It was making sure that there was funding and grants available for Greater Minnesota. It was a whole new way of increasing investment in Greater Minnesota that hadn't been done before. This was the governor's vision."[90]

"He called me up and said he would like to talk. The subject of the meeting was his vision of the Greater Minnesota Corporation. That was in 1986," recalled Bill Norris, the founder and former CEO of Control Data whom Perpich convinced to help him get the GMC up and running.

> But he talked fast. He described what he had in mind, which was to promote jobs, jobs, jobs through applied research, technology transfer, and product development. He had an order of magnitude in mind that surprised me. He was thinking of some organization that would ultimately reach a billion dollars in funding. He wanted it to be a public corporation independent of state government. His thinking was expansive. He had very big plans.
>
> He made a contract with the Stanford Research Institute to lay out the framework and mission of the Greater Minnesota Corporation. In retrospect, it might have been a little bit too ambitious. There was criticism it was unrealistic [but] it was ambitious, visionary.[91]

Perpich believed the GMC's success would not be short-term and hinged on the organization's ability to function like a private company, compete in the private sector, and attract private capital. Furthermore, it would need to be apolitical to withstand short-term political and economic vacillations.

The governor's goal of a $1 billion endowment that included public funding, along with the appointment of his chief of staff, Terry Montgomery, to lead the nascent enterprise, complicated both of those prerequisites.[92]

"I can assure this will not be a political board," Montgomery told reporters in August 1987 as he prepared to leave the governor's office after six and a half years as Perpich's top lieutenant.[93]

Despite the intentions of Perpich and Montgomery, the Greater Minnesota Corporation would become very political and very personal.

Perpich's animosity with the press and legislature—along with questions surrounding funding, mission, and accountability—left support for the GMC wavering over its first two years in existence. Still, hope for innovation and high-tech job creation started to materialize by 1989 as nearly $50 million annually from the newly created state lottery was earmarked to fund GMC's efforts.

The added capital launched Minnesota into the top tier of states in public funding of technology, an area in which Minnesota had lagged behind. National experts compared Minnesota's efforts under Perpich and the GMC to international models, placing Minnesota beside countries such as West Germany and Japan in their pioneering public–private investment in innovation, research, and technology.[94]

Then, on June 14, 1989, Perpich shocked everyone by announcing he would no longer promote the Greater Minnesota Corporation.

"I don't care what they [legislators] do," Perpich said. "I don't intend to spend any more of my time for the GMC. It's there for Greater Minnesota. If they don't want to defend it, so be it."[95]

The legislature had rebuffed Perpich's proposal of a constitutional amendment dedicating funding for GMC to support a $1 billion trust fund, preferring instead to pass a law committing half of the lottery's proceeds for five years to the corporation's economic development initiatives.

Perpich announced his intention to change the direction of the organization to get private funding for a "Class A" applied research institute to drive the efforts that would be "free of this circus we have upstairs," referring to the second-floor legislative chambers in the capitol. "With the legislative mentality, it's almost impossible to do anything long-term. When I'm gone, the GMC is gone."[96]

The temperamental remarks were off-the-cuff and stunned even those closest to the governor, something that was becoming increasingly common throughout Perpich's third term. The comments made headlines on the same day as the groundbreaking of the Mall of America.[97]

Later that year, the GMC suffered a near-fatal blow when Terry Montgomery was charged with sexually harassing a twenty-two-year-old woman who was pursuing an internship with the GMC.[98]

"That really, really hurt the Greater Minnesota Corporation," Norris remembered of the events surrounding Montgomery.

The scandal would bring down a dream. Montgomery abruptly resigned,
and the organization never fully recovered. Perpich later cited the failure of
the GMC to live up to the scale, scope, and impact of the farsighted vision he
once laid out as one of the greatest disappointments of his time as governor.[99]

Tax Showdown

Perhaps the most significant battle over taxes of Perpich's career came in 1989
when he again took on leaders of his own party, this time over the need for a
substantial overhaul of the property tax system. Perpich believed spending to
support school and local government aid created by the Minnesota Miracle
had become unsustainable a decade and a half after the legislature passed the
landmark bill. In early June, Perpich shocked many in his own party with his
veto of the legislature's $270 million property tax relief bill, with DFL house
speaker Robert Vanasek asking, "Has Rudy Perpich abandoned the people that
elected him?"

But as he often did, Perpich looked past the short-term political gains the
bill offered. Instead, he saw an opportunity and the necessity for long-term
reform of a system he likened to a runaway train. The veto was a significant
gamble, with members of the DFL openly questioning the sanity of their party's leader over the decision.[100]

"Where are the dollars going to come from? We need a system where state
government pays for the programs it can control while local government pays
for local spending," Perpich countered in Duluth as he kicked off a series of
meetings across the state to engage the public in the property-tax reform
discussion.[101]

Perpich believed the bill needed to provide more relief to commercial, industrial, and business properties. He also saw the property tax system as increasingly unsustainable, requiring long-term restructuring. He recognized
the short-term pain these measures would produce but believed failure to act
would put the state's future prosperity at risk.

After wrangling all summer, Perpich and the DFL-controlled legislature
agreed to a compromise bill during a special session in the last days of September to provide $383 million in property tax relief. The bill also established
a statewide recycling program, provided $110 million in business tax relief,
simplified the property tax system, and clarified the responsibilities of state
and local governments in taxing and spending decisions in an attempt to make
Minnesota government more accountable to taxpayers.[102]

The gamble over the 1989 property tax bill was pure Perpich. "Perpich Seems

Governor Rudy Perpich.
MNHS collections

to Be Tax Relief Bill's Biggest Political Winner," a headline in the *Star Tribune*
read. The maneuver marked yet another political rebirth after pundits had
written him off following a summer of criticism from friend and foe alike. By
the time he departed on a state fly-around to tout what the *Star Tribune* called
"the largest property tax relief package in state history," it was clear to everyone
that Perpich had dealt the cards and come up with aces. In the face of opposition from both of his party's leaders in the legislature, Vanasek in the house
and Moe in the senate, who both had openly acknowledged considering challenging him for the 1990 DFL endorsement, Perpich showed political courage
and conviction, rose above his self-interests, and stayed true to his intentions
of providing relief for businesses without rejecting farmers and homeowners,
whom he angered with his original veto. The political gamble paid off as well.

Dozens of DFL legislators who had criticized Perpich changed course after the compromise the governor had crafted and signed a petition urging him to run for an unprecedented fourth term, stating, "Minnesota needs your hand at the helm." Most telling was that Vanasek was among those who signed.[103]

Worlds Collide

Despite the follies and animosity of Perpich's third term, his final year in office included one of the country's most notable gestures of international diplomacy. It began, on February 26, 1990, with a letter from Perpich to Soviet Premier Mikhail Gorbachev, inviting the Russian leader to deliver a major address in Minnesota during a trip to the United States for a summit with President George H. W. Bush. Perpich hoped to link Minnesota businesses with emerging markets in the rapidly changing Soviet Union.[104]

"We even have a town called Moscow in Minnesota," Perpich wrote to Gorbachev.

"I traveled to those countries, I know them like the back of my hand," Perpich told the doubting press. "I think I would be able to develop a lot of trade between Minnesota and that whole bloc." The governor hoped to be clear that his invitation was more than a whimsical gesture.[105]

Three years younger than Perpich, Gorbachev was born into a peasant family in the rural region of Stavropol, near the Republic of Georgia. Like Perpich, he was a charismatic leader who had worked manual labor as a teenager and graduated with an advanced college degree before entering politics in his early twenties. Gorbachev considered himself a man of the people, and like Perpich, he was an optimist risk-taker who considered his wife his intellectual equal and his political partner.[106]

Lynn Anderson, Perpich's chief of staff, remembered Gorbachev as "a leader Rudy held in awe and respected because he was a visionary [and] was very misunderstood in his own country—like Rudy was in many, many ways in his own state."[107]

Gorbachev was a figure of increasing interest in America, credited with ending the Cold War after the fall of the Berlin Wall, and with it the Iron Curtain and decades of animosity between two of the world's great superpowers. Perpich saw opportunities for international goodwill and economic opportunity. He wanted to introduce Gorbachev, and by extension the international press, to the educational and cultural centers of Minnesota while promoting and leveraging the homegrown corporations that were already international leaders, such as Cargill, General Mills, Land O'Lakes, Pillsbury, Honeywell, 3M, Control Data, and Radisson Hotels.

Of course, ensuring the invitation reached Gorbachev was no simple matter. In March, Perpich first made his pitch over lunch with Soviet cinematographer Oleg Uralov. Uralov, who had direct access to the Soviet premier, was in Minneapolis because of ties to Bloomington-based Better Than Money Corp. The two hit it off, and Uralov brought Perpich's offer directly to Gorbachev upon his return to Russia.

Meanwhile, Control Data had close ties within the Soviet Union, where the company had done business with the Kremlin as far back as the Nixon administration. Control Data executives personally delivered Perpich's invitation to the Soviet Embassy in February 1990.[108]

Perpich also tapped Russian students studying at the University of Minnesota to write letters about their experience in Minnesota. The letters struck a chord with Gorbachev and his wife, Raisa, who wanted to visit with a "typical US family" on their trip to America.[109]

Predictably, the press ridiculed the governor and his invitation as another of his "goofy" ideas.

"Nobody believed that Gorbachev actually was going to come," the governor's brother Joseph said.[110]

Criticism was heard nationally. The *Kansas City Star* questioned whether the Soviet leader might mistake Minnesota's "North Star" motto for "no czar"—or perhaps Gorbachev was curious to know why any American would willingly live in the United States' equivalent of Siberia.[111]

"People laughed," recalled Anderson, "but in the back of their minds, they thought, 'Well, if anybody could pull it off, Rudy could pull it off.'"

Nobody was laughing when Anderson, in mid-May, received word from the US State Department and the Soviet Embassy that Gorbachev would accept Perpich's invitation.

"We had three weeks. We were wrapping up a legislative session, and we were getting ready to welcome an international leader."[112]

The timing was peculiar. Gorbachev was losing the confidence of people within parts of the Soviet Union in 1990, yet he was extremely popular among Americans. In May 1990, a Minnesota poll conducted two weeks before the visit showed 74 percent of Minnesotans approved of the way the Soviet president had performed as leader of the Soviet Union.[113]

By 1990, the Soviet Union was five years into what Gorbachev called "perestroika" and "glasnost," his restructuring of the Communist nation's political and economic systems with increased openness and transparency by allowing contested elections and a free press and instituting market reforms. He spoke of the need for multinational environmental action. His foreign policy promised to "make good on the potential of the socialist ideas" and "regain hope for a better future" that included the Soviet Union's common interests with democratic nations across the globe.[114]

Earlier that year, Gorbachev was named *Time*'s "Man of the Decade." He would be awarded a Nobel Peace Prize only months later. His visit to Minnesota in June 1990 centered more international attention on the state than at any time in its history to that point.[115]

When asked to explain Gorbachev's hold on Minnesotans' imaginations, former vice president Walter Mondale said, "He's had a pretty good couple of years for humankind. And they're grateful for the changes."[116]

The Soviet Premier Arrives

On June 3, an overcast and unseasonably cold and rainy day in the Twin Cities, thousands of Minnesotans lined the motorcade route to catch a glimpse of the man who gave them renewed "hope in a dusky world." Road signs were translated into Russian welcoming Gorbachev and his wife to Minnesota, and thousands of petunias and marigolds had been planted along the route.

While the motorcade made its way past cheering throngs, Mrs. Gorbachev asked the driver to make stops at Pepitos Deli and a Snyder's Drug store on the corner of Forty-Sixth Street and Nicollet Avenue, where she chatted with the clerk and bought Nintendo gum dispensers for her grandchildren.[117]

Rudy and Lola Perpich were with Mikhail and Raisa Gorbachev throughout their frenzied seven hours in Minnesota. The trip included a lunch of walleye and wild rice corn compote during a reception at the governor's residence, followed by tours of the capitol and the St. Paul Cathedral.

Then, Raisa and Lola departed for the home of Steve and Karen Watson in south Minneapolis. By the time they arrived, their party was seventy-five minutes behind schedule. Still, Raisa spent more than an hour with the Watsons and their four children, presenting each of them with a Russian picture book and an intricate teapot. The family presented Mrs. Gorbachev with a book of the Children's Theatre production of *Rembrandt Takes a Walk*, in which their daughter, Lisa, had performed in Moscow.

Raisa asked Karen, a part-time nurse, questions about the challenges of being a working mother, daycare, and family vacations. The visit was Raisa's attempt to better understand an average American family. When the group emerged from the house, both women, along with thirteen-year-old Lisa Watson, hugged and held hands before bidding an emotional farewell. A crowd of more than 5,000 waving and cheering people was still gathered.

Raisa approached a group of 125 children on a next-door lawn holding a homemade eighteen-foot banner that read "Good Neighbor = World Peace" signed by 3,000 area elementary school students. Mrs. Gorbachev asked for the sign as a token of her time in Minnesota.[118]

"I fell in love not only with them, but a thousand times with America and its people," Raisa told some of the nearly 3,000 journalists in town for the historic visit.[119]

While Raisa and Lola called on the Watsons, their husbands toured the headquarters of Control Data in Bloomington. When Gorbachev emerged from his limousine, he dismayed his KGB security detail—as he had done all day—when he approached the thousands of people cordoned off behind temporary fencing. When someone yelled, "How do you like Minnesota?" he replied, "Beautiful city, beautiful state. It looks like the middle of Russia."[120]

Seven short hours after their arrival, Mikhail and Raisa Gorbachev bid adieu before departing by plane for California. The warm connection between the Gorbachevs and the people of Minnesota on that cold June day in 1990 signified hope for a future of world peace and global cooperation that, unfortunately, would not be realized. Little more than a year after the visit, a coup attempt against Gorbachev by hard-line Communists led by Boris Yeltsin precipitated the collapse of the Soviet Union and the resignation of Gorbachev. Instead of Rudy Perpich's vision of Minnesota companies playing a major role in an increasingly open Soviet economy, widespread inflation and depression plagued the fifteen republics left in the wake of the collapse.[121]

The Gorbachev visit represented the best of what Rudy Perpich's governorship brought to Minnesota—a mixture of pride, optimism, and excitement. It was the heady international trade promised during the '82 campaign, audacity like that of the megamall in the summer of '85, and a connection to everyday Minnesotans that marked his entire time as governor. It was the story of immigrants and underdogs, education and jobs, and a world-class state all rolled into one.

And the whirlwind day was an unqualified success. A *New York Times* headline read, "Savoring the Afterglow of a World-Class Visit." In England, the *Guardian* ran a story about Perpich titled "The Man Who Put Minnesota on the Map."[122]

The day was an uninhibited success and the crowning moment of one of the greatest governorships in Minnesota history.

A week after the visit, Perpich addressed the DFL convention in his speech accepting their endorsement for a fourth term as governor:

"Soviet President Gorbachev came to Minnesota with a message of peace and friendship. . . . He saw what makes Minnesota and our country so great. . . . He saw an American family happy with their lives, appreciative for all they have. He saw Minnesota businesses that are competitive with the world. . . . He saw a state that works."[123]

On that day, the Soviet leader and the world saw what Rudy Perpich had seen all along.

CHAPTER 13

The 1990 Campaign

"From that point in the campaign, all hell broke loose."
—*Judge John Stanoch*

"Nobody can be a hero forever."
—*Al Zdon, editor,* Hibbing Daily Tribune

Rudy Perpich's decision to seek an unprecedented third full term as governor after having already served longer than any governor in state history did not come easily and was not without controversy. Many of those closest to him argued that he had created a legacy for the state that would only be diminished if he sought another four years in the governor's office. To them, he had nothing to prove and much to lose.

"Your legacy will be unlike that of any other governor in Minnesota, but your legacy will be cheapened if you run for another term. Go out with the horns blaring and the flags flying," Tom Triplett, then serving as finance commissioner, tried to reason with Perpich, but his pleas were in vain. "[He'd say,] We're not done. We're not done."[1]

"[He] couldn't quit. He couldn't say, 'I've shown the world I am a leader. I have shown the world that I am a great and good man, and now I need to let someone else be governor for a while.' He had to show them one more time. It's too bad because he didn't have to show them one more time," Lori Sturdevant remembered years later.[2]

But as he had throughout his political career, Perpich did have something to prove.

"His ideal job of his entire life was being governor of the state of Minnesota. He really loved the job and thought he could continue to do great things for Minnesota. So, I think he thought that just through the sheer force of presence, he was going to make it," remembered John Stanoch, whom Perpich asked to chair his 1990 reelection campaign. Stanoch had been considered for a position in Perpich's cabinet and was married to Ruth Esala Stanoch, who was finishing her term as chair of the Minnesota DFL. He had first met Perpich in the 1970s, when as a seventh grader, Stanoch interviewed Lieutenant Governor Perpich as part of a social studies history project.[3]

On October 8, 1989, Perpich led more than twenty reporters and a half dozen TV crews to the headwaters of the Mississippi for what he said would be a surprise announcement about his plans "for the rest of my life." The governor, looking relaxed in a sweater and slacks on the bright, crisp Minnesota fall day, had flown from St. Paul to Park Rapids before driving to Itasca State Park for the event.[4]

"I am standing at the headwaters of the Mississippi," Perpich told the crowd of approximately a hundred people who had gathered at the park for the announcement. "Like the Mississippi, the course of my administration is set. The basic themes of my administration have always been three: jobs, education, and the environment. Yet certainty does not mean stagnation. Like the Mississippi, my administration is self-renewing, ever-fresh, ever-vigorous, and always at the service of the people of Minnesota. I hope you will allow me to continue in your service as governor of our great state."[5]

After leading the capitol press corps on a four-hour excursion into Minnesota's north woods, Perpich delivered his seventy-six-word, forty-six-second statement without taking questions, leaving reporters confused and frustrated. As he walked to his car, Perpich told reporters that he had chosen the isolated location for the announcement because it would be "good for tourism" and allowed the press an opportunity to see the fall colors and breathe the fresh air of Itasca.[6]

Before his return trip to the capitol, he told reporters, "It doesn't make any difference to me" which Independent Republican he would face.[7]

"I think it's wonderful," state auditor Arne Carlson optimistically assessed the effects of Perpich's decision on his own ambitions. "It now allows my campaign to sell itself to the people of Minnesota. I think the people know Perpich and want to know what their options are."[8]

"I think that Rudy Perpich running for reelection is a little like the captain of the *Exxon Valdez* reapplying for his job as captain," said businessman Jon Grunseth, who would come to be known as the ultimate skipper of the sinking ship in Minnesota politics. "In this business, you've got to know when to hold them and know when to fold them. This guy has not read the mood of the people right."[9]

Friendly Competition

While GOP hopefuls were lining up, the announcement put Minnesota Democrats who had been positioning to succeed Perpich in an uncomfortable spot. Lieutenant Governor Marlene Johnson did not accompany Perpich to Itasca for the announcement. Instead, the governor's aides distributed a two-sentence statement that she would run for a third term in the number two position.[10]

Senate majority leader Roger Moe was not as reserved in his assessment of Perpich's decision.

"I believe I'm expressing the disappointment of a majority of Minnesotans over Governor Perpich's announcement that he intends to run again, especially in light of the fact that he has had a good administration and could step out on top," the Erskine DFLer said. "Minnesotans are looking for new faces."[11]

Mike Hatch, who was a member of Perpich's cabinet when the announcement was made, was more political. "I make no bones about it, I would like to be governor, [but] it would be out of character for me to divide the party. I just don't think it is good for the party, good for the state, and so, at this point in time, I support him."[12]

"At this point in time" gave Hatch's statement all the plasticity a seasoned politician needed. Three months later, in January 1990, Hatch resigned as commerce commissioner and announced he would challenge Perpich for the DFL endorsement.

"I like Rudy," Hatch said during his announcement. "But nothing is more futile than blind loyalty. And the winds of change are about us."[13]

The well-connected Hatch, who had served as the Minnesota DFL Party chair from 1980 to 1983 and as Perpich's Department of Commerce commissioner from 1983 to 1989, would try to persuade DFL delegates that it was "time for a change." The argument was especially compelling for numerous Democratic activists who would attend the party's convention in Minneapolis in June. To many, for as much reverence and affection as they held for the unpredictable Iron Ranger, ten years was enough for any one person in the governor's office. No previous Minnesota governor had served more than six.

Additionally, the issue of abortion was becoming increasingly divisive among party loyalists. During the 1980s, Minnesota's political activists had been sorting themselves into anti-abortion (Republican) and pro-choice (DFL) parties. Those shifts left Perpich increasingly isolated as an anti-abortion DFLer and strained his support among DFL feminists. They appreciated his record of appointing women and bolstering pay equity but did not trust him on the issue that increasingly mattered most to them: reproductive freedom.

In late January, Roger Moe announced that he would not challenge Perpich but made it equally clear that he felt the party needed new leadership and that the issue of abortion could cost the DFL control of the executive branch.

"The DFL governor cannot win reelection this year by waging the kinds of campaigns he did in his successful 1982 and 1986 races," Moe told reporters on January 29. "He will not win the 1990 gubernatorial race out of the back of a pickup."

Moe said Perpich would need to "show some very significant movement" on the issue of abortion. Not only was Perpich at odds with DFL delegates, Moe argued, but his views were "out of the mainstream of Minnesotans."[14]

Perpich and his campaign team recognized that eager Independent Republicans and passive-aggressive DFLers were not the only powerful currents running against them. Following Perpich's questionable handling of his announcement and his increasing tension with the Minnesota media, his rocky relationship with the press continued on a national stage. In January 1990, *Newsweek* ran an unflattering article referring to Perpich as "Governor Goofy." The attack introduced a coast-to-coast audience to the incomparable mixture of endearment and bewilderment with which many Minnesotans were growing weary. A January 1990 poll showed Perpich with an all-time low approval rating of 36 percent. Survey results that accompanied his announcement to run for another term were better for Perpich but still not the position an incumbent would find comfortable. Forty-nine percent of respondents thought that Perpich should not run for another term, while only 44 percent felt he should. More concerning for the populist who had built his political career on his ability to connect with everyday Minnesotans was that fewer than half of respondents agreed that Perpich "sides with the average citizen." An even smaller number felt he was "sympathetic to the conditions of the poor."[15]

Perpich believed the "Governor Goofy" attack was orchestrated by a *St. Paul Pioneer Press* reporter who had a toxic relationship with the governor and had fed the story to a bureau chief in Chicago with ties to *Newsweek*. His campaign realized that after the announcement, his increasingly poisonous relationship with the press would be even more tenuous. More importantly, they knew that the attacks against him were landing with voters.[16]

The Perpich team countered the attacks directly. The first ad of the 1990 campaign faced the growing criticism head-on.

"Critics call me goofy. They criticize the color of my hair. The way I speak. My clothes. Even the house and car," campaign manager John Stanoch remembered the governor appealing directly to voters. "But don't let them fool you, things are great in Minnesota."[17]

Perpich began the 1990 campaign with a straightforward message: he asked voters to focus on his record and what he had accomplished as governor rather than his personality. This theme was simple and effective in the early stages of the contest.

Stanoch quickly realized that Mike Hatch's support among DFL diehards was weaker than had been expected and that loyalty to Perpich among delegates was stronger than many had anticipated.[18]

When Perpich's lead in the delegate count was apparent on the eve of the June convention in Minneapolis, Hatch's campaign mounted a last-minute attempt to make abortion the central issue in the endorsement contest.

"I'm the pro-choice candidate," Hatch told convention-goers the day before balloting was set to begin.[19]

Perpich faced the issue of abortion unflinchingly. During a Q&A session, sharing the stage with Hatch, Perpich spoke to delegates directly.

"I am a pro-life governor," Stanoch remembered his candidate telling the convention crowd. But then Perpich pivoted quickly: "I am not just about the abortion issue. I am about jobs and education and health care."[20]

Perpich also had the support of several high-profile pro-choice leaders, whom his campaign used to political advantage. Perpich's name would be placed into nomination by Secretary of State Joan Growe. His lieutenant governor, Marlene Johnson, remained a strong political asset to a governor whose commitment to women's causes was being questioned by feminists at the convention.[21]

Stanoch remembered the decision to feature the governor's commitment to the cause of women through his actions, not his words.

"We thought, what could be better to show that this is a governor who has cared strongly about the issues involving women and children than to have the first [female] lieutenant governor in this state's history, his lieutenant governor, Marlene Johnson, up there answering questions," Stanoch recalled when Perpich took the stage arm in arm with Marlene Johnson. "And I will never forget the look in the Hatch campaign's eyes when they saw Rudy and Marlene going up there together. They were looking all over for their running mate. They had been one-upped by Governor Perpich once again."[22]

Perpich led on each of the first three ballots before going over the top and winning the DFL endorsement for governor on the fourth ballot with 64.4 percent of the delegates. It was a sweet affirmation of the good he had done for Minnesota and his party.[23]

"Rudy and Lola, instead of bringing them around the back, we brought them right up the center aisle of the convention, and they were surrounded by the delegates," Stanoch remembered of the winning candidate addressing the convention. "It was just a wonderful feeling and an indication that he was connected with the people."[24]

"I have worked hard, and Minnesota has worked hard," Perpich joyfully told the crowd. "Together, we have made this a state to be proud of."[25]

Before the convention adjourned and delegates returned to their respective corners of the state, Hatch announced plainly that he was not through challenging his old boss. "I'm going to run," Hatch announced his intentions for the September primary. "I've already said that."[26]

Perpich was unfazed by Hatch's announcement, believing his former commissioner had just lost his best chance to unseat him.

"He's thrown his Sunday punch, and we're still standing," Perpich, whose campaign played the *Rocky* theme song during demonstrations supporting their candidate throughout the convention, said of the Hatch primary challenge. Perpich also embraced the growing differences he saw within the DFL, including its endorsement of the liberal and relatively unknown Carlton College professor Paul Wellstone as the party's candidate for the US Senate.[27]

"We are partners," Perpich stated when asked if Wellstone's liberalism would negatively impact other DFLers on the November ballot. "I think we complement each other."[28]

The Perpich campaign felt good going into the primary, recognizing that Hatch was in a poor position following the convention and lacked a natural constituency without party endorsement. The Perpich team, with the strong support of labor and the reliable Eighth District, now added his party's backing to what looked like an unstoppable coalition. The campaign also hit Hatch hard over his wavering commitments. The former commissioner had originally said he would not run against his old boss. Then he said he would abide by the endorsement. Finally, he pledged not to go negative before launching ads criticizing his fellow Democrat's handling of the Terry Montgomery sexual harassment scandal, which had grown to include allegations by four women, along with Perpich's stance on abortion.[29]

"I never said that Warren Spannaus was the best governor in the history of the state. I never said I wasn't going to run against Warren Spannaus," the governor testily replied to comparisons of Hatch's challenge to Perpich's own 1982 primary battle against the DFL endorsee for governor that year, Attorney General Warren Spannaus. "I never said I wasn't going to go for the endorsement and if I didn't get the endorsement, that I wouldn't run. I never said I wasn't going to run any negative campaigns [before doing so]—I didn't run any negative campaigns; I kept my word. There's a big difference. And I didn't work for Warren Spannaus, by the way."[30]

While Hatch's campaign turned increasingly negative, Perpich remained positive, citing his achievements in job creation, education, and the environment. The triumph of the Gorbachev visit was fresh on the minds of voters. Rudy and Lola appeared together in ads with a simple message: "Together we're making Minnesota great."[31]

In the end, the primary wasn't close. Perpich defeated Hatch 55.5 percent to 42.2 percent.[32]

Perpich benefited from another strong showing on the Iron Range, where the voter turnout percentage was double that of the Twin Cities. Early returns showed he held a four-to-one advantage over his opponent in Virginia. But his support was not confined to one region of the state. The incumbent governor defeated his former commissioner in Burnsville, where Hatch resided, by a two-to-one margin.[33]

Rudy and Lola had campaigned in their hometown before driving their black Chevrolet Caprice to the Biwabik Town Hall, where they were two of the 574 registered voters to cast their ballots. They then visited Mary and Anton Perpich before returning to St. Paul.[34]

"You worked hard. We worked hard. Together, we made it," Perpich told cheering supporters at the Holiday Inn Metrodome in Minneapolis on primary night, continuing the disciplined, straightforward, and upbeat theme that had carried him to victories in the endorsement and primary contests. But he would be unable or unwilling to maintain this strategy in the general election.[35]

The Independent-Republican endorsee Jon Grunseth had trailed three-term state auditor Arne Carlson in opinion polls throughout the campaign, even after Carlson bypassed his party's endorsing convention. Yet Grunseth trounced the state auditor by 17 points—49 percent to 32 percent—in the IR primary.[36]

The abortion question was an issue in the IR primary as well, where Grunseth touted his pro-life stance in ads against the pro-choice Carlson. "It says to me that the pro-life community is stronger and works harder at its commitment than the pro-choice community," Grunseth campaign manager Leon Oistad reasoned after the election. Pro-choice Republicans were fast becoming an endangered species in Minnesota, and only a handful remained in elective office throughout the state. Furthermore, the party activists who voted in low-turnout IR primaries had become increasingly pro-life by 1990.

Carlson, who positioned himself as a moderate Republican more in line with mainstream Minnesotans than his increasingly conservative party, predicted that Independent Republicans would continue their poor showing in gubernatorial contests if a conservative such as Grunseth was the candidate in the general election. IRs had lost eight of the last eleven and four of the last five governor's races.[37]

Carlson told supporters that he had tried "to bring the moderate wing back into the party," but recognized his failure to do so as he delivered his concession speech shortly after midnight. About 340,000 voters cast IR ballots on September 9, out of a total eligible electorate of 3.1 million. DFL turnout was about 375,000, a total turnout of less than 25 percent.[38]

Perpich was surprised by the results of the IR primary. Like many, he assumed that Carlson's name recognition and twenty-year record as a legislator and state auditor would appeal to voters.

"Arne would have been tougher [in a general election] because he had more of the center, and that's where it is always decided, the center," Perpich said after learning of Grunseth's victory.[39]

He had anticipated a campaign between two public servants with extensive public records. He imagined a clean, hard-fought campaign focused on issues and policies with reasonable differences in political philosophy. He would be wrong.[40]

The fifty-six days between the September 11 primary and the November 6 general election would become the most bizarre, chaotic, and controversial election in Minnesota history.

Getting Personal

It started harmlessly enough, with Grunseth conducting the obligatory post-primary state fly-around. Perpich and his team met to discuss their strategy against the political newcomer. Without a record to contrast to their own, they went with what they knew: Grunseth was an executive with a chemical company running to be the governor of a state that valued a healthy environment. Perpich labeled his opponent as "Mr. Corporate Chemical" before Grunseth touched down at his first stop. The moniker stuck, and throughout the day, wherever Grunseth would travel, the press would ask him questions about his environmental record. Carlson also talked to reporters that morning, addressing his defeat and commenting at one point, "Wait until Rudy Perpich finds out about Jon Grunseth's environmental record."[41]

The day following the primary Arne Carlson received an unexpected call from Rudy Perpich. Perpich told Carlson he was the only Independent Republican who would have had a chance of defeating him in the November election. It was a prescient moment in which the visionary Perpich would come to wish that he was wrong.[42]

It was not the only contact between Carlson and the Perpich campaign. Shortly after his primary defeat, Carlson warned Perpich not to make the same mistake he had against Grunseth. Carlson accused his primary opponent of taking the low road while acknowledging the tardiness of his campaign's response. He urged Perpich to go on the offensive and not sit back and take the Grunseth attacks. Others were sending the governor a similar message.

"If you are going to run a campaign against this Grunseth fellow, you have to not allow yourself to be placed on the defensive the last two weeks," Stanoch remembered of the days following the primary. "People were speaking into the governor's ear, 'watch out for Grunseth.'"[43]

Less than two weeks into the general election campaign, a headline in the *Star Tribune* declared, "Perpich Campaign Now Accentuates the Negative."[44]

"He has made a career of obstructing states' power to protect their people from harmful chemicals," Perpich blasted his opponent at a capitol press conference standing next to a blown-up copy of Grunseth's lobbying registration.[45]

But the mud had not yet begun to be slung. A former Carlson campaign aide gave the Perpich team information and court documents including divorce papers from Grunseth's trial with his first wife, showing he had withheld court-ordered payments to his ex-wife and three daughters.[46]

"Here is stuff on Grunseth. Use it. We didn't. You better, or you will get beat," Stanoch remembered the Carlson campaign warning the Perpich staff.[47]

On September 29, two DFL legislators publicly accused Grunseth of failing to make child support payments to his family. On October 8, Perpich got on a plane and flew around the state, personally delivering copies of Grunseth's divorce papers to journalists.[48]

"If every Minnesotan had the opportunity to read through this, the campaign would be over. There would be no campaign," Perpich told reporters at the Duluth airport.[49]

Perpich was genuine in his belief that people would not vote for Jon Grunseth if they knew how he treated his wife and children. There was no moral grandstanding or holier-than-thou self-righteousness. Family was the core of Rudy Perpich's character.

Not everyone agreed with Perpich's decision to use Grunseth's divorce records and failure to pay child support as campaign material. Many close to the governor saw it as out of character for someone who prided himself on a career of clean, if rough-and-tumble, campaigns.

"This was not clean," Marlene Johnson would recount of the events of 1990 years later. "But even worse than that, it was a wrong strategy. I felt that it would not work and reflect badly on the governor."[50]

"He always said to us [that] he would never use anything that was negative that was not public record. He would never use family," remembered Lynn Anderson. "It became blurred in the public's mind because Grunseth very successfully pointed the finger back at us. . . . It became a personal attack on Jon Grunseth and his wife and family. It became an attack on divorce, which was never the issue."[51]

"But I think people need to place this in the context of Rudy Perpich and his connection with his family. He simply could not fathom how somebody could not pay child support for one of their children, and he really couldn't fathom how somebody could not do that even after he had been ordered by the court to do it—and still seemed to not be living up to that obligation. So, on a very personal level, I think it offended him," remembered John Stanoch.[52]

During the October 8 fly-around, Perpich told reporters that he would "go to my death before I'd take my family to court."[53]

Perpich's questionable decision to emphasize Grunseth's divorce records, which to some was bad form and to others was inconsistent with the above-the-fray uprightness with which he had conducted himself throughout his career, would provide his opponent the opportunity to raise uncertainties about the origins of the scandal that would, just days later, send shock waves through Minnesota's politics and beyond.

"And I would say from that point in the campaign, all hell broke loose," Stanoch succinctly summed up a campaign that was headed from bad to worse.[54]

October Surprises

While Perpich was flying around the state delivering copies of his opponent's court proceedings to reporters, the *Star Tribune* was working on a much bigger story on the IR candidate for governor.

On October 15 the headlines across Minnesota's largest paper read "Allegations Rock Governor's Race." The paper went on to detail allegations that Grunseth had tried to persuade four teenage girls to swim nude with him and his adult friends at a 1981 Fourth of July party at his home in Hastings. The girls included Grunseth's daughter and her friends, ages thirteen to sixteen at the time of the alleged activity.[55]

"Jon Grunseth and a couple of his friends came out and tried to coax us into taking off our suits and all go skinny dipping," one of the women, then twenty-two, told Minnesota Public Radio in October 1990.[56]

When one of the girls refused to take off her suit, the naked Grunseth chased the thirteen-year-old girl and blocked her in a corner of the pool. He then attempted to pull down the strap of her bathing suit with one hand while grabbing her breast with the other. The report also claimed Grunseth served alcohol to the girls at the party.[57]

The allegations were made in sworn affidavits by two of the girls and corroborated by a third, as well as by members of the rock 'n' roll band who performed at the party. Grunseth and his daughter denied the accusations, calling the charges "an outrage," "insane," and a politically motivated attack orchestrated by the Perpich campaign.[58]

"Rudy Perpich and his campaign have orchestrated this every step of the way," Grunseth told the press the day the allegations were first reported by the *Star Tribune*. "These are lies. Rudy Perpich knows they are lies, but Rudy Perpich is himself the supreme liar and will do anything to stay in office."[59]

"There is not a vase of flowers big enough to mask the stench coming from your campaign," Grunseth wrote in a letter to Perpich the night the exposé was released.[60]

Perpich and his campaign denied having any knowledge of the accusations prior to their release by the *Star Tribune*, which was verified by the newspaper's staff at the time and afterward.

"I mean, how could [he] say that I had anything [to do with that]? I mean, how could you orchestrate something like that?" said a flabbergasted Perpich to reporters as he tried to make sense of the situation. "I mean, how in your wild imagination? No. No one on my staff has had any contacts . . . with any of that."[61]

"I have no idea who these girls are. I've had no part in it. . . . I've heard all kinds of rumors, but that's beyond anything I've heard. The only thing we deal with is the public record. That's been my policy my whole political life."[62]

Lori Sturdevant was a political editor for the *Star Tribune* in 1990 and re-members the tension in the newsroom around the revelations that everyone realized would likely influence the election just three weeks away.

"I remember wishing that I could have, but of course, couldn't [have], told Rudy what we were working on a week earlier. Perpich was so far away from that information. If he had known, if he had had any smell of what was coming, he would have kept his mouth shut," Sturdevant recounted years later.[63]

But Perpich's decision to emphasize Grunseth's divorce records allowed his opponent to sow doubt about the new allegations' origins.

"It was uncharacteristic of Perpich to bring something personal like that into a campaign," Sturdevant reflected. "Either he was feeling desperate, like maybe he was in a losing situation, so he had to go negative, which was very unlike him, or maybe because Rudy was such a family man, he was greatly offended by someone who didn't live up to family obligations. And on that basis alone, he felt as though Grunseth should be disqualified from office. Maybe it's both. But, anyway, Rudy burbles all this out, outstate.

"I was wishing I could say, 'Keep your big mouth shut. We are on to something bigger than that.' But we had to play our cards as we had them to be played."[64]

"If he had known what was coming in the [*Star Tribune*], he never would have been flying around the state with Jon Grunseth's divorce papers. He would have been up canoeing in the Boundary Waters Canoe Area because the election would have been over," his campaign manager said, reflecting on the allegations that Perpich had prior knowledge of the charges. Stanoch remembered his candidate being "somber" and "subdued" when he learned of the accusations against his opponent.[65]

As the *Star Tribune* played its hand, the entire deck was about to be reshuffled. The final three weeks of the 1990 campaign for governor were a whirlwind of activity unmatched in Minnesota history.

Grunseth initially denied any wrongdoing and appeared to be completely tone-deaf to the seriousness of the allegations. He told reporters the day the story broke that if elected, he would take up residence at the governor's mansion only "if they install a swimming pool." The remark brought an audible gasp from his wife, Vicki Grunseth.[66]

He categorized the charges as a smear campaign and blamed Perpich and his team for orchestrating the political hit job. The day after the story was released, former governor and fellow Republican Elmer L. Andersen called on Grunseth to withdraw from the race and be replaced on the ballot by Arne Carlson "for the good of the party."[67]

But it was clear that the public's ability to perceive what was personal and what was fact, along with exactly what role the Perpich campaign played in the growing controversy, was diminishing by the day.

"Why are there so many dirty political things going around in the race for governor that have nothing to do with government?" eighth-grader Angie Rustand asked Perpich at a campaign stop in Fergus Falls on October 16, summing up what so many Minnesotans outside the political class were wondering.[68]

"The character of a person who runs for the position of governor is an important part of the public discussion as long as that comes from public records," Perpich defensively explained his earlier decision to bring the nonpayment of child support into the campaign. "This is not negative. It is a fact."[69]

Two days later, the IR's executive committee cast a vote of confidence in Grunseth after he passed a lie detector test. On October 21, Grunseth admitted to extramarital affairs during the "wild years" of his first marriage. When friends of the family and eyewitnesses corroborated the swimming pool story and similar behavior, Arne Carlson announced on October 22 that he was entering the race as a write-in candidate.[70]

"We are in this race. We are in it to the end," Carlson told cheering supporters at a capitol news conference. "We want to light a prairie fire throughout the entire state of Minnesota." Grunseth confirmed the next day that he was "in this campaign to stay."[71]

The turmoil within the IR was affecting races outside of the governor's contest. Polls suggested the disorder over Grunseth's departure was helping

Paul Wellstone's improbable candidacy against Republican US senator Rudy Boschwitz. Boschwitz, the perceived head of the IR, was assumed by many to be behind an effort within the party to force Grunseth out of the race.[72]

"We have a situation where two Republicans are running, and one Democrat is running," Boschwitz told reporters after Carlson began his write-in campaign. "Our base simply is not big enough to cut it in half. So . . . we're going to have to some way repair that situation."[73]

The pressure on Grunseth to withdraw from the race over multiple accusations of sexual impropriety was opposed most vehemently, ironically, by Christian conservatives within the Republican Party. Kathy Worre, a leader within that wing of the IR, said that many "pro-life, pro-family" voters were so furious with Boschwitz that they would rather elect his opponent, the liberal Wellstone.

"Rudy Boschwitz will lose, no matter what happens, whether [Grunseth] stays or leaves," Worre predicted.[74]

With less than two weeks until the election, as pressure from women's groups and fellow Republicans continued to mount, the GOP called a press conference on October 25, at which Grunseth was expected to withdraw from the contest. State TV and radio stations broadcast the event live across Minnesota.

Flanked by his wife, daughter, and running mate, Sharon Clark, the tarnished candidate addressed the crowd, his departure speech in hand.

"I came here tonight to withdraw from this race," he said to a crowd of mostly supporters, cheering as he ripped the speech in half. "But there has been an incredible outpouring of love and affection and support and prayer . . . beyond my wildest dreams. . . . We have the will and the wherewithal to finish this race."[75]

The next night, October 26, a televised debate featuring all three candidates was must-see TV. There were tense interactions between the candidates, but Perpich tried to keep the focus on his record as governor.

"What state is doing better than Minnesota?" Perpich repeatedly asked Carlson and Grunseth throughout the ninety-minute exchange.[76]

Driving home from the debate, Rudy turned to Lola and said, "Well mother, we're going to win this one."[77]

But the drama was far from over. On Sunday, nine days before the election, additional claims of Grunseth's extramarital affairs were published by the *Star Tribune*. Thirty-two-year-old Tamara Taylor maintained that she and Grunseth had carried on a nine-year sexual relationship that spanned both of his marriages and had ended in 1989, more than a year after he had entered the race for the Independent-Republican gubernatorial endorsement. This time, the pressure was too great, and the disgraced candidate finally relented.[78]

"There are three things that are extremely important to me: my wife, my family, first and foremost; the Republican Party; the people of Minnesota," Grunseth said in a statement announcing his withdrawal from the race the same day the final story was published.[79]

Grunseth's exit led to a chaotic end to what was already the most bizarre race in the history of Minnesota politics. Secretary of State Joan Growe had proactively informed reporters and the public that in the event of a major party candidate stepping down before an election, state law allowed the party up to four days before the election to name a replacement on the ballot. If they failed to do so, the second-place finisher in the primary would automatically become the candidate. On Tuesday, October 30, Independent Republicans, realizing it was too late in the process to back anyone other than Arne Carlson, reluctantly acquiesced to the liberal Republican as their candidate at the top of the state ticket. The following day Growe ordered that Carlson's name, along with his running mate, Joanell Dyrstad, appear on the ballot. It wasn't until November 1, five days before the election, that the Minnesota Supreme Court, in a 5–2 split decision, agreed with Growe and made the IR ticket official.[80]

End of Era

After thirty-five years and nineteen campaigns, the last week of the 1990 governor's race would be unlike any stretch in Rudy Perpich's political career. But some things would never change. In front of large rallies on university campuses and small gatherings at private residences—in gymnasiums, coffee shops, and nursing homes—Minnesota's supersalesman would make one final pitch to Minnesota voters, promising them and showing them that he would never lose touch with working people.

Four days before the election, Perpich was flying over the fields of the Seventh District on his way to visit farmers in the Red River Valley. He wore an expensive dark suit as he stared pensively out the window. He was uneasy and feeling a "flip." Something had changed that he couldn't put into words.

"It's the kind of feeling you get in your stomach only if you've been in this business a long time," Perpich said.

During the last days of the 1990 campaign, Perpich and Wellstone appeared together at rallies across the state. Wellstone told a gathering of more than five hundred supporters in St. Paul on the Sunday before the election that it would be a "moment of truth in Minnesota politics." Perpich, suppressing his instincts, fired up the crowd, predicting a "DFL landslide," before Wellstone embraced Perpich in a bear hug with the crowd chanting, "Wellstone, Wellstone, Wellstone."[81]

The following day, on the eve of the election, Rudy and Lola were back where everything started. They were in Hibbing, Chisholm, and Keewatin, where Perpich and his campaign team had bounced across the Iron Range with polka bands blaring from the backs of pickup trucks during his first campaigns for the school board and the state senate.

"Why change now?" Perpich asked rhetorically. "This is it. This is what Lola and I always do."[82]

On Election Day, Rudy and Lola voted at the Biwabik Town Hall before holding a rally at the Biwabik school. Later that day, returning home along St. Louis County Highway 4 from a rally at the University of Minnesota Duluth, Lola at his side, Rudy Perpich said softly, "I don't think it looks good, I have that feeling . . . ," his words trailing off as he stared out the window past the red dust and overburden of Minnesota's Iron Range. One last time, Rudy was right. On November 6, 1990, Arne Carlson defeated Rudy Perpich 50.1 percent to 46.8 percent.[83]

Epilogue

> "Rudy Perpich was a good governor, probably even a great one.
> But what really counts is that he was a good human being."
> —*Reverend Dennis Dease, president of the University of*
> *St. Thomas, in his eulogy to Governor Perpich*

The 1990 election results devastated Rudy Perpich. He had difficulty reckoning his rebuke by the people he had loved and served. In the hours after the painful results became evident, he seemed generous and strong. He comforted family, friends, and his campaign team before delivering a gracious concession speech congratulating his opponent. But in the following days and weeks, Perpich became increasingly bitter, prickly, and paranoid. He blamed the press and refused to speak with reporters. He complained of a Carlson conspiracy and publicly feuded with the incoming governor. He criticized Wellstone campaign workers and chastised the DFL for not supporting him.

Yet his characteristic impulsiveness and generosity were not squelched. Perpich delivered on a promise made to students at Hillcrest Lutheran Academy during the campaign. The school's band had been on the tarmac at 6:00 A.M. to welcome the governor with the "Minnesota Rouser" as Perpich's plane landed for his final "Capitol for a Day" in Fergus Falls on October 16, 1990. Perpich was so taken by the gesture that he invited the entire school to be his guests at the governor's residence. In December, students and faculty filled the home as special guests of the governor at a breakfast in their honor.[1]

Perpich's last day as governor was very much the same as his first. Like December 29, 1976, public events on Saturday, January 5, 1991, started with a Governor's Mass of Thanksgiving at St. Luke's Catholic Church on Summit Avenue, where a crowd of six hundred people paid tribute to Minnesota's governor and first lady with sustained applause. A reception with coffee and cookies followed the mass before Rudy and Lola crossed the street to welcome 3,500 Minnesotans from across the state to the residence for tours and a Polaroid photo with the first couple. The Perpich family stood in line for six hours to personally greet each visitor. Rudy spoke to the press for the first time since the day following his election defeat when he told the gathered media that his time as governor "was a blessing, it really was. . . . No regrets. . . . We've worked very, very, very hard. It was good. We gave it all we had."[2]

After leaving the governor's office, Perpich announced plans to work as a consultant to post-Soviet countries and private businesses in Eastern Europe. In April 1991, he retraced the path of his father and maternal grandparents when he moved his family to Croatia. He was offered the cabinet-level position of foreign affairs minister of the Republic of Croatia but ultimately declined the office over concerns that he could lose his US citizenship. Instead, he lived with Lola and Rudy Jr. in the capital of Croatia, Zagreb, working as a private consultant assisting the fledgling government in setting up a framework for democracy and privatization during the country's war for independence after Croatia declared its sovereignty on June 25, 1991.[3]

During his time in the former Yugoslavia, Perpich became ill and was diagnosed with cancer. He returned to New York, where he underwent surgery followed by chemotherapy. Perpich did not talk about his illness to anyone other than Lola, his children, and his brother Joseph, a physician. He returned to Europe believing he had beaten the disease. As conflict in the Balkans escalated, Perpich moved his family to Paris, France, in July 1992, where he continued working with foreign governments and on international trade projects. In 1993, Rudy and Lola returned to Minnesota to be nearer their first grandchild.

Perpich seemed awkward in retirement and was never comfortable being the elder statesman. He flirted with one more political comeback. Friends reported that his conversations inevitably turned to the next election. There were rumors he would run for the US Senate or for governor again in 1994. A twenty-four-foot sign on Howard Street in downtown Hibbing read, "RUDY PERPICH '94, Good for the Range, Great for Minnesota." He couldn't quit, continually insisting he had one more campaign left in him.[4]

On the Iron Range, there were buttons and T-shirts printed. The Monday Night group was meeting again. The RVs were ready to go. Everyone expected Perpich to announce another run when he appeared on WCCO radio on Tuesday, July 19, 1994. Perpich spent most of the hour characterizing the Carlson administration as a "caretaker administration," portraying the state as stagnant, and describing a series of events he would have pursued, including the Olympic Games, the World Cup soccer tournament, and a visit from Pope John Paul II.

Ron Gornick couldn't pick up WCCO at his home that morning, so he drove his truck to the Chisholm Baptist Church's parking lot, where he could tune in to the Boone and Erickson show.

"Come on, Rudy, announce this thing. Let's get it over with," thought Gornick. "By God, we are ready to go. We are ready to go on this campaign."[5]

Then, Perpich shocked everyone.

"I believe that Minnesota has fallen behind in the last four years, but not enough for people to recognize the urgency of innovation," he told his WCCO audience. "Thus, I have decided not to run for governor. Instead, I intend to continue to promote my ideas and run for governor in 1998."[6]

"I could have bawled right there," Gornick remembered. "I was already on that high, and others were on that high."

Perpich told friends and supporters that the times just weren't right. What he didn't tell them was that his cancer had returned.

"Listen, Gornick, in four years, we will be back in there. Don't worry. We will go strong," Perpich told his friend.[7]

"I didn't talk to him after the announcement," remembered Cathy Baudeck, who had worked on Perpich's '86 and '90 campaigns and served as a Perpich appointee to the state Board of Aging. "[Then] he drove in one day, unexpected, as he does. He said, 'I just couldn't feel it. I couldn't feel the campaign. We will look at '98.'

"And then it was the announcement on the radio."[8]

On September 21, 1995, at 12:05 P.M., Rudy Perpich died of colon cancer at the age of sixty-seven at his home in Minnetonka. One of Minnesota's most public men died a very private death; only a handful of people knew the former governor was sick. His public memorial service took place at the Basilica of St. Mary in downtown Minneapolis, drawing nearly 2,000 mourners. There was no reserved seating, so true to Perpich principle, the judges, administration officials, and politicians, including governors Wendell Anderson, Al Quie, and Arne Carlson, were seated among the people they served. Ninety-five-year-old Anton was there to lay his son to rest, making the trip from the nursing home in Hibbing where he resided with Mary, who was too frail to travel. George, Tony, and Joseph Perpich were pallbearers. Rudy Jr. comforted his mother, and Mary Sue delivered the most touching moment of the two-hour service when she said simply and emotionally, "Dad, thanks for so many incredible memories. Every day was a day in the sun with you."[9]

Following the service, not wanting to go home, former commissioners and staffers walked across Hennepin Avenue to the Minneapolis Community College. Thirty or forty former members of Perpich's administrations told stories and remembered their friend. Someone pointed out the cornerstone of the building, which read, "Built by the State of Minnesota, Rudy Perpich, Governor." The group laughed and reminisced about all the places across the state that shared a similar foundation.[10]

There was the building of the Minnesota History Center, the capitol complex redesign, and the Judicial Center renovation in St. Paul. There were national amateur sports facilities in Blaine and Biwabik. There was the Mall of America, the Center for Victims of Torture, and the World Trade Center. There was Iron World and the Minnesota Discovery Center on the Iron Range and the Metrodome in downtown Minneapolis. There was mine land reclamation and junkyard beautification, an arts high school, and numerous higher education research facilities across the state. Perpich was not solely responsible for all or any of these structures, but he was a driving force and a champion of what they collectively meant to Minnesota. They were part of a larger vision for the state that included the Super Bowl, the Gorbachev visit, the Special Olympics, and the Final Four.

Of course, there were misses. There were the chopsticks factory, the Saturn plant, and the Winter Olympics. But watching his childlike exuberance for the state he loved was part of the charm. If there was a chance for job creation or to put Minnesota in the spotlight, he was there.

Rudy Perpich was a builder and a dreamer. He was also a contradiction: the most public of men who chose to die a most private death. No governor in Minnesota history is so linked to one place, yet few championed the entire state as did Perpich. Intensely proud of his heritage, he was the son of immigrants who became Minnesota's first Catholic, Iron Range, and longest-serving governor. He was a risk-taker, a norm breaker, and a policy entrepreneur, yet there were no scandals or budget crises under his watch. He was prolabor without being antibusiness, forging a partnership with Minnesota's business leaders. He was the first to lose the state's highest office and come back to serve another term. He was the only governor to be kicked out of office by the voters twice. Yet thirty years later, he is widely regarded as one of Minnesota's best governors.

That's because of the enduring power of Perpich's vision for the state. He saw beyond a regional economy overly dependent on agriculture and mining. He described a future where Minnesota was a leader in the global marketplace, selling not only the state's traditional commodities like corn, wheat, timber, and ore but also technology, "brainpower," and the "good life" in Minnesota around the world.

He pursued that vision with enormous energy and a wellspring of ideas—sometimes genius, sometimes frivolous, but all indisputably Perpich.

"He had an idea a minute," remembered Mark Dayton, the Perpich mentee who would be elected governor in 2010—the first DFLer to succeed Perpich in twenty years. "Working for him was like waterskiing behind a super-speed

Governor Rudy Perpich playing bocce ball at the Minnesota State Fair. *Courtesy Minnesota Discovery Center*

boat. You were just trailing in the wake, holding on for dear life, hoping you could stay on your feet and keep up with him."[11]

As governor, Dayton often spoke about the inspiration he drew from Perpich. He posted on his office wall one of Perpich's adages: "None of us is as smart as all of us."

Under Perpich's leadership, the state's economy thrived, education went in a new direction, and the judiciary and state government were reshaped.

Many of Perpich's ideas centered on economic development, construction equipment, and jobs. But behind them was a deep conviction that government should positively influence people's lives—and a genuine love for people.

"I have never met anybody who was as good with people as Rudy Perpich," remembered Paul Wellstone, the US senator who himself is regarded as among the state's most empathetic political figures. "Nobody comes close to touching and being touched by ordinary people in Minnesota."[12]

Perpich believed that government's rightful role was to improve people's lives. It had done that for him, from financing his education on the G.I. Bill to providing him with his first pair of glasses. He advocated for an efficient and innovative government where competent leaders could do their jobs. He directed them to prioritize providing opportunities to the next generation.

He pushed the University of Minnesota to raise academic standards and focus on graduate-level research. He greatly expanded the Minnesota trade office and led a nation-setting trend of trade missions. He helped establish an environmental trust fund and chartered the Agriculture Utilization and Research Institute.

He put more women and minorities into government positions than any previous leader in state history. By the end of his run, he had appointed half of Minnesota's judges and more female commissioners and minority judges than any governor before him. He chose the state's first female lieutenant governor and appointed its first female supreme court justice. On his last day in office, he appointed Sandra Gardebring to the supreme court, making Minnesota the first state in the country with a majority of female justices on its high court.

Perpich loved being governor. More significantly, he understood what being governor meant and what a difference gubernatorial leadership could make for future generations. Perpich invested in the future because he could see that the dividends flowing from that investment would be required to keep improving, going forward, building, and innovating. Not all states have that. Rudy Perpich isn't solely responsible, but he deserves much credit for the enviable position Minnesotans find ourselves in today. He wasn't just paying today's bills; he was planning for an even better future.

Governor Rudy Perpich on a fishing excursion. *MNHS collections*

When designing the state capitol, architect Cass Gilbert reserved places for Minnesota's greatest governors above the doors in the governor's reception area. Rudy let it be known that he would have a place with them one day. If they ever decide to follow through on that plan at the capitol, there will be room for Rudy's boyhood political hero, Floyd B. Olson, for his progressive ideas that gave Minnesotans hope during the Depression and influence the DFL to this day. There will be room for the man Rudy befriended, Harold Stassen, who led Minnesota out of the Depression into a modern economy and laid out a progressive vision of Republican politics that shaped our state's policies for half a century. And there will be room for the immigrant son from the Iron Range who became governor.[13]

Acknowledgments

In October 2017, I joined a handful of outstate and metro mayors for a conversation in Bemidji on how rural–urban divisions were limiting our state's potential. There were no policy objectives or partisan affiliations, only an effort to build relationships and bridge divides.

It was the start of a personal journey to understand our state's history of overcoming political and geographic differences, leading me to historians and politicians, to conversations in small-town coffee shops, to the archives of the Minnesota Historical Society, and, ultimately, to a friendship with author and Minnesota's foremost political observer, Lori Sturdevant. I am grateful for Lori's friendship and belief in the voice of a small-town mayor from Greater Minnesota.

I shared my idea with Lori for a book about Minnesota's political history of the last half of the twentieth century: a state that worked. Governors like Wendell Anderson, Al Quie, and Arne Carlson forming partnerships and often friendships with legislators of the opposing party, such as Stanley Holmquist, Roger Moe, and Linda Berglin, to solve some of the state's most significant challenges such as the 1981–82 state budget crisis and to pass landmark legislation like the Minnesota Miracle and MinnesotaCare. Lori looked at my outline and said there was one major omission: the story of Rudy Perpich.

So started my quest, which led to my discovery of a collection of forty-one largely unpublished oral histories on Governor Perpich—of and by those who knew Rudy best—housed in the Iron Range Research Center in Chisholm, Minnesota. Thank you to the Minnesota Discovery Center and IRRC staff for helping me access the entire Rudy Perpich collection, often from two hundred miles away.

A special thank-you to the Bush Foundation for providing the fellowship that gave me the confidence to start this project, and to the Minnesota Historical Society's Legacy Grants program, which funded research on Rudy's early political career and the origins of his commitment to equity and justice, which helped me finish the project.

R. C. Drews once told me, "Books are never finished; they are merely abandoned." This book would have been abandoned long before it reached these pages if not for R. C.'s prodding, encouragement, stick-to-itiveness, and editing. R. C., I am indebted for everything you did to make this book a reality.

Much of this book was researched and written at the Fergus Falls Public Library. Thank you, Katelyn, for tracking down obscure titles, and Deb, for always helping with a smile! And to Gail, Kia, Krista, Arielle, and Emily—the best staff of the best public library in Minnesota.

I will never forget the call I received in early January 2022 from Ann Regan of the Minnesota Historical Society Press. I was driving my son to a hockey game, but I was eager to hear what she had to say. Ann, always wise and caring, told me to get to my destination before continuing our conversation. Those were the longest twenty miles of my life! When I reached the Alexandria rink and returned her call, she told me MNHS Press wanted to publish this book. Her thoughtful and practical advice continued throughout the remainder of her time at the press. To Ryan Hemmer and Shannon Pennefeather, thank you both for your kindness, patience, and guidance. It was this amateur's dream to work with such professionals.

To Anna Wasescha: I will always be grateful for your advice and encouragement.

To Rudy Jr. and Sue Perpich: thank you for reliving so many memories with me and for sharing your dad with Minnesota.

To Roger Moe, Joan Growe, Dave Durenberger, Marlene Johnson, Arne Carlson, Tom Berg, Chuck Slocum, Aaron Brown, Tom Anzelc, Al Zdon, Dean Urdahl, Mark Phillips, and Charlie Holmquist: thank you for sharing your time and knowledge of Minnesota history and politics.

A special thanks to Mark Dayton for your friendship and example of public service to Minnesota.

Thank you to my son Frank, my special research assistant and travel companion to the Iron Range Research Center, and all the young scriveners.

To my family, thanks for the memories, like the one of a beige Dodge Caravan, sporting slight rust colorization and a "Less Honkin', More Tonkin'" bumper sticker, rolling down a two-lane back road through a small Minnesota town, as the driver turns to the back seat and says, "Kids, let me tell you something about this place . . ."

"Dad, does it have to do with Rudy Perpich?" five voices groan in unison.

To Dove, Reno, Beatrice, Leo, and Frank: thank you for your curiosity and laughter, for keeping me young while giving me gray hairs, and for wearing matching Rudy! T-shirts with your dad. Always remember, "The best way to get somewhere is to go there." I hope one day you will read this book and appreciate the opportunities you had growing up in Minnesota—the pleasure of politics and connecting with your neighbors to improve the lives of others, as well as what Rudy Perpich has meant to Minnesota as a place for these things to happen. But most of all, I just hope you read the book.

Tessa, thanks for finishing my sentences and fulfilling my life.

Notes

See Bibliography for full citation details, including a list of interviews conducted for the Iron Range Research Center, for the Minnesota Historical Society, and by the author.

Abbreviation: MDC   Minnesota Discovery Center, Chisholm

Notes to Prologue: Inauguration

1. Barbara W. Sommer, Remembering Rudy: Excerpts from Governor Rudy Perpich Oral History Project and the Memorial Statements, 2000, Minnesota Governor Rudy Perpich Collection, Minnesota Discovery Center, Chisholm, MN (hereafter, Perpich Collection, MDC).
2. Alan Zdon, "Crowd Extends Best Wishes to Perpich," *Hibbing Daily Tribune*, December 30, 1976, 1.
3. Hunkie or Hunky: a derogatory term for Eastern European miners, common around the Iron Range and across the country in mining-centric communities.

Notes to Chapter 1: Heritage, Heroes, and Family
Opening quote: Anton and Mary Perpich interview.

1. Minnesota Compass, Iron Range Resources & Rehabilitation Service Area data.
2. Syramaki, "Iron Range Communities," 53.
3. Alex Tieberg, "A Brief History of Minnesota's Mesabi Iron Range," *MinnPost*, May 26, 2020; "United States Steel Corporation," Encyclopedia Britannica; Syramaki, "Iron Range Communities," 56.
4. Syramaki, "Iron Range Communities," 9–10, 57.
5. Syramaki, "Iron Range Communities," 11.
6. Edward Dana Durand, *Thirteenth Census of the United States Taken in the Year 1910*, 590.
7. Kraut, *The Huddled Masses*.
8. Minnesota State Senate, Constitution: Reforming Structure, Style and Form, Revisor of Statutes, 1974; Elazar, Gray, and Spano, *Minnesota Politics and Government*.
9. Elazar, Gray, and Spano, *Minnesota Politics and Government*, 10.

10. Elazar, Gray, and Spano, *Minnesota Politics and Government*, 11; Syramaki, "Iron Range Communities," 119; "Carson Lake Minnesota," Hibbing Historical Society and Museum.

11. Lubotina, "The Struggle for Control of Hibbing," 45.

12. Lubotina, "The Struggle for Control of Hibbing," 45.

13. "Won State-Wide Reputation in Political Circles," *Hibbing Daily News*, April 6, 1926.

14. Joseph Perpich interview, 3.

15. Anton and Mary Perpich interview.

16. Anton and Mary Perpich interview.

17. Joseph Perpich interview, 3.

18. Anton and Mary Perpich interview.

19. Ann Brown interview, 2.

Notes to Chapter 2: Growing Up in Carson Lake

Opening quotes: Associated Press, "Perpich Character Carved Out of Ethnic Background on Range," *Austin Daily Herald*, July 3, 1988, 2; Lori Sturdevant, "Rudy Perpich: Many of His Ideas Are Inspired by Experience," *Minneapolis Star and Tribune*, May 18, 1986, 6B.

1. Ann Brown interview, 7.

2. Kortenhof, *Potential and Paradox*.

3. Ann Brown interview, 5.

4. Anton and Mary would add two rooms to the house as the boys grew up, eventually relocating the house when the mining company decided to move Carson Lake in the early 1950s. They shifted the house to 4224 Fourth Avenue East, near St. Leo's Church, where they dug a basement, put in a bathroom, added on to the kitchen, and built a garage. They would own the home until Mary passed away in 1997.

5. Ann Brown interview, 6, 15; Rudy Perpich Jr. interview, 14.

6. Joseph Perpich interview, 2.

7. Floyd B. Olson served two additional terms (the governor was elected every two years until 1962), being reelected in 1932 and '34. His legacy benefited men and women across the state, including a progressive income tax, the state's first. He helped establish a social security program for older Minnesotans, equal pay for women, collective bargaining gains, a minimum wage, and unemployment insurance.

According to Minnesota historian Hy Berman, the merger of the Farmer-Labor and Democratic parties dates to a meeting between President Franklin D. Roosevelt and Governor Floyd Olson on August 8, 1934, in Rochester, Minnesota. FDR was in town to honor the Mayo brothers, who founded the Mayo Clinic. During the visit, the two leaders discussed the Minneapolis truckers strike, which would be resolved two weeks later on August 21 when a federally mediated settlement was ratified, essentially breaking employer hesitance to union organizing in Minneapolis.

But in addition to the strike, Berman alleged that Roosevelt and Olson struck a political arrangement in which Olson would ensure that no Farmer-Labor third party challenge would be mounted in Minnesota from FDR's left flank. In return, Roosevelt would not endorse the Democratic candidate in the 1934 election against Olson, and the Democrats would not run a candidate in Minnesota's 1936 gubernatorial contest.

Similar concerns from Roosevelt's inner circle surfaced in his 1940 and 1944 reelection bids, aiding the case that a single progressive party was needed in Minnesota.

Olson was mentioned as a competitor to FDR for the presidency in 1936, although he later decided to run for senator. It was not to be, however, as stomach cancer ended his political career and abruptly claimed his life.

In 1944, a thirty-three-year-old future Minneapolis mayor, US senator, and vice president named Hubert Humphrey served as the secretary of the Unity Convention that officially merged the two parties into the current Minnesota Democratic-Farmer-Labor Party. Berman and Weiner, *Professor Berman: The Last Lecture of Minnesota's Greatest Public Historian*, 67–69.

8. Iric Nathanson, "Gov. Olson, 80 Years Ago, Proposed Progressive Taxes and Unemployment Insurance," *MinnPost*, January 10, 2013.

9. Frank Ongaro Sr. interview, 12; George Rogich interview, 1. This view of the populist Farmer-Labor movement lasted until the Roosevelts came into power, at which time the New Deal and the Democratic Party became the savior of the working class: Rudy Perpich Jr. interview, 19.

10. George Rogich interview, 10, 1.

11. Joseph Perpich interview, 4.

12. Syramaki, "Iron Range Communities," 386.

13. Syramaki, "Iron Range Communities," 393.

14. Lubotina, "The Minnesota Farm-Labor Party," 23; US Congress, Congressional Record: Proceedings and Debates of the 90th United States Congress, 1967, A5481; Joseph Perpich interview, 5.

15. Rudy Perpich Jr. interview, 7.

16. Frank Ongaro Sr. interview, 2.

17. Norma McKanna interview, 2.

18. Frank Ongaro Sr. interview, 11.

19. Joseph Perpich interview, 3.

20. Sonja Hegman, "First Reading: Looking to the Past," *Session Weekly*, February 27, 2009, 3–4.

21. Norma McKanna interview, 2.

22. Ann Brown interview, 18.

23. The only prejudices Mary and Anton would allow were against those who criticized the Roosevelts. When Westbrook Pegler, a New Dealer who later soured on FDR's court-packing proposals and whose columns appeared in the *Hibbing Daily Tribune*, referred to Eleanor Roosevelt as "that woman," Anton threw the paper to the floor in disgust and started cursing: Joseph Perpich interview, 3–4.

24. Writers' Program of the Work Projects Administration, *The Minnesota Arrowhead Country*, xiv.
25. Syramaki, "Iron Range Communities," 360-62.
26. Syramaki, "Iron Range Communities," 378.
27. Frank Ongaro Sr. interview, 4.
28. Rudy Perpich Jr. interview, 16-17.
29. Frank Ongaro Sr. interview, 4.
30. Rudy Perpich Jr. interview, 23-24.
31. Joseph Perpich interview, 7.
32. Rudy Perpich Jr. interview, 23.
33. Joseph Perpich interview, 7.
34. Rudy Perpich Jr. interview, 22.

Notes to Chapter 3: The Senate Years
Opening quote: Norma McKanna interview, 5.

1. Joseph Perpich interview, 8.
2. Joseph Perpich interview, 7.
3. Ann Mastell interview, 1-2. Jack Fena would go on to serve as assistant St. Louis County attorney and twelve years in the state legislature, be appointed to the Minnesota Tax Court by Perpich during his first term as governor, and serve as a founding member of the Minnesota School for the Arts Board: "Fena, Jack Richard," Minnesota Legislative Reference Library, https://www.lrl.mn.gov/legdb/fulldetail?id=12789.
4. Ann Mastell interview, 1.
5. Joseph Perpich interview, 9.
6. Ann Mastell interview, 8; Rudy Perpich Jr. interview, 27.
7. Norma McKanna interview, 4.
8. Norma McKanna interview, 5.
9. Ann Brown interview, 24.
10. Joseph Perpich interview, 8-9.
11. Joseph Perpich interview, 9.
12. Elect Dr. Rudy Perpich, 1955, and Elect Dr. Rudy Perpich, n.d.—both Perpich Collection, MDC.
13. Karl F. Nolte, "An Appreciation," n.d., and "My Sincere Thanks," n.d.—both Perpich Collection, MDC; Ann Brown interview, 23.
14. George Rogich interview, 1; "Elect Dr. R. G. (Rudy) Perpich," n.d., Perpich Collection, MDC.
15. Rudy Perpich Jr. interview, 32.
16. Frank Ongaro Sr. interview, 6.
17. George Rogich interview, 14.
18. "Annual School Election," 1956, Perpich Collection, MDC; Rodney L. Halunen, "Ghost Towns and Locations of the Mesabi and the Inter-Urban Electric Line," 1966, p. 39, University Digital Conservancy, https://hdl.handle.net/11299/229672.

19. C. E. Taylor, "Dr. R. G. Perpich," Hibbing, MN, May 17, 1956, Perpich Collection, MDC.
20. Norma McKanna interview, 6.
21. Rudy Perpich Jr. interview, 30.
22. Frank Ongaro Sr. interview, 18.
23. Frank Ongaro Sr. interview, 5.
24. Norma McKanna interview, 5.
25. Rudy Perpich Jr. interview, 31.
26. George Rogich interview, 2.
27. The junior college opened its own campus in 1969, which remains today as the Hibbing campus of Minnesota North College: "Introducing Minnesota North College—Hibbing," Minnesota North College, https://minnesotanorth.edu/campuses/hibbing/, accessed July 1, 2024.

"Form College Foundation for Hibbing," *Hibbing Daily Tribune*, March 18, 1958. The first junior college in America was founded in 1901, and by 1914 only fourteen public junior colleges existed across the country: Drury, "Community Colleges in America." During his years as a state senator, Perpich would be instrumental in securing funding for an independent campus for the college, which opened in its current location in 1969. Today it is operated as Minnesota North College–Hibbing.
28. "Hibbing Re-Elects School Directors," n.d., Perpich Collection, MDC.
29. Rudy Perpich Jr. interview, 27.
30. Norma McKanna interview, 5.
31. George Rogich interview, 3.
32. Rudy Perpich Jr. interview, 27–28.
33. Ann Mastell interview, 8–9; Rudy Perpich Jr. interview, 33.
34. Rudy Perpich Jr. interview, 35–36.
35. Members of the Kiwanis, n.d., Perpich Collection, MDC.
36. R. G. Perpich, "Dear Mr. Kovacevich," n.d., Hibbing, MN, Perpich Collection, MDC.
37. George Rogich interview, 19.
38. Members of the Kiwanis, n.d., Perpich Collection, MDC.
39. "Radio Address," n.d., Perpich Collection, MDC.
40. Untitled campaign document, n.d., Perpich Collection, MDC.
41. "Dear Voter," n.d., Perpich Collection, MDC.
42. *New York Times*, August 3, 1975, F3; Jana Hollingsworth, "How Crucial Was the Iron Range to World War II?," *Minneapolis Star Tribune*, March 17, 2023, B5.
43. Department of Iron Range Resources and Rehabilitation, State of Minnesota, biennial report, 1962–1964, https://www.lrl.mn.gov/docs/2021/mandated/210608.pdf; Harold Schoelkopf, "Editor's Notebook," *St. Cloud Times*, May 22, 1962, 4.
44. Sam Romer, "Quarter of State Suffers as Whole Sets Job Record," *Minneapolis Star Tribune*, August 26, F9, F11.
45. "Rising Unemployment Seen for Iron Range," *Minneapolis Tribune*, December 2, 1962, 7.
46. Perpich speech to the Kiwanis Club, 1962, Perpich Collection, MDC.

236 NOTES TO PAGES 38–43

47. "Iron Range 33% Unemployed," n.d., Perpich Collection, MDC.
48. "Know Your Minnesota Legislature," *Minneapolis Star*, 1961.
49. Minnesota Historical Election Archive, State Senate, District 60, 1958; Elmer Peter Peterson, Minnesota Legislative Reference Library.
50. Norma McKanna interview, 6; Rudy Perpich Jr. interview, 33.
51. Elmer Peterson, "Prestige and Progress," 1962, Perpich Collection, MDC.
52. "The Range Needs a Change in the State Senate from the 63rd District," n.d.; R. G. Perpich, "My Grateful Appreciation," n.d.; and Members of the Kiwanis, n.d.—all Perpich Collection, MDC.
53. "A Man with a Plan!" n.d., and "Dear Voter," n.d.—both Perpich Collection, MDC.
54. Elmer Peterson, "Prestige and Progress," 1962, Perpich Collection, MDC.
55. Minnesota Historical Election Archive, State Senate, District 63, 1962.
56. The legislature met biannually until a state constitutional amendment was passed in 1972.
57. R. G. Perpich, "Dear Patient," Chisholm, MN, September 5, 1962.
58. Ann Mastell interview, 3.
59. Ann Mastell interview, 3, 8.
60. "Bill Proposes Tax Break for Mine Companies," *Minneapolis Star*, February 12, 1963; Star Statehouse Bureau, "War Declared on Tax Shift," *Minneapolis Star*, February 25, 1969.
61. Star Statehouse Bureau, "War Declared on Tax Shift," *Minneapolis Star*, February 25, 1969.
62. "Gas Boycott Proposed by Sen. Perpich," *Austin Daily Herald*, November 7, 1963; "Gasoline Prices Called Too High in State Area," *Minneapolis Star*, October 9, 1965; "Iron Range Residents Picket Gas Stations to Protest Prices," *Minneapolis Tribune*, July 17, 1968.
63. "Iron Range Residents Picket Gas Stations to Protest Prices," *Minneapolis Tribune*, July 17, 1968.
64. "State Senator Unhappy over Park Support," *Winona Daily News*, December 4, 1967; "Perpich Asks Help to Bar Canoe Area Mining," *St. Cloud Times*, January 21, 1970.
65. "Perpich Blasts Sen. Higgins' BCWA Views," *Winona Daily News*, February 2, 1970.
66. "Le Vander Blasted by Legislator," *Albert Lea Tribune*, July 2, 1967; "Feel Highway Agency Could Run Better," *Winona Daily News*, May 4, 1967.
67. "Feel Highway Agency Could Run Better," *Winona Daily News*, May 4, 1967.
68. Frank Wright, "Democrats," *Minneapolis Tribune* (Morning), November 8, 1966, 1, 6.
69. Frank Wright, "Democrats," *Minneapolis Tribune* (Morning), November 8, 1966, 1, 6.
70. Minnesota Historical Election Archive, Governor, 1966.
71. Norma McKanna interview, 9.

72. "Keith Asks Younger Leaders for DFL," *Winona Daily News*, November 11, 1966; Minnesota Legislative Reference Library, "Party Control of the Minnesota House of Representatives, 1951–present," https://www.lrl.mn.gov/history/caucus, accessed December 10, 2024.

73. Minnesota Secretary of State, 1966 General Election—Congress, Minnesota Legislative Reference Library. Their thirty-three-year-old brother George, a dentist in Chisholm, was busy establishing committees in communities across the Range to address homeowner tax relief: Al Woodruff, "Brothers Push Bills for Iron Range," *Minneapolis Star*, March 29, 1967.

74. Al Woodruff, "Brothers Push Bills for Iron Range," *Minneapolis Star*, March 29, 1967.

75. Al Woodruff, "Brothers Push Bills for Iron Range," *Minneapolis Star*, March 29, 1967.

76. Al Woodruff, "Brothers Push Bills for Iron Range," *Minneapolis Star*, March 29, 1967.

77. Vance Opperman interview, 1.

78. Vance Opperman interview, 2.

79. Rudy Perpich Jr. interview, 55.

80. Rudy Perpich Jr. interview, 55.

81. Rudy Perpich Jr. interview, 56.

82. Vance Opperman interview, 3.

83. Bernie Shellum, "The Perpich Brothers," *Minneapolis Tribune*, January 10, 1971, 1A, 17A.

84. Bernie Shellum, "The Perpich Brothers," *Minneapolis Tribune*, January 10, 1971, 1A, 17A.

85. Bernie Shellum, "The Perpich Brothers," *Minneapolis Tribune*, January 10, 1971, 1A, 17A.

86. Rudy Perpich Jr. interview, 34.

87. Rudy Perpich Jr. interview, 37.

Notes to Chapter 4: Statewide Office

Opening quote: Gary Lamppa interview, 11.

1. Rudy Perpich Jr. interview, 32–33.

2. Rudy G. Perpich, interview quote, *Minneapolis Tribune*, September 8, 1970, 12.

3. Rudy Perpich Jr. interview, 36.

4. Rudy Perpich Jr. interview, 46.

5. Frank Ongaro Sr. interview, 7.

6. Ted Smebakken, "DFL Fills Ticket," *Minneapolis Star*, June 29, 1970.

7. Rudy Perpich Jr. interview, 46.

8. Bernie Shellum, "Boo Urges Home Rule for Towns, Counties," *Minneapolis Tribune*, October 28, 1970.

9. "Political Roundup," *Minneapolis Star*, October 2, 1970, 7B.

10. Roger Moe interview, 4.

11. Ted Smebakken, "Poll Reports Head Leading by Slender 5%," *Minneapolis Star*, August 19, 1970.

12. Bruce Nelson, "Conservatives Refuse to Act on Lobbyists' Legislature: Perpich," *St. Cloud Times*, October 23, 1970.

13. Perpich for Lt. Governor, "RARE, BOLD COURAGE!" *St. Cloud Times*, November 2, 1970.

14. "Perpich Advocates Gross Earnings Tax," *Minneapolis Tribune*, July 21, 1970.

15. "Perpich Proposes Gross Earnings Tax," *Fergus Falls Daily Journal*, July 22, 1970; "Perpich Defends Tax Plan," *St. Cloud Times*, August 12, 1970.

16. "Perpich Proposes Senior-Citizen Agency," *Minneapolis Tribune*, October 25, 1970.

17. "DFL Candidates Receive ADA Nod," *La Crosse (WI) Tribune*, September 10, 1970.

18. "Maverick Millionaire Plunges into Political Campaign," *Mandan (ND) Morning Pioneer*, October 22, 1970.

19. "Paulucci TV 'Gift' Will Bar Perpich," *Minneapolis Star*, October 29, 1970.

20. Jim Klobuchar, "Paulucci Billboards Push Political 'Chop Suey,'" *Minneapolis Star*, October 21, 1970, 1, 4.

21. Jim Klobuchar, "Paulucci Billboards Push Political 'Chop Suey,'" *Minneapolis Star*, October 21, 1970, 1, 4.

22. Jim Klobuchar, "Paulucci Billboards Push Political 'Chop Suey,'" *Minneapolis Star*, October 21, 1970, 1, 4.

23. "Head, Boo and Forsythe," *Minneapolis Star*, October 29, 1970, 12, 14; "Douglas Head for Governor," *Minneapolis Tribune*, October 27, 1970.

24. "Canvassers Certify Election Result," *Minneapolis Tribune*, November 18, 1970.

25. Gene Lahammer, "DFL Set Up to Influence Politics of the '70s," *Winona Daily News*, November 5, 1970, 1, 13.

26. Peter Vanderpoel, "DFL Election Success Surprises Editors," *Minneapolis Tribune*, November 9, 1970.

27. Joseph Perpich interview, 11–12.

28. W. L. Anderson, "Campaign Financing Change Needed," *Winona Daily News*, December 10, 1970; Finlay Lewis, "HHH Top Spender in State Election," *Minneapolis Tribune*, December 13, 1970.

29. W. L. Anderson, "Campaign Financing Change Needed," *Winona Daily News*, December 10, 1970.

30. Bernie Shellum, "Anderson Appoints Kelm Top Aide, Indicates He'll Be State's No. 2 Man," *Minneapolis Tribune*, December 2, 1970.

31. Bernie Shellum, "Anderson Appoints Kelm Top Aide, Indicates He'll Be State's No. 2 Man," *Minneapolis Tribune*, December 2, 1970.

32. Gene Lahammer, "DFL Victory," *Winona Daily Star*, November 5, 1970; "Party Control of the Minnesota House of Representatives, 1951–present," Minnesota Legislative Reference Library.

33. "G.O.P. Wing Gains Seat in Minnesota," *Chicago Tribune*, January 14, 1971.

34. Steven Dornfeld, "DFL Takes Senate Control; Conservatives Vow Court Fight," *Minneapolis Tribune*, January 6, 1971.

35. Roger Moe interview, 5.

36. "Letter from Home," *Minneapolis Star*, January 11, 1971; Roger Moe interview, 5.

37. Gerry Nelson, "Conservatives Set to Complete Organization," *Winona Daily News*, January 14, 1971; Roger Moe interview, 7.

38. Gerry Nelson, "Perpich Denies Rift but Asks More Duties," *Winona Daily News*, February 11, 1971.

39. Bruce Nelson, "Perpich May Back Move to Abolish His Office," *St. Cloud Times*, February 11, 1971.

40. "Higher Sales, Income Taxes Help Boost State Spending $.5 Billion," *Minneapolis Star*, November 1, 1971.

41. John E. Haynes, "Wendell Anderson and the Minnesota Miracle," *Minneapolis Star Tribune*, July 19, 2016; Berg, *Minnesota's Miracle*, 32.

42. Tom Berg, interview by the author.

43. Berg, *Minnesota's Miracle*, 33.

44. Berg, *Minnesota's Miracle*, 33-34.

45. Tom Berg, interview by the author.

46. Berg, *Minnesota's Miracle*, 36.

47. Berg, *Minnesota's Miracle*, 38.

48. Dale Fetherling, "Legislators Ask Ouster of Water-Quality Official," *Minneapolis Tribune*, April 1971.

49. "Proposed Taconite Tax Hike Stirs Feud," *St. Cloud Times*, May 13, 1971.

50. "Taconite," *Minneapolis Tribune*, June 23, 1971; "Proposed Taconite Tax Hike Stirs Feud," *St. Cloud Times*, May 13, 1971.

51. C. Gordon Holte, "Conservative Tax Programs in Legislature Called Inadequate," *Winona Daily News*, June 16, 1971.

52. A mill rate is a term in taxes used to describe the amount payable per dollar of assessed value. One mill represents one dollar in taxes for $1,000 of assessed value.

53. Steven Dornfeld, "Tax Plan Retains Taconite Aid," *Minneapolis Tribune*, June 23, 1971, 3A.

54. Berg, *Minnesota's Miracle*, 40.

55. Pamela Miller, "With 'Minnesota Miracle,' Anderson Left His Mark on State," *Minneapolis Star Tribune*, 2016.

56. "Higher Sales, Income Taxes Help Boost State Spending $.5 Billion," *Minneapolis Star*, November 1, 1971; Berg, *Minnesota's Miracle*, 43.

57. Pamela Miller, "With 'Minnesota Miracle,' Anderson Left His Mark on State," *Minneapolis Star Tribune*, 2016.

58. Charlie Holmquist, interview by the author.

59. Charlie Holmquist, interview by the author.

60. Dean Urdahl, interview by the author.

61. Berg, *Minnesota's Miracle*, 44.

Notes to Chapter 5: Rivals, Reelection, and the Scandal-Fueled Recession of the Republican Party

Opening quote: Roger Moe interview, 9.

1. Bernie Shellum, "DFL, GOP Begin Battle for 1972 Legislative Races," *Minneapolis Tribune*, August 8, 1971.
2. Bernie Shellum, "DFL, GOP Begin Battle for 1972 Legislative Races," *Minneapolis Tribune*, August 8, 1971.
3. Bernie Shellum, "DFL, GOP Begin Battle for 1972 Legislative Races," *Minneapolis Tribune*, August 8, 1971.
4. Bernie Shellum, "The Perpich Brothers," *Minneapolis Tribune*, January 10, 1971, 1A, 17A.
5. Gary Lamppa interview, 5.
6. Joseph Perpich interview, 12.
7. "Perpich: Congress Should Protest Indochina Action," *Winona Daily News*, April 21, 1972.
8. Chuck Rathe, "It Says Here," *St. Cloud Times*, May 20, 1972.
9. "Perpich Fasting til War's End," *St. Cloud Times*, May 17, 1972.
10. Gerry Nelson, "Judges' New Redistricting Plan Creates Incumbent Contests," *Winona Daily News*, June 2, 1972.
11. "Perpich and Palmer Give Views on Remap," *Fergus Falls Daily Journal*, June 2, 1972.
12. "Perpich and Palmer Give Views on Remap," *Fergus Falls Daily Journal*, June 2, 1972.
13. "Palmer Won't Seek Re-Election," *Minneapolis Tribune*, June 29, 1972, 2B.
14. Berg, *Minnesota's Miracle*, 65.
15. "Lt. Gov. Rudy Perpich," *Minneapolis Tribune*, July 27, 1972.
16. Roger Moe interview, 8.
17. Berg, *Minnesota's Miracle*, 73, 74.
18. Minnesota Legislative Reference Library, State Constitutional Amendments Considered, 2024.
19. "Who'll Open the Senate? A Ditch in Time Gives DFLers the Jitters," *Minneapolis Star*, January 3, 1973.
20. Gerry Nelson, "Perpich Gets New Duties," *Minneapolis Tribune*, January 13, 1973.
21. Rudy Perpich Jr. interview, 40, 43; Barbara Rohde interview, 6.
22. "Perpich Gets New Job Duties," *St. Cloud Times*, January 13, 1973.
23. Roger Moe interview, 9.
24. Berg, *Minnesota's Miracle*, 84, 249. Between 1913 and 1974, candidates for the Minnesota legislature were elected either on nonpartisan ballots or without political party affiliation and caucused as either liberals or conservatives. The 1973 law change first took effect in the house in 1974 and the senate in 1976. For a comprehensive list of the successful legislation, see Berg, *Minnesota's Miracle*.
25. Roger Moe interview, 9.

26. Minnesota Legislative Reference Library, "Number of Bills Introduced and Laws Passed in the Minnesota Legislature, 1849–present."

27. "Perpich Criticizes Compromise over Cambodia Action," *Winona Daily News*, July 3, 1973.

28. "Perpich Raps Major Oil Companies," *St. Cloud Times*, January 25, 1974; Federal Reserve History, "Oil Shock of 1973–74," https://www.federalreservehistory.org/essays/oil-shock-of-1973-74, accessed September 1, 2023.

29. Rudy Perpich Jr. interview, 40.

30. Jack Coffman, "Death of Mine Chokes Town's Lake," *Minneapolis Tribune*, April 15, 1974.

31. Jack Coffman, "Death of Mine Chokes Town's Lake," *Minneapolis Tribune*, April 15, 1974. Unfortunately, this legislation never materialized, and the issues at Kelly Lake remain unsolved to this day.

32. "Lord Raps Reserve in Final Memo on Closing," *St. Cloud Daily Times*, May 13, 1974.

33. Lynn Anderson interview, 26.

34. "Blatnik Announces Plans to Retire," *St. Cloud Times*, February 11, 1974.

35. "Perpich Eyes Race for U.S. Congress," *Fergus Falls Daily Journal*, February 11, 1974; "Blatnik Announces Plans to Retire," *St. Cloud Times*, February 11, 1974.

36. "Perpich Eyes Race for U.S. Congress," *Fergus Falls Daily Journal*, February 11, 1974.

37. Finlay Lewis and Bernie Shellum, "Election Year Enlivened by Blatnik's Retirement," *Minneapolis Tribune*, February 12, 1974, 1A, 11A.

38. Finlay Lewis and Bernie Shellum, "Election Year Enlivened by Blatnik's Retirement," *Minneapolis Tribune*, February 12, 1974, 1A, 11A.

39. "Perpich Will Not Seek Blatnik's Seat," *St. Cloud Times*, February 13, 1974.

40. Bernie Shellum, "Rudy Perpich to Seek Reelection, Won't Run for Blatnik's Seat," *Minneapolis Tribune*, February 13, 1974.

41. Robert T. Scott and Richard Nordvold interview, 55.

42. Bernie Shellum, "Rudy Perpich to Seek Reelection, Won't Run for Blatnik's Seat," *Minneapolis Tribune*, February 13, 1974.

43. Finlay Lewis and Bernie Shellum, "Election Year Enlivened by Blatnik's Retirement," *Minneapolis Tribune*, February 12, 1974, 1A, 11A; "Eighth District DFLers Ready for Political Battle," *Fergus Falls Daily Journal*, May 10, 1974.

44. James Oberstar interview, 1.

45. James Oberstar interview, 2.

46. Alan Zdon interview, 1.

47. "In 30 Ballot Marathon Tony Perpich Endorsed for Congress," *St. Cloud Times*, May 13, 1974.

48. "In 30 Ballot Marathon Tony Perpich Endorsed for Congress," *St. Cloud Times*, May 13, 1974.

49. James Oberstar interview, 2.

50. Gary Lamppa interview, 10–11.

242   NOTES TO PAGES 70–76

51. Gordon Slovut, "Duluth GOPer Calls Oberstar 'Attractive Fellow,'" *Minneapolis Star*, September 12, 1974.
52. Gordon Slovut, "Duluth GOPer Calls Oberstar 'Attractive Fellow,'" *Minneapolis Star*, September 12, 1974.
53. "Rudy Perpich Refuses Flatly to Endorse Oberstar in 8th," *Minneapolis Star*, October 18, 1974.
54. "Oberstar Broke Faith, Mrs. Perpich Says," *Minneapolis Tribune*, November 1, 1974.
55. Joan Anderson Growe, Minnesota General Election Results—1974.
56. Bernie Shellum, "Rudy Perpich to Seek Reelection, Won't Run for Blatnik's Seat," *Minneapolis Tribune*, February 13, 1974.
57. "Loehr for Lt. Gov.?," *St. Cloud Times*, May 25, 1973.
58. "Anderson Announces Candidacy," *Fergus Falls Daily Journal*, April 30, 1974.
59. "State DFL Convention Opens Friday," *Fergus Falls Daily Journal*, June 10, 1974.
60. "DFL Tackles Controversial Issues," *Fergus Falls Daily Journal*, June 15, 1974.
61. Bernie Shellum, "DFL Chooses Joan Growe for State Post," *Minneapolis Tribune*, June 16, 1974, 1A, 11A. Republican Virginia Holm Bye—who was referred to in newspaper accounts and by party members at the 1952 state convention as Mrs. Mike Holm—was appointed by Governor Elmer Anderson in 1951 to succeed her deceased husband and was elected to the position in 1952.
62. Bernie Shellum, "DFL Chooses Joan Growe for State Post," *Minneapolis Tribune*, June 16, 1974, 1A, 11A.
63. Minnesota Legislative Reference Library, "Party Control of the Minnesota House of Representatives, 1951–present," https://www.lrl.mn.gov/history/caucus, accessed September 1, 2023; Jim Shoop, "Sweeps by DFL Puts Anderson in U.S. Picture," *Minneapolis Star*, November 6, 1974, 1A, 3A.
64. Bernie Shellum, "GOP Hurts Most by Lack of Republicans at Polls," *Minneapolis Tribune*, November 6, 1974, 1A, 7A.

Notes to Chapter 6: Party Planning and the Hubris of Wendell Anderson

Opening quote: Gary Lamppa interview, 9.

1. "Newsman Joins Perpich Staff," *Winona Daily News*, November 15, 1974.
2. "Perpich Seeks Changes for Handicapped," *Minneapolis Tribune*, January 22, 1975.
3. Roger Moe interview, 8.
4. "Appearances by Perpich Increasing," *Fergus Falls Daily Journal*, February 7, 1975.
5. Rudy Perpich Jr. interview, 54.
6. Barbara Rohde interview, 2.
7. "Bicentennial Community," *Fergus Falls Daily Journal*, April 9, 1975; "Grant County Plans Kickoff," *Fergus Falls Daily Journal*, June 16, 1975; "Lanesboro Bid for Bicentennial Designation OKed," *Winona Daily News*, September 30, 1975; *Minneapolis Tribune*, July 6, 1975; "Chisholm Makes Bicentennial Statement About Cass Lake," *Bemidji Pioneer*, November 13, 1976; "Special Events Set at Lanesboro," *Winona Daily News*, March 30, 1976.

8. "Perpich Presents Bicentennial Flag to Bagley," *Bemidji Pioneer*, May 5, 1976; "St. Benedict's Awarded Program," *St. Cloud Times*, April 7, 1976.

9. "Application Approved," *Fergus Falls Daily Journal*, June 12, 1974; "Bicentennial Plans," *Fergus Falls Daily Journal*, July 28, 1975; "New Bicentennial Community," *Fergus Falls Daily Journal*, July 23, 1975; "Eden Valley Attains Bicentennial Ranking," *St. Cloud Times*, October 3, 1975; "Perpich Supports Preston Tree Planting Program," *Winona Daily News*, March 31, 1976; Diane LeVasseur, "St. Cloud Unit Reveals Plans for Bicentennial," *St. Cloud Times*, February 20, 1975.

10. "Chisholm Makes Bicentennial Statement About Cass Lake," *Bemidji Pioneer*, November 13, 1976.

11. Nancy Paulu, "Small Town Throws Big Beer Bust," *Minneapolis Star*, February 12, 1976, 1A, 6A.

12. "6,000 Greet Wagons at Lake City," *Winona Daily News*, April 15, 1976.

13. Gary Lamppa interview, 9.

14. Roger Moe interview, 8.

15. Barbara Rohde interview, 3.

16. Eldon Brustuen interview, 19.

17. "Bill Monn," *St. Cloud Times*, December 22, 1975.

18. Barb Hunter, "What if Humphrey Weren't Senator," *Winona Daily News*, September 3, 1975.

19. "Frenzel Will Seek Reelection, Calls Race Against HHH 'Folly,'" *Minneapolis Star*, April 19, 1976.

20. Betty Wilson, "Perpich Says Democrats Will Choose Anderson," *Minneapolis Star*, October 22, 1975.

21. Dennis Cassano, "Anderson Denies Own, HHH Executive Bids," *Minneapolis Tribune*, October 24, 1975.

22. "Mondale Enters Limelight Again," *St. Cloud Times*, May 8, 1976.

23. Minnesota Secretary of State, 1962 General Election Canvassing Board Report, 521.

24. Betty Wilson and Eric Pianin, "Mondale Choice Hints Changes, Frenzel Sees GOP Opportunities," *Minneapolis Star*, July 15, 1976, 1A, 7A.

25. Betty Wilson and Eric Pianin, "Mondale Choice Hints Changes, Frenzel Sees GOP Opportunities," *Minneapolis Star*, July 15, 1976, 1A, 7A.

26. Betty Wilson, "Perpich Would Appoint Anderson to Senate," *Minneapolis Star*, July 23, 1976, 1A, 3A.

27. Betty Wilson, "Perpich Would Appoint Anderson to Senate," *Minneapolis Star*, July 23, 1976, 1A, 3A.

28. Betty Wilson, "Perpich Would Appoint Anderson to Senate," *Minneapolis Star*, July 23, 1976, 1A, 3A.

29. "Anderson Unworried about Future," *Winona Daily News*, August 8, 1976.

30. Eric Pianin and Betty Wilson, "Long-Lost Perpich Friends Jockey for a Place in Sun," *Minneapolis Star*, August 9, 1976, 1A, 4A.

31. Betty Wilson, "Perpich Says Carter Probably Won't Win," *Minneapolis Star*, September 28, 1976, 1A, 4A; Jim Klobuchar, "Rodeo Rider to Lead the Grand Ball," *Minneapolis Star*, November 10, 1976.

32. Betty Wilson, "Perpich Says Carter Probably Won't Win," *Minneapolis Star*, September 28, 1976, 1A, 4A; "Oberstar: A Candidate with No Opponent," *Minneapolis Tribune*, October 23, 1976.

33. Alan Zdon interview; Allen M. Fobes, "A Vote for Perpich," *Minneapolis Tribune*, October 11, 1976.

34. Nancy Paulu, "Perpich Now Thinks Carter Has Edge in Voting Race," *Minneapolis Star*, October 20, 1976.

35. "Perpich Would Appoint Anderson," *Bemidji Pioneer*, October 28, 1976.

36. Mike Padden, a faithless Republican from Washington state, cast his vote for president in favor of Ronald Reagan: Nina Agrawal, "All the Times in U.S. History That Members of the Electoral College Voted Their Own Way," *Los Angeles Times*, December 8, 2016.

37. Minnesota Secretary of State, "Minnesota Elections," 483, https://www.sos.state.mn.us/media/1364/chapter_10-minnesota_votes.pdf, accessed September 5, 2023.

38. "Perpich Would Appoint Anderson," *Bemidji Pioneer*, October 28, 1976.

39. Betty Wilson, "HHH Says He's in Good Condition," *Minneapolis Star*, October 30, 1976, 1A, 7A.

40. "Anderson Senate Bid Lauded," *St. Cloud Times*, November 5, 1976; "Advice Split on Move to Senate by Anderson," *St. Cloud Times*, November 9, 1976.

41. Alan Zdon interview, 20–21.

42. "Anderson to Take Senate Seat," *St. Cloud Times*, November 10, 1976.

43. Betty Wilson, "'Admirer' of Anderson Will Now Try on His Shoes," *Minneapolis Star*, November 10, 1976, 1A, 8A.

44. Barbara Rohde interview, 7–8.

45. "Perpich Rises with 'Firsts,'" *St. Cloud Times*, November 11, 1976.

46. "Perpich Brings Unique Style to Governorship," *Fergus Falls Daily Journal*, November 11, 1976.

47. Betty Wilson, "'Learning' Perpich Sets Goals for Term," *Minneapolis Star*, November 22, 1976, 1A, 5A; Jim Adams, "New PCA Head Might Be a Woman," *Minneapolis Star*, November 18, 1976, 1A, 7A; "Perpich to Employ Citizen Advocate," *Minneapolis Tribune*, November 26, 1976, 1A, 11A.

48. Betty Wilson, "'Learning' Perpich Sets Goals for Term," *Minneapolis Star*, November 22, 1976, 1A, 5A.

49. In a 1973 campaign finance disclosure, Perpich listed his family's net worth as $69,001.88, along with 289 contributions totaling $11,717 for the year, which was used to finally retire his 1970 campaign debt. Perpich listed a homestead valued at $35,077 located fifty miles north of Duluth on Lake Esquagama, as well as $32,200 for his home in Hibbing, which he had rented out since moving his family to the Twin Cities in January of that year. He listed a total of $2,112 in securities including 93 shares of Dayton Hudson stock owned by his children,

as well as 300 shares of Circuit Science and 100 shares of Bison Instruments he owned with Lola. "Contributors Listed—Perpich Says Net Worth Is $69,001," *Minneapolis Star*, December 27, 1973.

50. "Rudy Perpich, Minnesota's Designated Governor: 'I Refuse to Ride in Parades,'" *Minneapolis Tribune*, November 28, 1976, 1B, 7B.

51. Robert T. Scott and Richard Nordvold interview, 57; John Stanoch interview, 18.

52. "Reserve Mining to Be Top Priority for Perpich," *Fergus Falls Daily Journal*, December 1, 1976.

53. "Perpich Taps Moderate as Chief Aide," *Minneapolis Star*, December 6, 1976, 1A, 5A. The decision to appoint Montgomery would have long-term consequences for Perpich. See Chapter 12 for more information.

54. "Rules Enforcement Major Priority of Next PCA Director," *Minneapolis Tribune*, December 18, 1976.

55. Sandra Gardebring interview, 2–3.

56. Wilson, *Rudy! The People's Governor*, 78.

57. Robert T. Scott and Richard Nordvold interview, 56.

58. "Anderson Stayed Away from Controversy," *Fergus Falls Daily Journal*, December 29, 1976.

59. "Perpich's Inaugural Down-to-Earth," *St. Cloud Times*, December 29, 1976; Betty Wilson, "Perpich Inaugural Brief and Simple," *Minneapolis Tribune*, December 29, 1976, 1A, 5A; Steven Dornfeld, "Perpich Assumes Office in Low-Key Public Ceremony," *Minneapolis Star*, December 30, 1976, 1A, 3A.

60. Betty Wilson, "Perpich Inaugural Brief and Simple," *Minneapolis Tribune*, December 29, 1976, 1A, 5A.

Notes to Chapter 7: Governor Perpich

Opening quote: Jim Klobuchar, "Rodeo Rider to Lead the Grand Ball," *Minneapolis Star*, November 10, 1976.

1. Lynn Anderson interview, 16.

2. Mark Dayton interview, 1–2.

3. "Perpich Works in Style Appreciated by Voters," *Fergus Falls Daily Journal*, February 7, 1977, 1, 20; Steven Dornfeld, "I've Got Bad News for You: I'm Pulling the Coffee Machine Plug," *Minneapolis Tribune*, March 13, 1977, 1A, 11A; Alan Zdon interview, 24.

4. Robert T. Scott and Richard Nordvold interview, 14.

5. Terry Montgomery interview, 7–8.

6. Bill Monn, "With a 'Hi-yo Silver Bay,' It's the Lone Iron Ranger," *St. Cloud Times*, March 23, 1977.

7. Steven Dornfeld, "I've Got Bad News for You: I'm Pulling the Coffee Machine Plug," *Minneapolis Tribune*, March 13, 1977, 1A, 11A; Frank Ongaro Sr. interview, 10.

8. "Perpich Works in Style Appreciated by Voters," *Fergus Falls Daily Journal*, February 7, 1977, 1, 20. Mike Menning switched parties after leaving the senate in

1982 and was an unsuccessful Independent-Republican candidate for governor in 1986.

9. "Perpich Works in Style Appreciated by Voters," *Fergus Falls Daily Journal*, February 7, 1977, 1, 20.

10. "Perpich Answers Critics of His Style," *Minneapolis Tribune*, March 18, 1977, 1A, 5A.

11. Lynn Anderson interview, 2–3.

12. "Perpich Offers Rural Job Aid Plan," *St. Cloud Times*, January 5, 1977, 1, 2; Betty Wilson, "Perpich Says He'll Push Energy-Saving Program," *Minneapolis Star*, January 5, 1977, 1A, 10A.

13. Betty Wilson, "Perpich Says He'll Push Energy-Saving Program," *Minneapolis Star*, January 5, 1977, 1A, 10A.

14. Terry Montgomery interview, 5.

15. Roger Moe interview, 10.

16. "Perpich Offers Rural Job Aid Plan," *St. Cloud Times*, January 5, 1977, 1, 2.

17. Betty Wilson, "Perpich Says He'll Push Energy-Saving Program," *Minneapolis Star*, January 5, 1977, 1A, 10A.

18. "The Governed Tell Governor What's on Their Minds," *Minneapolis Tribune*, January 6, 1977; Betty Wilson, "Perpich Says He'll Push Energy-Saving Program," *Minneapolis Star*, January 5, 1977, 1A, 10A.

19. Terry Montgomery interview, 4.

20. Steven R. Anderson, "Power Line Controversy," MNopedia.

21. Dave Peters, "Perpich Seeks Line Hearings," *St. Cloud Times*, January 5, 1977; "Guard Asked to Protect Surveyors," *Winona Daily News*, January 5, 1977.

22. Jack Coffman, "Legislators to Hear Power-Line Dispute; Perpich Optimistic," *Minneapolis Tribune*, January 6, 1977.

23. Casper and Wellstone, *Powerline*, 165.

24. Blair Charnley, "Governor Visits Power-Line Opponents," *Minneapolis Star*, January 12, 1977, 1A, 10A.

25. Terry Montgomery interview, 4.

26. Terry Montgomery interview, 9.

27. Blair Charnley, "Governor Visits Power-Line Opponents," *Minneapolis Star*, January 12, 1977, 1A, 10A.

28. Jack Coffman and Steve Dornfeld, "Perpich Slips Unescorted into Power-Line Area," *Minneapolis Tribune*, January 12, 1977, 1A, 12A.

29. "Perpich Stops Included Visits in Fergus Area," *Fergus Falls Daily Journal*, January 12, 1977.

30. Casper and Wellstone, *Powerline*, 168.

    Hibbing Daily Tribune editor Alan Zdon recalls one of those trips:

    "We got back to the mansion about nine o'clock that night, and every department head was waiting for a meeting that night in the residence," remembered Zdon. "They had been waiting for some time for us to cruise in from where he was out doing stuff with the power lines and meeting with people in coffee shops and things.

"He had been out there several times. He went to three or four coffee shops and just talked to people. Met with politicians. We came back and he went into a staff meeting that went on for two hours. The rest of us are just dead. So, now, two hours of meetings and he is right in the middle running everything. At about eleven o'clock, he met with people that had been waiting for him for hours. There were a couple of union guys from the Range. So, at midnight, we took the two union guys and drove all the way to Minneapolis because there was a certain type of pizza that he liked.

"We went to this pizza place in downtown Minneapolis and then drove all the way back. Now it is like one-thirty in the morning and finally, his day is done. I slept in the residence. I woke up at about five in the morning and I thought, 'I am going to show him.' So, I actually made it down to the dining room at probably five twenty or somewhere around there. I was eating breakfast when he came down. He was a little miffed that I beat him down there. But he wasn't more than ten minutes after me.

"Then, over to the capitol, and he had a meeting schedule starting at about seven-thirty, every fifteen minutes, until about two when they had some big meeting scheduled. What it reminded me of in later reading was how Lincoln used to hold concessions with people or have the open White House. Anybody that wanted to see Rudy could get in to see him. He met with somebody every fifteen minutes. They would usher them in and usher them out. I sat there until about eleven in the morning and probably a dozen people had come in and out by that time. Finally, my ride was there to take me back to the Range.

"He was just building up speed. And I got in that car that these guys were driving, that was the two union guys from the Range, and I got in the back seat and I don't think we even drove out of the parking lot of the capitol and I was asleep. I slept all the way home. I was totally exhausted. When I wrote the story, I invented a phrase that I thought would really catch on. Of course, it never did. But the headline of the story was "Perpichual Motion." I thought that was so clever. But he had more energy than almost anybody I have ever met. Probably more than anybody I have ever met. He just never quit. He was always flying." Alan Zdon interview, 24–25.

31. Blair Charnley, "Governor Visits Power-Line Opponents," *Minneapolis Star*, January 12, 1977, 1A, 10A.
32. Lynn Anderson interview, 19.
33. Blair Charnley, "Perpich Tells Plan to Open Posts to All," *Minneapolis Star*, January 15, 1977, 1A, 2A.
34. Sturdevant, *Her Honor*, 96, 101; Wilson, *Rudy! The People's Governor*, 78.
35. Ray Bohn interview, 5.
36. "Perpich Backs Increase for Women's Sports Aid," *Minneapolis Star*, January 25, 1977.
37. George White, "Perpich: Will Pick Woman for Court," *Minneapolis Tribune*, January 16, 1977, 1A, 9A.

38. George White, "Perpich: Will Pick Woman for Court," *Minneapolis Tribune*, January 16, 1977, 1A, 9A.
39. George White, "Perpich: Will Pick Woman for Court," *Minneapolis Tribune*, January 16, 1977, 1A, 9A.
40. Sturdevant, *Her Honor*, 98–99.
41. Sturdevant, *Her Honor*, 100–101.
42. Sturdevant, *Her Honor*, 101; Gwenyth Jones, "Women Lawyers Push 7 as Court Candidates," *Minneapolis Star*, May 13, 1977.
43. Sturdevant, *Her Honor*, 102.
44. Doug Stone, "Ms. Wahl Hopes to Please Her Rooters," *Minneapolis Tribune*, June 13, 1977, 1A, 6A.
45. Gwenyth Jones, "She Hopes to Enrich Court View," *Minneapolis Star*, June 21, 1977.
46. Ray Bohn interview, 5.
47. Sturdevant, *Her Honor*, 104.
48. Bill Monn, "Woman Named to State Supreme Court," *St. Cloud Times*, June 4, 1977.
49. Brenda Ingersoll, "Ms. Wahl Is Named to State High Court," *Minneapolis Star*, June 4, 1977, 1A, 2A; Harley Sorenson, "Rosalie Wahl Named to State High Court," *Minneapolis Tribune*, June 4, 1977, 1A, 11A.
50. Sturdevant, *Her Honor*, 107; Rosalie E. Wahl, "Memories of a New Supreme Court Justice," *Minneapolis Star*, June 7, 1977.
51. Brenda Ingersoll, "Ms. Wahl Is Named to State High Court," *Minneapolis Star*, June 4, 1977, 1A, 2A; Harley Sorenson, "Rosalie Wahl Named to State High Court," *Minneapolis Tribune*, June 4, 1977, 1A, 11A; Doug Stone, "Ms. Wahl Hopes to Please Her Rooters," *Minneapolis Tribune*, June 13, 1977, 1A, 6A.
52. Minnesota State Law Library, "Rosalie E. Wahl, Associate Justice 1977–1994," https://mncourts.libguides.com/wahl, accessed May 10, 2024. For a more detailed account of the process to nominate Rosalie Wahl, including the other candidates considered for the historic appointment, see Lori Sturdevant's 2014 book, *Her Honor*, particularly chapter 5, "Ready to Soar."
53. Jim Adams, "No Violence, Vows Perpich," *Minneapolis Star*, March 16, 1977; Casper and Wellstone, *Powerline*, 168–69.
54. Casper and Wellstone, *Powerline*, 171–74.
55. Casper and Wellstone, *Powerline*, 178.
56. Casper and Wellstone, *Powerline*, 191.
57. Casper and Wellstone, *Powerline*, 201–2.
58. Casper and Wellstone, *Powerline*, 202–3.
59. Casper and Wellstone, *Powerline*, 211.
60. Casper and Wellstone, *Powerline*, 217–18.
61. Casper and Wellstone, *Powerline*, 220–22, 225.
62. Casper and Wellstone, *Powerline*, 244.
63. With Minnesota's gubernatorial election as a backdrop, five 150-foot towers were toppled between August and December 1978, in a desperate attempt by

NOTES TO PAGES 103–9

the protestors to stop the power line. But their efforts were in vain. On August 1, 1979, the cooperative power line officially went into operation. By September 1980, a total of fourteen towers had fallen along the line. Casper and Wellstone, *Powerline*, 278–87.

64. Casper and Wellstone, *Powerline*, 248–49.
65. Thane Peterson, "In State Primary, the Secondary Is Very Crowded," *Minneapolis Tribune*, August 27, 1978, 1A, 6A; Casper and Wellstone, *Powerline*, 249.
66. Casper and Wellstone, *Powerline*, 254.
67. Paul Wellstone interview, 1–2.

Notes to Chapter 8: The Minnesota Massacre
Opening quote: Lynn Anderson interview, 3.

1. Eric Pianin and Betty Wilson, "GOP Sees Gains if DFL Brawls," *Minneapolis Star*, August 9, 1976, 1A, 4A.
2. Betty Wilson and Eric Pianin, "Long-Lost Perpich Friends Jockey for a Place in Sun," *Minneapolis Star*, August 9, 1976, 1A, 4A.
3. Blair Charnley, "Perpich Hot on the Trail," *Minneapolis Star*, July 18, 1977, 1A, 4A.
4. Blair Charnley, "Perpich Hot on the Trail," *Minneapolis Star*, July 18, 1977, 1A, 4A.
5. Gerry Nelson, "Perpich Portrays Himself as Plain Folks," *Minneapolis Tribune*, September 29, 1977.
6. Berg, *Minnesota's Miracle*, 196.
7. Berg, *Minnesota's Miracle*, 197.
8. Quote from Berg, *Minnesota's Miracle*, 196–98.
9. Berg, *Minnesota's Miracle*, 198.
10. Berg, *Minnesota's Miracle*, 201.
11. Gerry Nelson, "Perpich Asks U.S. Aid for Roads to Voyageurs," *Minneapolis Star*, May 4, 1978.
12. Betty Wilson, "Fraser Foes 'Draft' Alternate Candidate," *Minneapolis Star*, May 8, 1978, 1A, 4A.
13. Betty Wilson, "Fraser Foes 'Draft' Alternate Candidate," *Minneapolis Star*, May 8, 1978, 1A, 4A; Joseph Begich interview, 8.
14. Berg, *Minnesota's Miracle*, 201–2.
15. "Perpich Endorsed on First Ballot; Olson Given Nod," *Winona Daily News*, June 4, 1978.
16. Lynn Anderson interview, 15.
17. Gerry Nelson, "Abortion, BWCA Are Major DFL Hurdles for 1978 Convention," *Austin Daily Herald*, June 2, 1978.
18. Mondale and Hage, *The Good Fight*, 196; Berg, *Minnesota's Miracle*, 202.
19. Betty Wilson, "Primary Voting May Sway State's Politics for Years," *Minneapolis Star*, September 11, 1978.
20. Berg, *Minnesota's Miracle*, 203.

21. Gerry Nelson, "Voters Ask: What Makes Rudy Run?," *St. Cloud Times*, August 21, 1978, 1, 12.

22. Betty Wilson, "Perpich Hopes Back Roads Lead to Victory," *Minneapolis Star*, October 17, 1978, 9A, 10A.

23. Steven Dornfeld, "Not All in DFL Party Are Comfortable with Perpich's Popularity," *Minneapolis Tribune*, December 25, 1977, 1A, 9A.

24. Betty Wilson, "DFLers Beef to Perpich," *Minneapolis Star*, November 8, 1977, 1A, 2A.

25. Lori Sturdevant, "Martin Sabo: The Making of the Modern Legislature," unpublished manuscript, forthcoming in 2025 from the Minnesota Historical Society Press.

26. Rudy Perpich, op-ed, *Minneapolis Star Tribune*, November 5, 1977, 6.

27. Steven Dornfeld, "Not All in DFL Party Are Comfortable with Perpich's Popularity," *Minneapolis Tribune*, December 25, 1977, 1A, 9A.

28. Steve Brandt, "Perpich Prides Himself on Organization," *Minneapolis Tribune*, October 22, 1978, 1A, 6A.

29. Tom Triplett interview, 6.

30. Steven Dornfeld, "Perpich's Legislative Record Spotty," *Minneapolis Tribune*, May 29, 1977, 1B, 11B.

31. "Perpich Orders Economy Measure," *St. Cloud Times*, June 30, 1977; Gerry Nelson, "Voters Ask: What Makes Rudy Run?," *St. Cloud Times*, August 21, 1978, 1, 12.

32. Steve Brandt, "Perpich Prides Himself on Organization," *Minneapolis Tribune*, October 22, 1978, 1A, 6A.

33. Lynn Anderson interview, 7.

34. Roger Moe interview, 11.

35. Terry Montgomery interview, 7.

36. Tom Triplett interview, 5.

37. Betty Wilson, "Perpich Hopes Back Roads Lead to Victory," *Minneapolis Star*, October 17, 1978, 9A, 10A.

38. Betty Wilson, "Perpich Hopes Back Roads Lead to Victory," *Minneapolis Star*, October 17, 1978, 9A, 10A.

39. Betty Wilson, "Perpich Hopes Back Roads Lead to Victory," *Minneapolis Star*, October 17, 1978, 9A, 10A.

40. "BWCA Bill Signed by President," *Austin Daily Herald*, October 24, 1978.

41. Dave Anderson, "N. Minnesotans Unite, Say They 'Can't Take Any More,'" *Minneapolis Star*, October 12, 1978; Dave Anderson, "Perpich Taken to Task as Citizen Groups Form Coalition," *Minneapolis Tribune*, October 12, 1978.

42. Terry Montgomery interview, 5.

43. Steve Brandt, "Perpich Prides Himself on Organization," *Minneapolis Tribune*, October 22, 1978, 1A, 6A.

44. Stephen Alnes, "Rudy Perpich for Governor," *Minneapolis Star*, October 13, 1978.

45. Steven Dornfeld and Nick Coleman, "DFLers Boo Carter Loudly When He Supports Short," *Minneapolis Tribune*, October 22, 1978, 1A, 10A.

46. Gerry Nelson, "Perpich 'Very, Very Optimistic,' Quie Says He's 'Satisfied,'"
    Winona Daily News, October 23, 1978, 1, 2.

47. Gerry Nelson, "Perpich 'Very, Very Optimistic,' Quie Says He's 'Satisfied,'"
    Winona Daily News, October 23, 1978, 1, 2.

48. Bill Monn, "Quie Attacks Perpich on Issues and Governor's Image, Style,"
    St. Cloud Times, October 27, 1978, 1, 17.

49. Bill Monn, "Quie Attacks Perpich on Issues and Governor's Image, Style,"
    St. Cloud Times, October 27, 1978, 1, 17.

50. Bill Monn, "Quie Attacks Perpich on Issues and Governor's Image, Style,"
    St. Cloud Times, October 27, 1978, 1, 17.

51. Betty Wilson, "Gov. Quie? The Congressman Has Faith," *Minneapolis Star*,
    October 17, 1978, 9A, 10A.

52. Betty Wilson, "Gov. Quie? The Congressman Has Faith," *Minneapolis Star*,
    October 17, 1978, 9A, 10A.

53. Lori Sturdevant, "Perpich Alleges 'Gutter Politics,'" *Minneapolis Tribune*,
    November 2, 1978, 1B, 5B.

54. Pearlstein, Colson, and Moe, *Riding into the Sunrise*, 154–55.

55. Berg, *Minnesota's Miracle*, 207–8.

56. Steven Dornfeld, "The How and Why of Minnesota's Vote," *Minneapolis Tribune*,
    November 8, 1978, 1A, 20A.

57. Berg, *Minnesota's Miracle*, 209–11.

58. Roger Moe interview, 13. Moe's figures here are a little strong, but inflation in
    1978 was around 9 percent, with interest on home mortgages reaching double-
    digit figures by the year's end.

59. "Debate a Battle in Perpich's 'War' on MCCL," 7.

60. Patrick Marx, "Mrs. Perpich Blasts Quie for Tactics in Campaign," *Minneapolis
    Star*, December 1, 1978; David Phelps, "Perpich's Wife Says Quie Used Religious
    Beliefs for Political Gain," *Minneapolis Tribune*, December 2, 1978.

61. Gretchen Quie to Governor and Mrs. Perpich, December 10, 1978, Perpich
    Collection, MDC.

Notes to Chapter 9: Rudy Returns and Minnesota Pivots
Opening quote: Lynn Anderson interview, 20.

1. Mary Sue Perpich Bifulk interview, 14.
2. Rudy Perpich Jr. interview, 68.
3. Norma McKanna interview, 19.
4. Norbert Berg interview, 1.
5. Norbert Berg interview, 1–2.
6. William C. Norris interview, 1.
7. Norbert Berg interview, 2.
8. Norbert Berg interview, 2.
9. Norbert Berg interview, 2–3.
10. Norbert Berg interview, 3–6.

11. Rudy Perpich Jr. interview, 74.
12. Lynn Anderson interview, 21.
13. Lynn Anderson interview, 2.
14. Rudy Perpich Jr. interview, 71.
15. Norbert Berg interview, 4.
16. Mary Sue Perpich Bifulk interview, 12.
17. Ron Gornick interview, 4.
18. Robert T. Scott and Richard Nordvold interview, 37.
19. Ron Gornick interview, 5.
20. Lori Sturdevant, "Perpich Returns, Says He's Changed," *Minneapolis Tribune*, April 11, 1982.
21. Lori Sturdevant, "Perpich Returns, Says He's Changed," *Minneapolis Tribune*, April 11, 1982.
22. Lori Sturdevant interview, 7.
23. Wilson, *Rudy! The People's Governor*, 309.
24. Eldon Brustuen interview, 25.
25. "Debate a Battle in Perpich's 'War' on MCCL," 7.
26. Rochelle Olson, "'Giant of Minnesota Politics' Former Attorney General Warren Spannaus Dies," *Minneapolis Star Tribune*, November 27, 2017; Eldon Brustuen interview, 11.
27. Lori Sturdevant, "Spannaus Wins DFL Endorsement by Large Margin," *Minneapolis Star and Tribune*, June 6, 1982, 1A.
28. Rudy Perpich Jr. interview, 77.
29. Eldon Brustuen interview, 6.
30. Gary Lamppa interview, 21; Eldon Brustuen interview, 35.
31. Robert T. Scott and Richard Nordvold interview, 41.
32. Frank Ongaro Sr. interview, 19; Gary Lamppa interview, 21; Eldon Brustuen interview, 21.
33. Robert T. Scott and Richard Nordvold interview, 45.
34. Joseph Perpich interview, 4.
35. Rudy Perpich Jr. interview, 91, 108; "Emily Anne (Staples) Tuttle," *Minneapolis Star Tribune*, February 11, 2018, 15B.
36. Lori Sturdevant, "Spannaus Chooses Rep. Carl Johnson; Feminists Unhappy," *Minneapolis Star and Tribune*, May 26, 1982, 1A.
37. Lori Sturdevant and Betty Wilson, "Perpich, Spannaus Bid with Iron Range Aid Plans," *Minneapolis Star and Tribune*, June 8, 1982, 3C.
38. Marlene Johnson interview, 8.
39. Marlene Johnson interview, 10.
40. Marlene Johnson interview, 10.
41. Lori Sturdevant interview, 7–8.
42. Mai Na M. Lee, "Hmong and Hmong Americans in Minnesota," MNopedia; Lynn Anderson interview.
43. Paul Wellstone interview, 5.
44. Robert T. Scott and Richard Nordvold interview, 46.

45. Gary Lamppa interview, 22; Philip Landborg interview, 11–12.
46. Ron Gornick interview, 11.
47. *Hibbing Daily Tribune* editor Alan Zdon remembered Range voters having the potential to swing an election, as he believed they did with John F. Kennedy in 1960. After winning the Minnesota primary by just over 22,000 votes, Kennedy remarked upon his return to Hibbing: "I must say I would not have missed coming to the strongest Democratic area that I have seen in this campaign. I used to think they were pretty good in South Boston, but we are going to send them out here for indoctrination." Alan Zdon interview, 18–19; John F. Kennedy speech at Hibbing, October 2, 1960, Papers of John F. Kennedy, Pre-Presidential Papers, Senate Files, Speeches and the Press, Speech Files, 1953–1960, Hibbing, Minnesota, 2 October 1960, JFKSEN-0912-030, John F. Kennedy Presidential Library and Museum.
48. Minnesota Secretary of State, "Minnesota Election Results: Primary Election and General Election," 1982.
49. Gary Lamppa interview, 22; Robert T. Scott and Richard Nordvold interview, 44; Minnesota Secretary of State, "Minnesota Election Results: Primary Election and General Election," 1982.
50. Tom Triplett interview, 9.
51. Mark Dayton interview, 4–5.
52. Minnesota Secretary of State, "Minnesota Election Results: Primary Election and General Election," 1982.
53. Rudy Perpich Jr. interview, 88.

Notes to Chapter 10: The Education Governor

Opening quote: Lori Sturdevant, "Perpich Vows Bold Economic Steps," *Minneapolis Star and Tribune*, January 5, 1983, 1A, 5A.

1. Lynn Anderson interview, 28.
2. Lori Sturdevant, "Calls for Innovation on School Budgets," *Minneapolis Star and Tribune*, January 4, 1983, 1A, 4A.
3. Lori Sturdevant, "Calls for Innovation on School Budgets," *Minneapolis Star and Tribune*, January 4, 1983, 1A, 4A.
4. Ruth Randall interview, 23.
5. Betty Wilson, "900-Plus Lobbyists Scramble for Share of Slim State Pickings," *Minneapolis Star and Tribune*, January 4, 1983, 1A, 4A.
6. Lori Sturdevant, "Perpich Vows Bold Economic Steps," *Minneapolis Star and Tribune*, January 5, 1983, 1A, 5A.
7. Lori Sturdevant, "Perpich Vows Bold Economic Steps," *Minneapolis Star and Tribune*, January 5, 1983, 1A, 5A.
8. Lori Sturdevant, "Perpich Vows Bold Economic Steps," *Minneapolis Star and Tribune*, January 5, 1983, 1A, 5A.
9. Lori Sturdevant and Betty Wilson, "Perpich Seeks New Partnership for Recovery," *Minneapolis Star and Tribune*, January 6, 1983.

10. Lori Sturdevant, "Perpich Vows Bold Economic Steps," *Minneapolis Star and Tribune*, January 5, 1983, 1A, 5A.
11. Lori Sturdevant and Betty Wilson, "Perpich Seeks New Partnership for Recovery," *Minneapolis Star and Tribune*, January 6, 1983.
12. Lori Sturdevant and Betty Wilson, "Perpich Seeks New Partnership for Recovery," *Minneapolis Star and Tribune*, January 6, 1983.
13. Lori Sturdevant, "Perpich Offers $9.8 Billion Budget," *Minneapolis Star and Tribune*, February 16, 1983, 1A, 14A.
14. Ray Bohn interview, 3, 9, 11.
15. Mark Dayton interview, 6–7.
16. Lori Sturdevant interview, 14.
17. Lori Sturdevant, "Perpich Starts Soft-Sell of Budget by Answering Questions Around State," *Minneapolis Star and Tribune*, February 17, 1983, 3B, 8B.
18. Lori Sturdevant, "Perpich Starts Soft-Sell of Budget by Answering Questions Around State," *Minneapolis Star and Tribune*, February 17, 1983, 3B, 8B.
19. Lori Sturdevant, "This Time, Perpich Rode Close Herd on Lawmakers," *Minneapolis Tribune*, May 29, 1983, 1A, 4A.
20. Lori Sturdevant, "This Time, Perpich Rode Close Herd on Lawmakers," *Minneapolis Tribune*, May 29, 1983, 1A, 4A.
21. Lori Sturdevant, "This Time, Perpich Rode Close Herd on Lawmakers," *Minneapolis Tribune*, May 29, 1983, 1A, 4A.
22. Lori Sturdevant, "This Time, Perpich Rode Close Herd on Lawmakers," *Minneapolis Tribune*, May 29, 1983, 1A, 4A.
23. "Governor Warns of School Closings," *Austin Daily Herald*, September 6, 1984.
24. Lynn Anderson interview, 9.
25. Lynn Anderson interview, 22–23.
26. Tom Triplett interview, 9.
27. Lynn Anderson interview, 22–23.
28. Ray Bohn interview, 10.
29. Lynn Anderson interview, 24.
30. Nancy Paulu, "Rosemount Superintendent New State Education Commissioner," *Minneapolis Star and Tribune*, May 18, 1983, 3B, 4B.
31. Ruth Randall interview, 2.
32. Nancy Paulu, "Rosemount Superintendent New State Education Commissioner," *Minneapolis Star and Tribune*, May 18, 1983, 3B, 4B.
33. Ruth Randall interview, 15.
34. Rudy Perpich Jr. interview, 67, 98.
35. Mary Jane Smetanka, "Perpich Vows to Shut Poor Schools," *Minneapolis Star and Tribune*, September 6, 1984.
36. Ruth Randall interview, 26, 30.
37. Lori Sturdevant, "Perpich Unveils School Plan," *Minneapolis Star and Tribune*, January 5, 1985, 1A, 8A. "Access to Excellence" was also the name of a University of Minnesota initiative which started as "Commitment to Focus" by President Ken Keller in the mid-1980s, with the program's name changed to "Access to

Excellence" by his successor, Nils Hasselmo: Andrew Tellijohn, "U Looks Back On," *Minnesota Daily*, March 13, 1998.

38. Lori Sturdevant, "Perpich Unveils School Plan," *Minneapolis Star and Tribune*, January 5, 1985, 1A, 8A.

39. Lynn Anderson interview, 11.

40. Lori Sturdevant, "Perpich Unveils School Plan," *Minneapolis Star and Tribune*, January 5, 1985, 1A, 8A.

41. Barbara Rohde interview, 17.

42. Lynn Anderson interview, 28.

43. Editorial Board, "A First Task for the School-Choice Task Force," *Minneapolis Star and Tribune*, October 9, 1985.

44. Mary Jane Smetanka, "School-of-Choice Proposal Unpopular with Small Districts," *Minneapolis Star and Tribune*, January 16, 1985, 3B, 12B.

45. Mary Jane Smetanka, "State Panel Offers Its Own School Plan," *Minneapolis Star and Tribune*, February 22, 1985, 1B, 2B.

46. Lori Sturdevant, "House IR Leader Levi Able to Win Friends, Influence People," *Minneapolis Star and Tribune*, May 16, 1985, 1B, 4B.

47. Lori Sturdevant, "Perpich Unveils School Plan," *Minneapolis Star and Tribune*, January 5, 1985, 1A, 8A.

48. Ruth Randall interview, 10.

49. Lynn Anderson interview, 29.

50. Lori Sturdevant, "Perpich School Plan Clears House Hurdle," *Minneapolis Star and Tribune*, March 28, 1985, 1A, 9A.

51. Lori Sturdevant, "Perpich, Lehr Join Forces to Sell Open Enrollment Education Plan," *Minneapolis Star and Tribune*, April 13, 1985.

52. Lori Sturdevant, "Open-Enrollment Plan Is Hanging by a Thread," *Minneapolis Star and Tribune*, April 25, 1985, 1B, 4B.

53. Lori Sturdevant, "Whatever Lawmakers Do, Open Enrollment Is Winner for Perpich," *Minneapolis Star and Tribune*, April 25, 1985, 1B, 4B.

54. Lori Sturdevant, "Open-Enrollment Plan Is Hanging by a Thread," *Minneapolis Star and Tribune*, April 25, 1985, 1B, 4B.

55. Lynn Anderson interview, 8.

56. Jack B. Coffman, "Legislators Cool to Plan for Arts High School," *Minneapolis Star and Tribune*, March 24, 1984, 1B, 7B.

57. Ruth Randall interview, 35–36.

58. Lynn Anderson interview, 28.

59. Ray Bohn interview, 29.

60. Lori Sturdevant, "Perpich Would Put Pupils in College Early," *Minneapolis Star and Tribune*, March 1, 1985.

61. Snider, "Minnesota Backs Nation's First 'Choice' System."

62. Lori Sturdevant, "Arts High School Plan Seems to Be Evolving into a Bargaining Chip," *Minneapolis Star and Tribune*, June 5, 1985; Lori Sturdevant, "Education Aid Bill Is Approved, but Grumbling Persists," *Minneapolis Star and Tribune*, June 21, 1985.

63. Ruth Randall interview, 10–12.
64. Lori Sturdevant, "Perpich Signs Education Bills, Lists Schools as 1986 Priority," *Minneapolis Star and Tribune*, April 17, 2024, 1B, 18B.
65. Lori Sturdevant, "Perpich Signs Education Bills, Lists Schools as 1986 Priority," *Minneapolis Star and Tribune*, April 17, 2024, 1B, 18B.
66. Ruth Randall interview, 38–39.
67. Jeff Wood, "Open Up 'Model' School," *St. Cloud Times*, November 14, 1985, 1A, 10A.
68. Ruth Randall interview, 14.
69. Lynn Anderson interview, 28.
70. Editorial Board, "A First Task for the School-Choice Task Force," *Minneapolis Star and Tribune*, October 9, 1985; Paul Gustafson, "Perpich: School Aid Cuts Could Be Canceled," *Minneapolis Star and Tribune*, February 6, 1986.
71. Paul Gustafson, "Perpich Asks 170 Districts to Try Open Enrollment Voluntarily," *Minneapolis Star and Tribune*, August 17, 1985, 1B, 14B.
72. Gregor W. Pinney, "Perpich Abandons Open Enrollment Plan," *Minneapolis Star and Tribune*, May 21, 1986, 1B, 2B.
73. Gregor W. Pinney, "Perpich Abandons Open Enrollment Plan," *Minneapolis Star and Tribune*, May 21, 1986, 1B, 2B.
74. Joe Kimball and Randy Furst, "State Teachers' Unions Back Perpich," *Minneapolis Star and Tribune*, August 7, 1986.
75. Betty Wilson, "State to Give Parents Choice of Public Schools," *Minneapolis Star Tribune* (St. Paul edition), May 7, 1988, 1B, 11B. That same year, Perpich signed the Minnesota American Indian Education Act into law. His compassion and belief in education as an equalizer were behind the legislation, which provided state grants to supplement federal funding, eliminating funding discrepancies between Native American schools and public schools receiving state aid.

"He knew the Native Americans did suffer in many ways because of high unemployment and the lack of education," recalled Ruth Randall, who had three Native American PhDs serving under her in the Minnesota Department of Education. "And he believed that for them, as for others, education was a very key part of that. Jobs, jobs, jobs. How education affects jobs makes a difference."

In addition to providing state aid to Native American schools, the new program made grants for postsecondary preparation, undergraduate students, and teacher training, created adult basic education programs, and established Native-led parent advisory committees. The law also developed licensure and provided funding for Native American language and culture education "relevant to the needs, interests, and cultural heritage of" and to "provide positive reinforcement of the self-image of American Indian pupils." Ruth Randall interview, 14; Minnesota Revisor of Statutes, 124D.74 American Indian Education Programs.
76. Rudy Perpich Jr. interview, 97.
77. Lynn Anderson interview, 29; Rudy Perpich Jr. interview, 98.
78. Lynn Anderson interview, 29.

79. Lynn Anderson interview, 29.
80. Betty Wilson, "State to Give Parents Choice of Public Schools," *Minneapolis Star Tribune* (St. Paul Edition), May 7, 1988, 1B, 11B.

Notes to Chapter 11: Labor, Latimer, and Supersalesman Rudy Perpich
Opening quote: Lori Sturdevant, "Perpich Vows Bold Economic Steps," *Minneapolis Star and Tribune*, January 5, 1983, 1A, 5A.

1. "Recession of 1981–1982," Federal Reserve History.
2. Al Quie interview, 21; and Wayne Burggraaff interview, 12—both Minnesota Historical Society.
3. Minnesota Management and Budget, "Historical Expenditure: General Fund and All Funds."
4. Jon Holten, "NE. Minnesota Jobless Rate 18.5% in July," *Minneapolis Star and Tribune*, September 8, 1982, 3C, 4C.
5. "President Steps Out of Role as Spending Cutter in NYC Visit," *Minneapolis Star*, September 7, 1981; "Quie Says Jobs Necessary, or Else," *Austin Daily Herald*, January 13, 1982, 1, 2; Tyler Marshall, "Once Socialist Sri Lanka Now Woos Western Firms," *Minneapolis Star*, January 19, 1981.
6. Lori Sturdevant, "Perpich Enters Governor's Race," *Minneapolis Star and Tribune*, April 23, 1982, 1A, 7A.
7. Mark Dayton interview, 9.
8. Betty Wilson, "Perpich Puts Jobs at Top of His List of Priorities for 1983 Legislature," *Minneapolis Star and Tribune*, January 3, 1983.
9. Joseph Alexander interview, 25.
10. Betty Wilson, "Perpich Puts Jobs at Top of His List of Priorities for 1983 Legislature," *Minneapolis Star and Tribune*, January 3, 1983.
11. Lynn Anderson interview, 9.
12. Roger Moe interview, 19.
13. Lori Sturdevant, "Perpich Vows Bold Economic Steps," *Minneapolis Star and Tribune*, January 5, 1983, 1A, 5A.
14. Lori Sturdevant interview, 10, 13.
15. Lori Sturdevant, "State's Budget Options Are All Painful," *Minneapolis Tribune*, January 2, 1983, 1A, 10A.
16. Lori Sturdevant, "State's Budget Options Are All Painful," *Minneapolis Tribune*, January 2, 1983, 1A, 10A; Betty Wilson, "Perpich Puts Jobs at Top of His List of Priorities for 1983 Legislature," *Minneapolis Star and Tribune*, January 3, 1983.
17. Betty Wilson, "State Divisions Voted $1 Billion by Legislature," *Minneapolis Star and Tribune*, May 24, 1983, 1B, 2B.
18. Mark Dayton interview, 9. When Butler Taconite in Keewatin closed in 1985 due to a Wheeling-Pittsburgh Steel Chapter 11 bankruptcy restructuring, leaving 450 workers unemployed, Perpich did his best to persuade company management to reconsider. But it was clear that corporate leaders had made their decision, and there wasn't any possibility of their reopening the plant.

"The following week, [Perpich] went up to the Range and brought all of his commissioners who were involved in any aspect of that situation—job retraining, relocation services, human services, welfare, unemployment, economic development—and we all walked into the high school auditorium in Keewatin," Dayton remembered vividly.

"There must have been four hundred men, women, and children sitting in the stands. He knew going in there that he didn't have any magic to pull out, but he was willing to go there because he was the governor and he knew that they were depending on him. And as he said later, in a situation like that, all you could do was put your arm around people and cry with them. It took a lot of courage and, even more so, a huge amount of compassion on his part to wade into those kinds of situations which most politicians would avoid.

"Rudy was always willing to go after something even if it might blow up in his face and even if it might leave him with a public failure. He cared more about the possibility of succeeding and what that would do for the people of Minnesota than he cared about the pundits and the critics being able to say, 'Here's another one of these attempts that didn't succeed.' That was not only part of his genius but also a great part of his character." Mark Dayton interview, 9–10.

19. "Perpich Wants Atom-Smasher Project in State," *St. Cloud Times*, November 16, 1983. The small town of Waxahachie, Texas, thirty miles south of Dallas, was chosen as the site for the project. Construction started in 1987, but the supercollider was ultimately canceled by Congress in October 1993 after costs to complete the project soared to more than $11 billion. David Appell, "The Supercollider That Never Was."

20. "Perpich Signs Bill to Help Lure Saturn Plant to State," *St. Cloud Times*, May 25, 1985; Garber and Fausey, "Today's Jobs at Yesterday's Wages"; General Motors, "Spring Hill Manufacturing," https://www.gm.com/company/facilities/spring-hill, accessed July 7, 2024.

21. "Perpich, Lindau Promote Mega-Mall Around State," *Albert Lea Tribune*, September 5, 1985.

22. "State Surplus Is Higher Than Originally Predicted," *Austin Daily Herald*, July 22, 1984. The groundwork for the drastic turnaround was laid when lame-duck governor Al Quie allowed an income-tax surcharge to become law in January 1982, going against his campaign pledges, the advice of many in his party, and political pundits at the time: Lori Sturdevant, "Gov. Quie Showed a Lame Duck's Advantages," *Minneapolis Star Tribune*, September 20, 2008.

23. Mary R. Sandok, "Perpich Goals Draw Praise," *Austin Daily Herald*, January 11, 1985.

24. Lori Sturdevant, "Perpich Starting Expanded Campaign to Promote State in Foreign Markets," *Minneapolis Star and Tribune*, March 7, 1983, 3B, 4B.

25. Lori Sturdevant, "Perpich Starting Expanded Campaign to Promote State in Foreign Markets," *Minneapolis Star and Tribune*, March 7, 1983, 3B, 4B.

26. Eldon Brustuen interview, 53–54.

27. "Perpich: State on Right Track," *St. Cloud Times*, December 22, 1983; Lori Sturdevant, "Perpich Starting Expanded Campaign to Promote State in Foreign Markets," *Minneapolis Star and Tribune*, March 7, 1983, 3B, 4B.

28. Lynn Anderson interview, 13–14.

29. "Trade Travel Draws Some Praise," *Albert Lea Tribune*, January 2, 1985.

30. Joseph Alexander interview, 12.

31. Terry Montgomery interview, 14.

32. Eldon Brustuen interview, 53–56.

33. Norbert Berg interview, 14–16.

34. Susan Marks, "Hormel Strike, 1985–1986," MNopedia.

35. Boyce, Edwards, and Wetzel, "Slaughterhouse Fight."

36. "A Timeline of the Hormel Strike," *Austin Daily Herald*, August 15, 2010.

37. Boyce, Edwards, and Wetzel, "Slaughterhouse Fight."

38. Lori Sturdevant, "When Guard Assistance Was Sought, Perpich Was Prepared," *Minneapolis Star and Tribune*, January 21, 1986, 1A, 10A.

39. Mark Andersen, "Perpich Gains Commitment from Both Sides to Meet, Talk," *Austin Daily Herald*, February 5, 1985.

40. Joe Samargia interview, 22.

41. "P-9 Begins Strike," *Austin Daily Herald*, August 18, 1985; Boyce, Edwards, and Wetzel, "Slaughterhouse Fight."

42. "A Timeline of the Hormel Strike," *Austin Daily Herald*, August 15, 2010.

43. Susan Marks, "Hormel Strike, 1985–1986," MNopedia; "A Timeline of the Hormel Strike," *Austin Daily Herald*, August 15, 2010.

44. Rudy Perpich, "Perpich's Statement on Activating National Guard," *Minneapolis Star and Tribune*, January 21, 1986.

45. Robert Whereatt, Neal St. Anthony, and Conrad deFiebre, "Barricade at Hormel Prompts Action," *Minneapolis Star and Tribune*, January 21, 1986, 1A, 10A.

46. "Hormel Strike Heads Labor Scene," *Albert Lea Evening Tribune*, December 31, 1986.

47. Lori Sturdevant, "When Guard Assistance Was Sought, Perpich Was Prepared," *Minneapolis Star and Tribune*, January 21, 1986, 1A, 10A.

48. Lori Sturdevant, "When Guard Assistance Was Sought, Perpich Was Prepared," *Minneapolis Star and Tribune*, January 21, 1986, 1A, 10A.

49. Lori Sturdevant, "When Guard Assistance Was Sought, Perpich Was Prepared," *Minneapolis Star and Tribune*, January 21, 1986, 1A, 10A.

50. Lee Bonorden, "Goodnature Blasts Actions by Mayor," *Austin Daily Herald*, January 30, 1986; "Perpich Reduces National Guard at Hormel Plant," *Austin Daily Herald*, January 29, 1986.

51. "Perpich Orders Guard Removed by Week's End," *Austin Daily Herald*, February 18, 1986.

52. Lori Sturdevant, "Perpich Calls House Budget Bill 'Outrage,'" *Minneapolis Star and Tribune*, February 27, 1986, 1B, 4B.

53. Tom Anzelc, interview by the author. While serving as lieutenant governor, Rudy would bound into a room of strangers and declare, "Hi. I'm Floyd Olson!": Eldon Brustuen interview, 1. The policies and campaigns of Olson and others, along with Rudy's involvement with them even as a child, left a lasting impression.

54. "A Timeline of the Hormel Strike," *Austin Daily Herald*, August 15, 2010; Susan Marks, "Hormel Strike, 1985–1986," MNopedia.

55. "A Timeline of the Hormel Strike," *Austin Daily Herald*, August 15, 2010; Susan Marks, "Hormel Strike, 1985–1986," MNopedia.

56. Dave Hage, "A Look at History, Issues of Dispute," *Minneapolis Star and Tribune*, February 3, 1986, 8A, 9A.

57. Tom Berg interview, 37.

58. Lori Sturdevant, "Perpich May Be Forced to Mend Ties to Labor," *Minneapolis Star and Tribune*, March 6, 1986, 1A, 12A.

59. Joe Samargia interview, 16.

60. Betty Wilson and Dennis J. McGrath, "Perpich Vetoes Jobless Bill, Calls It 'Unfair, Unbalanced,'" *Minneapolis Star and Tribune*, March 23, 1986, 1A, 10A.

61. Joe Samargia interview, 17.

62. Betty Wilson and Dennis J. McGrath, "Perpich Vetoes Jobless Bill, Calls It 'Unfair, Unbalanced,'" *Minneapolis Star and Tribune*, March 23, 1986, 1A, 10A.

63. Lori Sturdevant, "Perpich May Be Forced to Mend Ties to Labor," *Minneapolis Star and Tribune*, March 6, 1986, 1A, 12A.

64. Betty Wilson and Dennis J. McGrath, "Perpich Vetoes Jobless Bill, Calls It 'Unfair, Unbalanced,'" *Minneapolis Star and Tribune*, March 23, 1986, 1A, 10A.

65. Lori Sturdevant, "Perpich May Be Forced to Mend Ties to Labor," *Minneapolis Star and Tribune*, March 6, 1986, 1A, 12A.

66. Kevin Duchschere, "Lion of St. Paul Still Roars," *Minneapolis Star Tribune*, February 7, 2015, B1, B6.

67. Lori Sturdevant, "Governorship Looks Good to Latimer, but Will He Run?," *Minneapolis Star and Tribune*, January 14, 1985, 11A, 14A.

68. Lori Sturdevant, "Latimer to End Suspense Tonight," *Minneapolis Star and Tribune*, February 22, 1985, 1B, 4B.

69. Lori Sturdevant, "It's Official: Latimer to Run for a Sixth Term," *Minneapolis Star and Tribune*, February 23, 1985, 1B, 7B; Lori Sturdevant, "Latimer Leans Toward Taking on Perpich in Primary," *Minneapolis Star and Tribune*, March 13, 1986.

70. Betty Wilson and Dennis J. McGrath, "Perpich Vetoes Jobless Bill, Calls It 'Unfair, Unbalanced,'" *Minneapolis Star and Tribune*, March 23, 1986, 1A, 10A.

71. Lori Sturdevant, "Latimer Could Be Strong Foe for Perpich, Ratings Indicate," *Minneapolis Star and Tribune*, December 22, 1985, 1A, 4A.

72. Betty Wilson, "Perpich Upbeat About State's Economy in 1986," *Minneapolis Star and Tribune*, December 19, 1985, 1B, 10B.

73. Lori Sturdevant, "Latimer's Challenge Puts Fire in Perpich's Campaign," *Minneapolis Star and Tribune*, December 22, 1985.

74. Lori Sturdevant, "Latimer's Challenge Puts Fire in Perpich's Campaign," *Minneapolis Star and Tribune*, December 22, 1985.

75. Lori Sturdevant, "Latimer's Challenge Puts Fire in Perpich's Campaign," *Minneapolis Star and Tribune*, December 22, 1985.

76. Lori Sturdevant, "Latimer's Challenge Puts Fire in Perpich's Campaign," *Minneapolis Star and Tribune*, December 22, 1985.

77. Betty Wilson and Lori Sturdevant, "Both Sides Applaud Governor's Proposal," *Minneapolis Star and Tribune*, January 11, 1985, 1A, 10A.

78. Betty Wilson and Lori Sturdevant, "Both Sides Applaud Governor's Proposal," *Minneapolis Star and Tribune*, January 11, 1985, 1A, 10A.

79. Tom Triplett interview, 15.

80. Lori Sturdevant, "Neither Perpich nor Latimer Make Plea to Caucuses," *Minneapolis Star and Tribune*, March 16, 1986.

81. "Latimer Announces Bid for Governor," *St. Cloud Times*, April 1, 1986, 1B, 2B.

82. Lori Sturdevant, "Instinct Guided Latimer to Campaign Decision," *Minneapolis Star and Tribune*, April 2, 1986, 1B, 5B.

83. Betty Wilson, "Perpich Will Seek DFL Help for Campaign," *Minneapolis Star and Tribune*, April 12, 1986, 1B, 2B.

84. Betty Wilson, "Perpich Will Seek DFL Help for Campaign," *Minneapolis Star and Tribune*, April 12, 1986, 1B, 2B.

85. Lori Sturdevant, "Perpich Calls Latimer, Jennings Too Extreme to Be Elected," *Minneapolis Star and Tribune*, April 15, 1986.

86. Lori Sturdevant, "Perpich Given Nod by DFL Delegates," *Minneapolis Star and Tribune*, June 14, 1986, 1A, 10A.

87. Lori Sturdevant, "Sen. Biden Says America Is Ready for the Democratic Party's Message," *Minneapolis Star and Tribune*, June 14, 1986.

88. Lori Sturdevant, "Perpich Given Nod by DFL Delegates," *Minneapolis Star and Tribune*, June 14, 1986, 1A, 10A.

89. Robert Whereatt, "3 Candidates Attack Perpich After Reserve Mining Layoffs," *Minneapolis Star and Tribune*, July 25, 1986.

90. Minnesota Secretary of State, Minnesota Election Results 1986: Primary Election and General Election; Betty Wilson and Robert Whereatt, "Perpich, Ludeman Nominated," *Minneapolis Star and Tribune*, September 10, 1986, 1A, 10A.

91. Betty Wilson and Robert Whereatt, "Perpich, Ludeman Nominated," *Minneapolis Star and Tribune*, September 10, 1986, 1A, 10A.

92. Tom Berg interview, 25.

93. Lori Sturdevant, "Ludeman Faces Dual Difficulties in Trying to Oust Perpich," *Minneapolis Star and Tribune*, September 10, 1986, 1A, 11A.

94. Betty Wilson, "Governor's Coattails of Uncertain Help to DFL," *Minneapolis Star and Tribune*, November 5, 1986, 1A, 4A.

95. Lori Sturdevant, "Perpich Has Big Lead over Ludeman," *Minneapolis Star and Tribune*, October 12, 1986, 1A, 4A.

96. Betty Wilson, "Perpich Calls for Election of More DFL Legislators," *Minneapolis Star and Tribune*, November 2, 1986, 1B, 9B.

97. Joe Kimball, "Perpich Compiles List of Firms Aided During Last 3 Years," *Minneapolis Star and Tribune*, October 4, 1986, 1A, 7A. Perpich's list was printed in full in the October 4, 1986, edition of the *Minneapolis Star and Tribune* and includes businesses like Farmstead Foods of Albert Lea; Telex of Blue Earth; Hibbing Enterprises of Hibbing; Nordic Boat Company of Little Falls; and North Star Foods of St. Charles: Rudy G. Perpich, "List of Companies Assisted by Perpich, State," *Minneapolis Star and Tribune*, October 4, 1986.

98. Betty Wilson, "Perpich Calls for Election of More DFL Legislators," *Minneapolis Star and Tribune*, November 2, 1986, 1B, 9B.

99. Betty Wilson, "Ludeman Was Facing Formidable Statewide Political Machine," *Minneapolis Star and Tribune*, November 5, 1986.

100. Minnesota Secretary of State, Minnesota Election Results 1986: Primary Election and General Election; Betty Wilson, "Governor's Coattails of Uncertain Help to DFL," *Minneapolis Star and Tribune*, November 5, 1986, 1A, 4A.

101. Minnesota Legislative Reference Library, "Party Control of the Minnesota Senate, 1951–present," and "Party Control of the Minnesota House of Representatives, 1951–present."

102. Betty Wilson, "Governor's Coattails of Uncertain Help to DFL," *Minneapolis Star and Tribune*, November 5, 1986, 1A, 4A; Minnesota Historical Election Archive, Arne Carlson.

103. Betty Wilson, "Governor's Coattails of Uncertain Help to DFL," *Minneapolis Star and Tribune*, November 5, 1986, 1A, 4A.

104. Lynn Anderson interview, 36; Eldon Brustuen interview, 49; Terry Montgomery interview, 29.

105. Dane Smith and Betty Wilson, "Perpich Hopes to Focus on State's Jobs, 'Brainpower,'" *Minneapolis Star and Tribune*, November 5, 1986, 1B, 4B; Betty Wilson, "Governor's Coattails of Uncertain Help to DFL," *Minneapolis Star and Tribune*, November 5, 1986, 1A, 4A.

106. Lori Sturdevant, "Debate in '86 Governor Race to Be Familiar," *Minneapolis Star and Tribune*, November 10, 1985, 1B, 9B; Dane Smith and Betty Wilson, "Perpich Hopes to Focus on State's Jobs, 'Brainpower,'" *Minneapolis Star and Tribune*, November 5, 1986, 1B, 4B.

107. Dane Smith and Betty Wilson, "Perpich Hopes to Focus on State's Jobs, 'Brainpower,'" *Minneapolis Star and Tribune*, November 5, 1986, 1B, 4B.

108. Dane Smith and Betty Wilson, "Perpich Hopes to Focus on State's Jobs, 'Brainpower,'" *Minneapolis Star and Tribune*, November 5, 1986, 1B, 4B.

109. Dane Smith and Betty Wilson, "Perpich Hopes to Focus on State's Jobs, 'Brainpower,'" *Minneapolis Star and Tribune*, November 5, 1986, 1B, 4B.

110. Dane Smith and Betty Wilson, "Perpich Hopes to Focus on State's Jobs, 'Brainpower,'" *Minneapolis Star and Tribune*, November 5, 1986, 1B, 4B.

NOTES TO PAGES 178–82

Notes to Chapter 12: Hits and Misses

Opening quotes: Rudy G. Perpich, "The State of the State," 1987, Minnesota Legislative Reference Library; Jim Klobuchar, "Rodeo Rider to Lead the Grand Ball," *Minneapolis Star*, November 10, 1976.

1. Rudy G. Perpich, "The State of the State," 1987, Minnesota Legislative Reference Library.
2. Minnesota Department of Revenue, "Minnesota Tax Reform: Report to the Legislature and the Citizens of Minnesota," January 1987, https://www.lrl.mn.gov/docs/pre2003/other/870128.pdf, accessed December 10, 2024.
3. Mark Haveman, "Gov. Walz Relied on Old Budget Toolbox When We Need Redesign," *Minneapolis Star Tribune* Opinion Exchange, March 7, 2019.
4. Betty Wilson, "Critics of Perpich Tax-Cut Plan Fear Trims in Services," *Minneapolis Star Tribune*, January 15, 1985, 1B; Betty Wilson, "Perpich Says Special Session Improved Jobs Climate," *Minneapolis Star Tribune*, June 23, 1985, 8A.
5. Betty Wilson and Robert Whereatt, "Tax Reform Tops Perpich Priorities," *Minneapolis Star and Tribune*, January 8, 1987, 1A, 6A; Mark Haveman, "Gov. Walz Relied on Old Budget Toolbox When We Need Redesign," *Minneapolis Star Tribune* Opinion Exchange, March 7, 2019.
6. Dane Smith, "Some IR Legislators Praise Perpich Plan," *Minneapolis Star Tribune*, January 8, 1987, 1A.
7. Dane Smith, "Perpich's View of Future Research and Hard Work," *Minneapolis Star Tribune*, January 28, 1987, 5A; Associated Press, "Parts of State Tax Plan Get IR Support," *St. Cloud Times*, January 16, 1987, 2C.
8. Dane Smith, "Some IR Legislators Praise Perpich Plan," *Minneapolis Star and Tribune*, January 8, 1987, 1A, 6A; Betty Wilson and Robert Whereatt, "Tax Reform Tops Perpich Priorities," *Minneapolis Star and Tribune*, January 8, 1987, 1A, 6A.
9. Betty Wilson and Robert Whereatt, "Tax Reform Tops Perpich Priorities," *Minneapolis Star and Tribune*, January 8, 1987, 1A, 6A.
10. Betty Wilson, "Perpich Praises 'Great' Session," *Minneapolis Star and Tribune*, May 20, 1987, 1A; Betty Wilson, "Perpich Cites 'Equity;' IRs Call It 'Callous' as '87 Session," *Minneapolis Star and Tribune*, May 19, 1987, 1A, 8A.
11. Betty Wilson, "Perpich Praises 'Great' Session," *Minneapolis Star and Tribune*, May 20, 1987, 1A, 8A.
12. Lynn Anderson interview, 36.
13. Dane Smith, "The Perpiches: The Governor and a Family of Advisers," *Minneapolis Star and Tribune*, November 30, 1986, 1A, 4A, 5A.
14. Dane Smith, "The Perpiches: The Governor and a Family of Advisers," *Minneapolis Star and Tribune*, November 30, 1986, 1A, 4A, 5A.
15. Dane Smith, "The Perpiches: The Governor and a Family of Advisers," *Minneapolis Star and Tribune*, November 30, 1986, 1A, 4A, 5A.
16. Lori Sturdevant interview, 18–19.
17. Roger Moe interview, 18–19.

18. Lori Sturdevant interview, 20.
19. Betty Wilson, "Is Perpich Losing His Political Touch?," *Minneapolis Star and Tribune*, September 13, 1987, 1A, 13A.
20. Betty Wilson, "Is Perpich Losing His Political Touch?," *Minneapolis Star and Tribune*, September 13, 1987, 1A, 13A.
21. Betty Wilson, "Is Perpich Losing His Political Touch?," *Minneapolis Star and Tribune*, September 13, 1987, 1A, 13A.
22. Betty Wilson, "Is Perpich Losing His Political Touch?," *Minneapolis Star and Tribune*, September 13, 1987, 1A, 13A.
23. Lori Sturdevant interview, 16.
24. Betty Wilson, "Is Perpich Losing His Political Touch?," *Minneapolis Star and Tribune*, September 13, 1987, 1A, 13A.
25. Alan Zdon interview, 12–13.
26. Marlene Johnson interview, 54–55.
27. Rudy Perpich Jr. interview, 142.
28. "Perpich to Lead Effort for Torture Center Funds," *Albert Lea Tribune*, May 15, 1985.
29. Terry Montgomery interview, 32.
30. Lynn Anderson interview, 10.
31. "Perpich to Lead Effort for Torture Center Funds," *Albert Lea Tribune*, May 15, 1985.
32. Gregor W. Pinney, "Torture-Victim Center Opens at Edge of 'U' Campus," *Minneapolis Star and Tribune*, May 29, 1987, 1B, 4B.
33. Shannon Prather, "Torture Victims Find Healing, Solace at Center," *Minneapolis Star Tribune*, February 26, 2017, B1, B9; Center for Victims of Torture, "CVT Overview," https://www.cvt.org/wp-content/uploads/cvt_overview_feb_2022_final.pdf; Center for Victims of Torture, "Our History," https://www.cvt.org/about-us/our-history, accessed December 10, 2024.
34. Tom Triplett interview, 11.
35. Terry Montgomery interview, 25.
36. Lynn Anderson interview, 31; Ron Gornick interview, 38.
37. Harvey Mackay interview, 2–3.
38. The speech was carried by WCCO and Mackay gave a copy to Hubert H. Humphrey, who borrowed the line in an address to the state legislature and has since been credited for the line: Harvey Mackay interview, 2–3.
39. Harvey Mackay interview, 6.
40. Harvey Mackay interview, 11.
41. Harvey Mackay interview, 10.
42. Ron Gornick interview, 31.
43. Marilyn Carlson Nelson interview, 2.
44. Ron Gornick interview, 33.
45. Marilyn Carlson Nelson interview, 2–3.
46. Marilyn Carlson Nelson interview, 14; Iric Nathanson, "Looking Back at the 1992 Super Bowl, in 'a City That Does Winter Right,'" *MinnPost*, May 28, 2014.

47. Marilyn Carlson Nelson interview, 2, 14.

48. Marilyn Carlson Nelson interview, 15.

49. Gary Lamppa interview, 26.

50. Jimmy Lovrien, "35 Years Ago, the World's Best Cross-Country Skiers Competed in Biwabik," *Duluth News Tribune*, December 12, 2020.

51. "Perpich, Keller Make 1991 Final Four Pitch," *St. Cloud Daily Times*, July 8, 1986.

52. Ron Gornick interview, 37.

53. Marilyn Carlson Nelson interview, 7–8.

54. Betty Wilson, "Perpich Says Trip to Vienna Is Aimed at Investors," *Minneapolis Star and Tribune*, October 30, 1985, 1B, 7B.

55. Betty Wilson, "Perpich Says Trip to Vienna Is Aimed at Investors," *Minneapolis Star and Tribune*, October 30, 1985, 1B, 7B.

56. Betty Wilson, "Perpich Says Trip to Vienna Is Aimed at Investors," *Minneapolis Star and Tribune*, October 30, 1985, 1B, 7B.

57. Betty Wilson, "Perpich Says Trip to Vienna Is Aimed at Investors," *Minneapolis Star and Tribune*, October 30, 1985, 1B, 7B.

58. Lori Sturdevant interview, 17.

59. Lori Sturdevant interview, 17.

60. Lori Sturdevant interview, 17.

61. "Minnesota College Living Out Bubble's Burst in Akita," *Japan Times*, October 6, 1997.

62. Lynn Anderson interview, 33–34.

63. Eldon Brustuen interview, 70–71.

64. Lori Sturdevant interview, 15.

65. Lori Sturdevant, "Megamall Indebted to Stassen," *Minneapolis Star Tribune*, April 13, 1997.

66. Lori Sturdevant, "Megamall Indebted to Stassen," *Minneapolis Star Tribune*, April 13, 1997.

67. Lori Sturdevant, "Perpich Ignored Office-Seeker, Picked Stassen," *Minneapolis Star and Tribune*, July 19, 1983, 3B, 4B.

68. Lori Sturdevant, "Perpich Ignored Office-Seeker, Picked Stassen," *Minneapolis Star and Tribune*, July 19, 1983, 3B, 4B.

69. Lori Sturdevant interview, 15.

70. Betty Wilson and R. T. Rybak, "An Excited Perpich Backs Met Project," *Minneapolis Star and Tribune*, July 14, 1985, 1B, 8B.

71. Terry Montgomery interview, 25–26.

72. Betty Wilson, "Perpich's Mega-Mall Role Gives DFL Jitters," *Minneapolis Star and Tribune*, August 24, 1985, 1A, 5A.

73. Betty Wilson, "Perpich's Mega-Mall Role Gives DFL Jitters," *Minneapolis Star and Tribune*, August 24, 1985, 1A, 5A.

74. Betty Wilson, "Perpich's Mega-Mall Role Gives DFL Jitters," *Minneapolis Star and Tribune*, August 24, 1985, 1A, 5A.

75. Laurie Blake and Lori Sturdevant, "Reports Say Mega-Mall Won't Help State," *Minneapolis Star and Tribune*, October 30, 1985, 1B, 5B.

76. Gregor W. Pinney, "Perpich Heatedly Defends Mega-Mall," *Minneapolis Star and Tribune*, January 11, 1986.
77. Gregor W. Pinney, "Perpich Heatedly Defends Mega-Mall," *Minneapolis Star and Tribune*, January 11, 1986.
78. Mall of America, "About Mall of America," https://www.mallofamerica.com/about, accessed June 13, 2024.
79. Eldon Brustuen interview, 58.
80. "Perpich to Leave for 'Down Under,'" *Winona Daily News*, October 25, 1983.
81. Eldon Brustuen interview, 59.
82. Eldon Brustuen interview, 59.
83. Minnesota World Trade Center, "Welcome to the Minnesota World Trade Center," https://www.lrl.mn.gov/docs/2012/other/120085.pdf. Renamed Wells Fargo Place in 2003, it remains the tallest building in St. Paul.
84. Minnesota World Trade Center, "Welcome to the Minnesota World Trade Center," https://www.lrl.mn.gov/docs/2012/other/120085.pdf.
85. Eldon Brustuen interview, 61.
86. Betty Wilson, "Perpich Repeats Decision to Skip Opening," *Minneapolis Star Tribune*, September 9, 1987.
87. "Perpich Won't Attend Opening," *Winona Daily News*, September 4, 1987.
88. Marlene Johnson interview, 54.
89. Office of the Legislative Auditor, "Greater Minnesota Corporation: Structure and Accountability," 1991.
90. Lynn Anderson interview, 2–3.
91. William C. Norris interview, 14.
92. Lori Sturdevant, "State Job-Creation Effort No 'Quick Fix,'" *Minneapolis Star Tribune*, August 4, 1987, 3B, 4B.
93. Lori Sturdevant, "State Job-Creation Effort No 'Quick Fix,'" *Minneapolis Star Tribune*, August 4, 1987, 3B, 4B.
94. "2 Years Later, GMC Still Lacks Solid Backing," *St. Cloud Times*, August 28, 1989.
95. Betty Wilson, "Perpich Ends His Support of Rural Economic Program," *Minneapolis Star Tribune*, June 15, 1989, 1A, 15A.
96. Anthony Neely, "Mega-Hopes Prevail at Mall Groundbreaking," *Minneapolis Star Tribune*, June 15, 1989, 1A, 19A.
97. Anthony Neely, "Mega-Hopes Prevail at Mall Groundbreaking," *Minneapolis Star Tribune*, June 15, 1989, 1A, 19A.
98. "Montgomery Resigns Amid Inquiry," *St. Cloud Times*, December 12, 1989.
99. William C. Norris interview, 15.
100. Betty Wilson, "Governor's Veto Angers DFL's Legislative Leaders," *Minneapolis Star Tribune*, June 4, 1989, 4A.
101. Associated Press, "Perpich Kicks Off Property Tax Meetings," *St. Cloud Times*, June 29, 1989, 2B.

102. Betty Wilson, "Bill Includes Reform That Begins in 1991," *Minneapolis Star Tribune*, September 30, 1989, 1A, 6A.

103. Dennis J. McGrath, "Perpich Seems to Be Tax Relief Bill's Biggest Political Winner," *Minneapolis Star Tribune*, September 30, 1989, 7B.

104. Betty Wilson, "Perpich Invites Gorbachev to State," *Minneapolis Star Tribune*, March 9, 1990, 1A, 14A.

105. Betty Wilson, "Perpich Invites Gorbachev to State," *Minneapolis Star Tribune*, March 9, 1990, 1A, 14A; Gaut and Neff, "Red Stars over Minnesota."

106. "The Life of Gorbachev," *Minneapolis Star Tribune*, June 3, 1990; Gaut and Neff, "Red Stars over Minnesota."

107. Lynn Anderson interview, 15.

108. Dennis J. McGrath and Betty Wilson, "Shoes Shining, State Puts Best Foot Forward," *Minneapolis Star Tribune*, June 3, 1990; William C. Norris interview, 18; Gaut and Neff, "Red Stars over Minnesota."

109. Dan Oberdorfer, "Family Hopes Gorbachev Will Feel at Home," *Minneapolis Star Tribune*, May 24, 1990; Harvey Mackay interview, 17.

110. Joseph Perpich interview, 17.

111. "Mottos Explain Minnesota-Soviet Affinity," *Minneapolis Star Tribune*, May 24, 1990.

112. Lynn Anderson interview, 11.

113. Chuck Haga, "Gorbachev Has Critics, but He's Popular Figure Here," *Minneapolis Star Tribune*, June 3, 1990, 16A, 17A.

114. Gaut and Neff, "Red Stars over Minnesota."

115. Eric Black, "Making History," *Minneapolis Star Tribune*, June 3, 1990.

116. David Peterson, "From 1:50 Until 8:22 We See His Personal Glasnost," *Minneapolis Star Tribune*, June 4, 1990, 16–19A; David Phelps, Josephine Marcoty, and Susan E. Peterson, "Gorbachev Tells Business Leaders to Seize the Moment," *Minneapolis Star Tribune*, June 4, 1990, 16–17A.

117. Dennis J. McGrath, "Gorbachev Warms a Cold Day," *Minneapolis Star Tribune*, June 4, 1990, 3A, 14A.; Gaut and Neff, "Red Stars over Minnesota."

118. Jim Dawson and Robert Franklin, "Visit Anything but Typical for 'Typical' Family," *Minneapolis Star Tribune*, June 4, 1990, 18–19A; Donald Woutat, "Charming, Charmed Raisa Steals Show," *Minneapolis Star Tribune*, June 4, 1990, 18–19A.

119. Donald Woutat, "Charming, Charmed Raisa Steals Show," *Minneapolis Star Tribune*, June 4, 1990, 18–19A.

120. David Peterson, "From 1:50 Until 8:22 We See His Personal Glasnost," *Minneapolis Star Tribune*, June 4, 1990, 16–19A.

121. Gaut and Neff, "Red Stars over Minnesota"; US State Department, Office of the Historian, "The Collapse of the Soviet Union."

122. Gaut and Neff, "Red Stars over Minnesota."

123. "Here Are Excerpts of Speeches by Hatch, Johnson, Perpich," *Minneapolis Star Tribune*, June 10, 1990.

Notes to Chapter 13: The 1990 Campaign

Opening quotes: John Stanoch interview, 22; Alan Zdon interview, 13.

1. Tom Triplett interview, 17.
2. Lori Sturdevant interview, 25.
3. John Stanoch interview, 1–3.
4. Betty Wilson, "Perpich Says He Will Run Again; Marlene Johnson Will Remain on the Ticket," *Minneapolis Star Tribune*, October 9, 1989, 1, 8.
5. Text of speech, *Minneapolis Star Tribune*, October 9, 1989, 8.
6. Betty Wilson, "Perpich Says He Will Run Again; Marlene Johnson Will Remain on the Ticket," *Minneapolis Star Tribune*, October 9, 1989, 1, 8.
7. Betty Wilson, "Perpich Says He Will Run Again; Marlene Johnson Will Remain on the Ticket," *Minneapolis Star Tribune*, October 9, 1989, 8.
8. Robert Whereatt and Gregor W. Pinney, "When Perpich Spoke, a Dozen Rivals Listened Closely," *Minneapolis Star Tribune*, October 9, 1989, 8.
9. Robert Whereatt and Gregor W. Pinney, "When Perpich Spoke, a Dozen Rivals Listened Closely," *Minneapolis Star Tribune*, October 9, 1989, 8–9.
10. Betty Wilson, "Perpich Says He Will Run Again; Marlene Johnson Will Remain on the Ticket," *Minneapolis Star Tribune*, October 9, 1989, 1, 8.
11. Robert Whereatt and Gregor W. Pinney, "When Perpich Spoke, a Dozen Rivals Listened Closely," *Minneapolis Star Tribune*, October 9, 1989, 8.
12. Robert Whereatt and Gregor W. Pinney, "When Perpich Spoke, a Dozen Rivals Listened Closely," *Minneapolis Star Tribune*, October 9, 1989, 8.
13. Betty Wilson, "The Fight's On: Hatch to Challenge Perpich for DFL Endorsement," *Minneapolis Star Tribune*, January 22, 1990, 1B.
14. "Moe Drops Bid for Governorship," *St. Cloud Times*, January 30, 1990, 10, 12.
15. Associated Press, "Perpich's Rating Near All-Time Low," *Albert Lea Tribune*, July 30, 1990; "Minnesota Poll: Public Split Evenly on Fourth Term for Perpich," *Minneapolis Star Tribune*, October 9, 1989, 8, 9.
16. Rudy Perpich Jr. interview, 149.
17. John Stanoch interview, 7.
18. John Stanoch interview, 13.
19. Betty Wilson, "Perpich–Hatch Race Shadowed by Abortion," *Minneapolis Star Tribune*, June 9, 1990, 1B.
20. John Stanoch interview, 17.
21. Betty Wilson, "Perpich–Hatch Race Shadowed by Abortion," *Minneapolis Star Tribune*, June 9, 1990, 4B.
22. John Stanoch interview, 14.
23. Betty Wilson and Robert Whereatt, "Perpich Wins Endorsement on 4th Ballot," *Minneapolis Star Tribune*, June 10, 1990, 1A.
24. John Stanoch interview, 14.
25. Betty Wilson and Robert Whereatt, "Perpich Wins Endorsement on 4th Ballot," *Minneapolis Star Tribune*, June 10, 1990, 1A.
26. Betty Wilson and Robert Whereatt, "Perpich Wins Endorsement on 4th Ballot," *Minneapolis Star Tribune*, June 10, 1990, 1A.

27. Betty Wilson and Robert Whereatt, "Perpich Wins Endorsement on 4th Ballot," *Minneapolis Star Tribune*, June 10, 1990, 20A.
28. Betty Wilson and Robert Whereatt, "Perpich Wins Endorsement on 4th Ballot," *Minneapolis Star Tribune*, June 10, 1990, 20A.
29. John Stanoch interview, 20; Bill McCallister, "Governor Primary Is a 2-Party Slugfest," *St. Cloud Times*, September 9, 1990, 4A.
30. Bill McCallister, "Governor Primary Is a 2-Party Slugfest," *St. Cloud Times*, September 9, 1990, 4A.
31. Betty Wilson, "It's Perpich vs. Grunseth: Wellstone Beats Nichols for DFL Senate Nomination; Governor Wins DFL Nomination for 4th Term," *Minneapolis Star Tribune*, September 12, 1990, 9.
32. Minnesota Secretary of State, Minnesota Election Results 1990: Primary Election and General Election, https://www.lrl.mn.gov/archive/sessions/ electionresults/1990-09-11-p-sec.pdf.
33. Betty Wilson, "It's Perpich vs. Grunseth: Wellstone Beats Nichols for DFL Senate Nomination; Governor Wins DFL Nomination for 4th Term," *Minneapolis Star Tribune*, September 12, 1990, 14A; Rob Hotakainen, "Once Again, Perpich Benefits from Solidarity of Iron Range," *Minneapolis Star Tribune*, September 12, 1990, 14A.
34. Rob Hotakainen, "Once Again, Perpich Benefits from Solidarity of Iron Range," *Minneapolis Star Tribune*, September 12, 1990, 14A.
35. Betty Wilson, "It's Perpich vs. Grunseth: Wellstone Beats Nichols for DFL Senate Nomination; Governor Wins DFL Nomination for 4th Term," *Minneapolis Star Tribune*, September 12, 1990, 1.
36. Robert Whereatt, "It's Perpich vs. Grunseth; Wellstone Beats Nichols for DFL Senate Nomination; IR Nominee Lost Polls, but Won the Vote," *Minneapolis Star Tribune*, September 12, 1990, 1; Minnesota Secretary of State, Minnesota Election Results 1990: Primary Election and General Election, https://www.lrl .mn.gov/archive/sessions/electionresults/1990-09-11-p-sec.pdf.
37. Robert Whereatt, "It's Perpich vs. Grunseth; Wellstone Beats Nichols for DFL Senate Nomination; IR Nominee Lost Polls, but Won the Vote," *Minneapolis Star Tribune*, September 12, 1990, 1, 14.
38. Robert Whereatt, "It's Perpich vs. Grunseth; Wellstone Beats Nichols for DFL Senate Nomination; IR Nominee Lost Polls, but Won the Vote," *Minneapolis Star Tribune*, September 12, 1990, 1; Minnesota Secretary of State, Elections Division, "Minnesota Election Statistics, 1950–2020," https://www.sos.state.mn.us/ media/4395/minnesota-election-statistics-1950-to-2020.pdf.
39. Randy Furst and Rob Hotakainen, "Governor's Race Begins to Shape Up: Perpich Aims to Attract Centrists," *Minneapolis Star Tribune*, September 13, 1990, 1B.
40. John Stanoch interview, 19.
41. John Stanoch interview, 22.
42. Jim Parsons, "For Arne Carlson, Reality of Loss Is Hard to Swallow," *Minneapolis Star Tribune*, September 13, 1990, 17A.

43. John Stanoch interview, 21–22.
44. Betty Wilson, "Best Laid Plans of Politicians . . . : Perpich Launches Attack; IR Aide Claims Reversal," *Minneapolis Star Tribune*, September 22, 1990, 1B.
45. Betty Wilson, "Best Laid Plans of Politicians . . . : Perpich Launches Attack; IR Aide Claims Reversal," *Minneapolis Star Tribune*, September 22, 1990, 5B.
46. Betty Wilson and Bill McAuliffe, "Perpich Intensifies Attack on Grunseth," *Minneapolis Star Tribune*, October 9, 1990, 1A; John Stanoch interview, 23.
47. John Stanoch interview, 23.
48. "Controversy," *Minneapolis Star Tribune*, October 26, 1990, 18A.
49. Betty Wilson and Bill McAuliffe, "Perpich Intensifies Attack on Grunseth," *Minneapolis Star Tribune*, October 9, 1990, 1A.
50. Marlene Johnson interview, 61.
51. Lynn Anderson interview, 16–17.
52. John Stanoch interview, 20–21.
53. Dane Smith, "Strategy Raises Eyebrows, But Could Be Savvy," *Minneapolis Star Tribune*, October 9, 1990, 1.
54. John Stanoch interview, 22.
55. Allen Short, "Allegations Rock Governor's Race: 2 Women Claim Improper Behavior by Grunseth at '81 Party; He Denies It," *Minneapolis Star Tribune*, October 15, 1990, 1.
56. Curtis Gilbert, "Recent Race Tame Compared to 1990 Gubernatorial Contest," MPR News, November 5, 2010, https://www.mprnews.org/story/2010/11/04/carlson-grunset-revisited.
57. Allen Short, "Allegations Rock Governor's Race: 2 Women Claim Improper Behavior by Grunseth at '81 Party; He Denies It," *Minneapolis Star Tribune*, October 15, 1990, 1.
58. Allen Short, "Allegations Rock Governor's Race: 2 Women Claim Improper Behavior by Grunseth at '81 Party; He Denies It," *Minneapolis Star Tribune*, October 15, 1990, 6.
59. Allen Short, "Grunseth Vows to Stay in Race; Criticizes Lack of Time to Respond," *Minneapolis Star Tribune*, October 16, 1990, 12.
60. "Grunseth's Letter Sent to Perpich," *Minneapolis Star Tribune*, October 15, 1990, 5.
61. Curtis Gilbert, "Recent Race Tame Compared to 1990 Gubernatorial Contest," MPR News, November 5, 2010, https://www.mprnews.org/story/2010/11/04/carlson-grunset-revisited.
62. Allen Short, "Allegations Rock Governor's Race: 2 Women Claim Improper Behavior by Grunseth at '81 Party; He Denies It," *Minneapolis Star Tribune*, October 15, 1990, 6.
63. Lori Sturdevant interview, 25.
64. Lori Sturdevant interview, 25.
65. John Stanoch interview, 23, 25.
66. Kim Ode, "Behind the Image, Few Really Knew Him: Grunseth Seen as a Fresh Face in Statewide Race," *Minneapolis Star Tribune*, October 29, 1990, 10A.

67. "Controversy Has Dogged Grunseth Campaign," *Minneapolis Star Tribune*, October 26, 1990.
68. Betty Wilson, "Perpich on Defensive, but IR Area is Friendly," *Minneapolis Star Tribune*, October 17, 1990, 1B.
69. Betty Wilson, "Perpich on Defensive, but IR Area is Friendly," *Minneapolis Star Tribune*, October 17, 1990, 1B, 7B.
70. "Controversy Has Dogged Grunseth Campaign," *Minneapolis Star Tribune*, October 26, 1990.
71. Betty Wilson, Dane Smith, and Randy Furst, "Carlson Entry Tightens Race: Poll Shows Only 6 Points Separate Grunseth, Perpich: Write-in Begun by Auditor," *Minneapolis Star Tribune*, October 23, 1990, 1A; "Controversy Has Dogged Grunseth Campaign," *Minneapolis Star Tribune*, October 26, 1990.
72. Curtis Gilbert, "Recent Race Tame Compared to 1990 Gubernatorial Contest," MPR News, November 5, 2010, https://www.mprnews.org/story/2010/11/04/carlson-grunset-revisited.
73. Betty Wilson, "Grunseth Wavers but Stays In; He Says 'Incredible' Support Altered Plan to Quit; Ludeman Had Waited in the Wings," *Minneapolis Star Tribune*, October 26, 1990, 18.
74. Betty Wilson, "Grunseth Wavers but Stays In; He Says 'Incredible' Support Altered Plan to Quit; Ludeman Had Waited in the Wings," *Minneapolis Star Tribune*, October 26, 1990, 18.
    Paul Wellstone defeated Rudy Boschwitz in the 1990 US Senate race 50.5 percent to 47.9 percent. Wellstone went on to serve two terms in the Senate. He died along with his wife, daughter, three campaign workers, and two pilots when their plane crashed while trying to land in Eveleth, Minnesota, on October 25, 2002, during his reelection campaign. Wellstone had decided to skip a rally and fundraiser in Minneapolis and instead head to the Iron Range in order to attend the funeral of Martin Rukavina, the father of Virginia state legislator and longtime Wellstone ally Tom Rukavina. Aaron Brown, "Sen. Paul Wellstone and the Portents of His Death, Two Decades Later," Minnesota Reformer, October 24, 2022; Minnesota Election Results 1990: Primary Election and General Election, https://www.lrl.mn.gov/archive/sessions/electionresults/1990-09-11-p-sec.pdf.
75. Rob Hotakainen, "Grunseth Backers Mad at Other Rudy," *Minneapolis Star Tribune*, October 26, 1990, 1A; Curtis Gilbert, "Recent Race Tame Compared to 1990 Gubernatorial Contest," MPR News, November 5, 2010, https://www.mprnews.org/story/2010/11/04/carlson-grunset-revisited.
76. Betty Wilson, "Debate's Focus Is State Finances; Candidates All Lament Tone of Campaign," *Minneapolis Star Tribune*, October 27, 1990, 1A.
77. Curtis Gilbert, "Recent Race Tame Compared to 1990 Gubernatorial Contest," MPR News, November 5, 2010, https://www.mprnews.org/story/2010/11/04/carlson-grunset-revisited; John Stanoch interview, 27.
78. Allen Short and Paul McEnroe, "When Did Grunseth's Wild Years End? Woman Claims Affair into '89; He Says It Was over 'Long Ago,'" *Minneapolis Star Tribune*, October 28, 1990, 1; Curtis Gilbert, "Recent Race Tame Compared to 1990

Gubernatorial Contest," MPR News, November 5, 2010, https://www.mprnews
.org/story/2010/11/04/carlson-grunset-revisited.
79. Campaign Statement, *Minneapolis Star Tribune*, October 29, 1990, 1A.
80. Robert Whereatt, "IR Team Is Carlson-Dyrstad; Justices Reject Clark's Challenge," *Minneapolis Star Tribune*, November 2, 1990, 1A; Growe and Sturdevant,
Turnout, 130–33; Betty Wilson, "IR Panel Ponders Next Step; Decision Today
May Put Carlson on Ballot; Some Still Would Like Ticket Led by Clark," *Minneapolis Star Tribune*, October 30, 1990, 1A.
81. Norman Draper and Paul McEnroe, "Late Entry Turns Marathon for Governor
into a One-Week Sprint," *Minneapolis Star Tribune*, November 5, 1990, 1A, 12A;
Robert Scott and Richard Nordvold interview, 64.
82. Norman Draper and Paul McEnroe, "Late Entry Turns Marathon for Governor
into a One-Week Sprint," *Minneapolis Star Tribune*, November 5, 1990, 13A;
Robert Scott and Richard Nordvold interview, 64.
83. Robert Scott and Richard Nordvold interview, 64. This stretch of highway would
later be named "Rudy Perpich Memorial Drive": John A. Weeks III, "Minnesota
Named Highways," http://www.johnweeks.com/highway/mnnamedhighways/
index.html, accessed December 11, 2024.

Notes to Epilogue
Opening quote: Robert Whereatt, "A Good Governor . . . a Good Human Being,"
Minneapolis Star Tribune, September 26, 1995, 1A, 11A.

1. John Stanoch interview, 34; "Memories of Rudy Perpich," [letters sent to Perpich
family after Rudy's death], 1996, Minnesota Historical Society.
2. Dane Smith, "Thousands Bid Perpiches Adieu," *Minneapolis Star Tribune*, January 6, 1991, 1B, 7B.
3. Robert Whereatt, "Perpich Has Moved In, Croatian Reports Say," *Minneapolis
Star Tribune*, April 12, 1991, 1B, 5B.
4. Lori Sturdevant interview, 27; "Rudy Perpich Retrospective, with Commentary
from Hy Berman," *Midday*, September 22, 1995, Minnesota Public Radio,
https://archive.mpr.org/stories/1995/09/22/rudy-Perpich-retrospective-with
-commentary-from-hy-berman.
5. Ron Gornick interview, 42–43.
6. "Rudy Perpich Retrospective, with Commentary from Hy Berman," *Midday*,
September 22, 1995, Minnesota Public Radio, https://archive.mpr.org/stories/
1995/09/22/rudy-Perpich-retrospective-with-commentary-from-hy-berman.
7. Ron Gornick interview, 43.
8. Cathy Baudeck interview, 20, 21.
9. Robert Whereatt, "A Good Governor . . . a Good Human Being," *Minneapolis
Star Tribune*, September 26, 1995, 1A, 11A.
10. John Stanoch interview, 35.
11. Mark Dayton interview, 11–12.
12. Paul Wellstone interview, 4, 9.
13. Lori Sturdevant interview, 29.

Bibliography

Archives and Oral Histories

Hibbing Historical Society and Museum, Hibbing, MN.
Iron Range Research Center/Minnesota Discovery Center, Chisholm, MN.
    Governor Rudy Perpich Oral History Project. Edited by Barbara W. Sommer.
        Alexander, Joseph
        Anderson, Lynn
        Baudeck, Cathy
        Begich, Joseph
        Berg, Norbert
        Berg, Thomas "Tom"
        Bifulk, M. S. P.
        Bohn, Ray
        Brown, Ann
        Brustuen, Eldon
        Dayton, Mark
        Gardebring, Sandra
        Gornick, Ron
        Johnson, Marlene
        Lamppa, Gary
        Landborg, Philip R.
        Mackay, Harvey
        Mastell, Ann
        McKanna, Norma
        Moe, Roger
        Montgomery, Terry
        Nelson, Marilyn Carlson
        Norris, William C. "Bill"
        Oberstar, James
        Ongaro, Frank Sr.
        Opperman, Vance
        Perpich, Joseph
        Perpich, Rudy Jr.

Randall, Ruth
Rogich, George
Rohde, Barbara
Samargia, Joe
Scott, Robert T., and Nordvold, Richard
Stanoch, John
Sturdevant, Lori
Triplett, Tom
Wellstone, Paul
Zdon, Alan
Iron Range Interpretative Program Oral History Collection.
    Perpich, Anton (1899–1996) and Mary (1911–1997), March 24, 1977.
Rudy G. Perpich Collection.
    Sommer, Barbara W. Remembering Rudy: Excerpts from Governor Rudy
        Perpich Oral History Project and the Memorial Statements. 2000.
John F. Kennedy Presidential Library and Museum, Boston, MA.
Minnesota Historical Society, St. Paul, MN.
    Oral History Interview Project. Mark Haidet and Hyman Berman. 1983.
    Burggraaff, Wayne
    Quie, Al
Minnesota Legislative Library, St. Paul, MN.
Perpich: A Truly Minnesota Original Research Project. Benjamin M. Schierer,
    2020–23.
    Anzelc, Tom
    Berg, Tom
    Holmquist, Charlie
    Urdahl, Dean
    Zdon, Alan
State of Minnesota, St. Paul, MN.
    Minnesota Management and Budget
    Minnesota Revisor of Statutes
    Minnesota Secretary of State
    Minnesota State Law Library
    Office of the Legislative Auditor

Newspapers

Albert Lea Evening Tribune
Albert Lea Tribune
Austin Daily Herald
Bemidji Pioneer
Chicago Tribune
Duluth News Tribune
Fergus Falls Daily Journal

Hibbing Daily News
Hibbing Daily Tribune
Japan Times
La Crosse (WI) Tribune
Los Angeles Times
Mandan (ND) Morning Pioneer
Minneapolis Star
Minneapolis Star and Tribune
Minneapolis Star Tribune
Minneapolis Tribune
Minnesota Daily
MinnPost
New York Times
St. Cloud Daily Times
St. Cloud Times
Winona Daily News
Winona Daily Star

Online Sources

The Center for Victims of Torture. https://www.cvt.org.
Encyclopedia Britannica. https://www.britannica.com.
Federal Reserve History. https://www.federalreservehistory.org.
General Motors, Spring Hill Manufacturing. https://www.gm.com/company/ facilities/spring-hill.
Mall of America. https://www.mallofamerica.com.
Minnesota Compass. https://www.mncompass.org.
Minnesota Historical Election Archive, University of Minnesota. https://mn .electionarchives.lib.umn.edu.
Minnesota North College. https://minnesotanorth.edu.
MNopedia. https://www.mnopedia.org.
Office of the Historian. US State Department. https://history.state.gov.

Published Sources

Appell, David. "The Supercollider That Never Was." *Scientific American*, October 15, 2013.
Berg, Tom. *Minnesota's Miracle: Learning from the Government That Worked*. Minneapolis: University of Minnesota Press, 2012.
Berman, Hyman, and Jay Weiner. *Professor Berman: The Last Lecture of Minnesota's Greatest Public Historian*. Minneapolis: University of Minnesota Press, 2019.
Boyce, Steven, Jake Edwards, and Tom Wetzel. "Slaughterhouse Fight: A Look at the Hormel Strike." *Ideas & Action* 7 (1986).

Casper, Barry M., and Paul David Wellstone. *Powerline: The First Battle of America's Energy War.* Amherst: University of Massachusetts Press, 1981.

"Debate a Battle in Perpich's 'War' on MCCL." *Minnesota Citizens Concerned for Life Newsletter* (October 1979): 7.

Drury, Richard L. "Community Colleges in America: A Historical Perspective." *Inquiry* 8, no. 1 (2003).

Elazar, Daniel J., Virginia Gray, and Wyman Spano. *Minnesota Politics and Government.* Politics and Governments of the American States. Lincoln: University of Nebraska Press, 1999.

Garber, Carter, and Verna Fausey. "Today's Jobs at Yesterday's Wages: GM's Saturn Auto Plant Arrives in Spring Hill, Tennessee." *Southern Changes* 8, no. 4 (1986).

Gaut, Greg, and Marsha Neff. "Red Stars over Minnesota." *Minnesota History* (Winter 2009): 346–59.

Growe, Joan Anderson, with Lori Sturdevant. *Turnout: Making Minnesota the State That Votes.* Minnesota Historical Society Press, 2020.

Kortenhof, Kurt. *Potential and Paradox: A Gateway to Minnesota's Past.* St. Paul: Minnesota Libraries Publishing Project, 2022.

Kraut, Alan M. *The Huddled Masses: The Immigrant in American Society, 1880–1921.* The American History Series. Arlington Heights, IL: Harlan Davidson, 1982.

Lubotina, Paul. "The Minnesota Farm-Labor Party: The Role of Third Parties in the Americanization of European Labor Radicals in the Great Lakes Region." *Upper Country: A Journal of the Lake Superior Region* 4 (2016).

Lubotina, Paul. "The Struggle for Control of Hibbing: The People's Perspective." *Upper Country: A Journal of the Lake Superior Region* (2015): 45–55.

Mayer, George H. *The Political Career of Floyd B. Olson.* Minneapolis: University of Minnesota Press, 1951.

Mondale, Walter F., and Dave Hage. *The Good Fight: A Life in Liberal Politics.* New York: Scribner, 2010.

Pearlstein, Mitchell B., Charles W. Colson, and Roger D. Moe. *Riding into the Sunrise: Al Quie: A Life of Faith, Service and Civility.* Lakeville, MN: Pogo Press, 2008.

Snider, William. "Minnesota Backs Nation's First 'Choice' System." *Education Week,* May 4, 1988.

Sturdevant, Lori. *Her Honor: Rosalie Wahl and the Minnesota Women's Movement.* St. Paul: Minnesota Historical Society Press, 2014.

Syramaki, John. "Iron Range Communities." PhD diss, Yale University, 1940.

US Congress. *Congressional Record: Proceedings and Debates of the 90th United States Congress.* Washington, DC: US Government Printing Office, 1967.

"Welcome to the Minnesota World Trade Center." St. Paul: Minnesota World Trade Center. https://www.lrl.mn.gov/docs/2012/other/120085.pdf.

Wilson, Betty. *Rudy! The People's Governor.* Minneapolis, MN: Nodin Press, 2005.

Writers' Program of the Work Projects Administration and Minnesota Arrowhead Association. *The Minnesota Arrowhead Country.* American Guide Series. Chicago, IL: A. Whitman & Co., 1941.

Index

Page numbers in *italic* refer to images or captions.

 **Ben Schierer** served two terms as mayor of Fergus Falls, Minnesota. A former Bush Fellow and NewDEAL Leader, he received his master's of public administration degree from the Hubert H. Humphrey Institute.